MW00469659

Sunbelt Justice

Critical Perspectives on Crime and Law

Edited by Markus D. Dubber

Sunbelt Justice

ARIZONA AND THE TRANSFORMATION OF AMERICAN PUNISHMENT

Mona Lynch

Stanford Law Books
An Imprint of Stanford University Press
Stanford, California

Stanford University Press
Stanford, California

Printed in the United States of America on acid-free, archival-quality paper

Library of Congress Cataloging-in-Publication Data

Lynch, Mona Pauline.
  Sunbelt justice : Arizona and the transformation of American punishment / Mona Lynch.
     p. cm. — (Critical perspectives on crime and law)
  Includes bibliographical references and index.
  ISBN 978-0-8047-6284-7 (cloth : alk. paper) — ISBN 978-0-8047-6285-4 (pbk. : alk. paper)
  1. Imprisonment—Arizona—History. 2. Punishment—Arizona—History. 3. Criminal
justice, Administration of—Arizona—History. I. Title. II. Series: Critical perspectives on
crime and law.
  HV9475.A6L96 2009
  364.609791—dc22
                                    2009011175

Typeset by Bruce Lundquist in 10/14 Minion

For my father and for Greg

CONTENTS

ACKNOWLEDGMENTS

THIS BOOK WOULD NOT HAVE BEEN POSSIBLE without the help and support of numerous people. Much of the inspiration for the project has come through lively conversations and exchanges about punishment, Arizona, and lots of other things with many friends and colleagues over the past decade. Among those people are Vanessa Barker, Katherine Beckett, Jennifer Culbert, Alessandro DeGiorgi, Malcolm Feeley, Ben Fleury-Steiner, David Garland, David Theo Goldberg, Steve Herbert, Tim Kaufman-Osborne, Ann Lucas, Michael Musheno, Richard Perry, Joan Petersilia, Austin Sarat, and Loic Wacquant. A special, special thanks goes to two very good friends and colleagues who put in way too much of their time reading drafts of this book, giving me advice whenever I asked for it, and generally acting as sounding boards for me: Jonathan Simon and Frank Zimring. Their insights provided depth and complexity to my arguments that otherwise would have been absent.

San Jose State University and the University of California, Irvine, were very supportive of this project, financially and otherwise, and it is due to the wonderful working environment at those institutions that I have been able to complete this book. I was also privileged to spend a productive semester during the earliest stages of writing at the Center for the Study of Law and Society at the University of California, Berkeley. This is a true haven for law and society scholars thanks to Lauren Edelman and Rosann Greenspan.

I owe a huge debt of gratitude to the National Science Foundation, Law and Social Science Program, which provided the crucial funding for the research. I am also indebted to the archivists at the Arizona State Archives, especially Wendi Goen and Melanie Sturgeon, and to Paul King at the Institute for Governmental Studies library at UC Berkeley, for their assistance in helping me track down numerous documents. I had excellent research assistance from Nathan Coben and Diego Jara-Simkin at different stages of the project, and I am very grateful for their help. As I finalized the writing of this book, I benefited immensely from the guidance and advice of my editor, Kate Wahl, and assistant editor Joa Suorez at Stanford University Press, as well as from the comments of the anonymous reviewers.

Central to the research was the generous cooperation and assistance provided by the Arizona Department of Corrections, which opened its doors to me when I asked in 2001. Many people in that organization gave much of their time as I gathered information and materials in the early stages of the project. I also thank all of those who allowed me to interview them about their experiences; these accounts added much to the project and helped me to understand more deeply the processes at work in Arizona.

On a final note, I am immensely grateful for several people who have been so important and inspiring to me in this endeavor and in my life. Craig Haney has been my mentor and teacher since I was an undergraduate, and his brilliant, thoughtful, and deeply caring work on the problems of crime and punishment has served as a model to which I can only aspire. My love and thanks go to my children, Nathan and Molly, and the rest of my family, who are my foundation. I am especially and completely indebted to my husband and best friend, Gregory Coben, who has been a constant source of love, inspiration, and support and to whom this book is dedicated. Without him, this project would not have been nearly as much fun. Finally, I thank my father, Thomas Lynch, to whom this book is also dedicated and who has been my hero since before I can remember.

Sunbelt Justice

INTRODUCTION

From the Reformative Project to
the Warehousing Solution

IT IS NO LONGER NEWS that over the past three decades, the use of incarceration in many Western nations has exploded, most dramatically in the United States. This phenomenon, at least in the United States, would have been hard to predict even five years before it began during the late 1970s, given that a budding movement away from the prison as a central penal response to criminal offending seemed to be under way at that time and the use of incarceration in the United States had, for decades, been quite stable. From 1929 to 1967, the U.S. state and federal prison incarceration rate hovered around 100 prisoners per 100,000 population (Bureau of Justice Statistics, 1998), so there was little to forecast the explosion in prison population to come. Indeed, beginning in the mid-1960s through the early 1970s, the imprisonment rate in this country began a slow but consistent decline, which seemed to signify a new horizon in penology that moved corrections away from isolated total institutions and back into less restrictive community settings. This downward trend fit with what was happening in a number of state institutions and was predicted by many as the logical outcome of the turmoil that was brewing around punishment ideals and practices (Scull, 1977).

The consequences of this turmoil within corrections took several forms. The most significant alternative to the prison that appeared to be emerging was what is known as "community corrections" or community-based control (Cohen, 1979). The ideology underlying this movement spoke of the involvement of family, schools, peers, neighborhoods, the police, and an array of community professionals in keeping criminal offenders in line within communities rather than isolated in segregated penal institutions. Although the

1

new community-based forms of intervention did not threaten to completely replace the prison, there were clear signs that incarceration rates would remain static, if not continue to decline, as the prison became a cardinal point—a last resort—on the continuum of social control rather than a primary option for penal intervention (Cohen, 1979; Scull, 1977, 1983).

The decarceration trend, though, was short-lived. By the late 1970s, the U.S. prison population began a rather sharp ascent, and this acceleration, it turned out, has continued (although it has slowed since the late 1990s) into the twenty-first century. Consequently, a mere 25 years after what looked like the demise, or at least the diminution of incarceration, the national imprisonment rate had nearly quintupled to 410 prisoners per 100,000 population (Bureau of Justice Statistics, 1998). By the end of 2006, more than 1.5 million people were in state and federal prisons in the United States—about 1.1 million more than were incarcerated just 25 years earlier (Sabol, Couture, and Harrison, 2007; Gilliard and Beck, 1995).[1]

Although the incarceration explosion was a conundrum in itself, it was not the only indication of paradigmatic penal change. Almost concurrent with the start of the imprisonment boom was a notable break with the underlying rationale for the penal institution itself. As a number of observers have pointed out, during the 1970s, faith in the rehabilitative ideal that had prevailed in penology for the past century began to erode among criminal justice practitioners, academics, and policymakers (Allen, 1981; Garland, 2001; Martinson, 1974). The often cited (and often mis-cited) article by Robert Martinson titled "What Works?" (1974) exemplified the growing skepticism about the legitimacy of rehabilitation; the answer for many to the "what works?" question, and for very different reasons, tended to be "nothing" when it came to reforming offenders. Ultimately, the prison as a sociolegal institution was roundly criticized from all sides as, at best, ineffectual and misguided in its pursuits and, in more biting attacks from the left, as a racist, class-biased tool of the elite used to subjugate members of marginalized groups. Thus, there was a deep irony at the heart of this penological phenomenon: the expansion of a practice that had almost simultaneously lost much of its meaning and purpose.

This fracture in the accepted "account" (Simon, 1993) of the prison's purpose appears to have contributed to a second, equally important transformation in state punishment: the broad (re)adoption of deliberately harsh penal techniques and institutional conditions by jurisdictions in many parts of the United States. Many contemporary prisons have become, by design, little more than human warehouses filled with a segment of the population for which there is no investment in reformation or rehabilitation (Robertson, 1997). Within these new "no-frills" prisons, policies and procedures are implemented that aim to punish more deeply than the sentence of imprisonment itself. In recent decades, we have seen the imposition of "hard labor" requirements behind bars, the return of chain gangs, vastly expanded use of solitary confinement within "super" maximum-security (supermax) facilities, new restrictions on intrainstitutional rights and privileges, the removal of recreational equipment and facilities, and the elimination of inmate programs, among other developments. Thus, as Craig Haney (1998: 27) has observed, the late twentieth-century "punishment wave" has been characterized by a generalized "devolving standards of decency" within the U.S. penal system.

Concurrent with the population explosion and qualitative changes to institutional life inside prisons, the racial and ethnic composition of the U.S. prison population also changed significantly. The relative percentage of minorities in prison, especially of African Americans, grew steadily from 1960 to the present, with the sharpest increase beginning around 1980 (Beck and Mumola, 1999; Tonry, 1995). This demographic shift is largely a product of changes in sentencing strategies, particularly those aimed at drug offenders. The number of nonwhites in prison for nonviolent drug offenses far outstrips the number of whites so imprisoned, and as a number of state legislatures, as well the U.S. Congress, began passing legislation that ratcheted up sentence lengths for drug-related offenses during the 1970s and 1980s, the racial disparities among state and federal prison populations grew accordingly (Blumstein and Beck, 1999; Provine, 2007).

This book directly confronts these late modern transformations of state punishment by closely examining the mechanics of change in one state—Arizona—over the second half of the twentieth century. I explore how a state-level polity was able to move from maintaining a modest and stable level of dependence on imprisonment over its history to making the costly investment in massive prison expansion over just several decades, and I illustrate how this state became a national trend-setting leader in delivering harsh punishment. The book, though, is not simply a narrative history of penal developments in a single jurisdiction. Rather, it situates the story of one state within a sociolegal and cultural theoretical framework that explicates how punishment functions during a moment of paradigm transformation. In doing so, it aims to elucidate the interconnections between late modern penal change and broader geopolitical and cultural changes that have occurred in post–World War II America, especially the rise of the "New Right" in the Sunbelt Southwest.

WHY ARIZONA?

Arizona is an exemplary case for understanding these paradoxical but none-theless dramatic changes in penal ideals, policies, and practices for several reasons. First, the timing of the bureaucratization of the state's penal system reveals how changing understandings of criminality and penal intervention at a broader level were translated into policy and practice. Indeed, the estab-lishment of Arizona's Department of Corrections in 1968 perfectly coincided with the beginning of the end for the rehabilitative penal philosophy that had shaped many punishment practices in the United States for most of the twen-tieth century. Rehabilitation was not institutionally rooted in the state, so its introduction with the modernizing of the system through bureaucratization guaranteed its fragile status. As will be detailed in the coming chapters, Ari-zona had historically embraced a punitive approach to lawbreakers, so the correctionalist philosophy was imported and introduced to the state with the new department's first several directors. However, within two decades of its inception, this department had abandoned its flirtation with rehabilitation and had come to exemplify the model of the harsh, postrehabilitative mass incarcerative warehouse-style prison system that had come to prevail in juris-dictions across the nation.

Second, the prison system's sheer growth over the last quarter of the twentieth century represents a hallmark example of the broader trends de-scribed above. Arizona's rate of imprisonment ballooned from a low of 75 per 100,000 citizens in 1971 to 515 per 100,000 by the turn of the twenty-first century, and the prison population multiplied from 878 inmates in 1950 to almost 26,510 by 2000 (U.S. Department of Commerce, 1958; Beck and Har-rison, 2001; see Figure 1 and the appendix). After the state's incarceration rate had hovered for decades near the national average (generally just above it), by 1975, increases in that rate began to significantly outstrip the growth in the national imprisonment rate. In every year from 1984 through the pres-ent, Arizona has been among the top 10 of the 50 states in terms of rate of incarceration.

Third, the qualitative changes in punishment that have occurred in the late twentieth century are also clearly evident in Arizona, and indeed the state

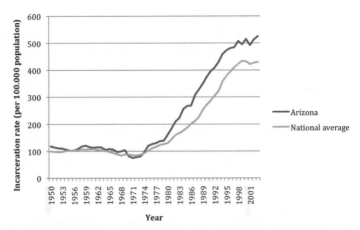

Figure 1. Incarceration rates: Arizona and the national average, 1955–2003. The national rate is the average of U.S. state prison rates, excluding federal prisons and local jails. From U.S. Census Bureau, Statistical Abstract of the United States, 1950–94; Bureau of Justice Statistics, Prisoners in 1994, and following years to 2003.

was both an innovator and a leader in implementing many of the "get-tough" practices that characterize contemporary punishment. For instance, Arizona was home to the first state-level newly constructed (as opposed to retrofitted) supermax facility in the country (it opened in 1987), and as of 1999, it had the second highest percentage of bed space devoted to such units in the nation (King, 1999). It was also one of the first states to reintroduce chain gangs to the prison and to institute a range of fees charged to inmates for various living expenses, among other such trends. From 1984 to 2003, the leadership of the Arizona Department of Corrections consistently boasted about the department's "success" in providing economical, no-frills accommodations for its incarcerated population and spent proportionately little of its budget on programming resources for inmates.

Finally, Arizona provides an interesting example of the racialization of punishment. Unlike the pattern in many states that embraced and then retreated from rehabilitation (Flanagan, Clark, Aziz, and Szelest, 1990; Haney, 2006), Arizona has had a high and consistent rate of minority overrepresentation behind bars, relative to the state's general population. So although the national trend indicates that the share of minorities in prison began to rise rapidly as rehabilitation began its descent as a reigning logic, this case study suggests the possibility that there were places without a long-standing commitment to re-

Table 1 Overall incarceration rate vs. African American incarceration rate in Arizona, 1960–2000

Year	% African American general population	African American incarceration rate (per 100,000 population)	Overall incarceration rate (per 100,000 population)	Ratio of African American to overall rate
1960	3	783	115	6.81
1970	3	689	81	8.51
1980	3	911	161	5.66
1990	3	2,107	389	5.42
2000	3	2,493	515	4.84

SOURCES: U.S. Department of Commerce, 1962, 1972, 1982, 2003; Arizona Department of Corrections annual reports (1980, 1990, 2000); Arizona State Prison biannual report (1960); Arizona State Prison annual report (1970).

habilitation that had earlier patterns of minority overrepresentation strikingly similar to the contemporary national trends (see the appendix). Nationwide, the relative share of whites in the prison population has slowly decreased since the late 1950s, but in Arizona, a state with an African American general population share of just 3 percent, African Americans have been consistently, and strikingly, overrepresented in the prison population (see Table 1).

SUNBELT JUSTICE AND THE SPECIFICITIES OF PLACE

Beyond its penal significance as a state, Arizona also illuminates an important yet understudied regional phenomenon: Sunbelt justice. As William Frey (2002) has argued, region has become an increasingly significant analytic distinction—supplanting the categories of urban, suburban, and rural—for understanding U.S. cultural demography. He suggests that there has been a "fading of these local cultural boundaries in favor of increasingly sharp regional ones," especially in the area that he calls the New Sunbelt (Frey, 2002: 349), or the high-growth states of the 1990s that include those states running from Virginia to Georgia on the southeast coast and Arizona, Nevada, and Colorado in the West. Ever since the concept was popularized in the late 1960s, there has been considerable academic debate over whether the states and subregions of the South and Southwest that are said to make up the Sunbelt form a unified regional entity (e.g., Browning and Gesler, 1979; Abbott, 1990). However, as an analytical framework, the Sunbelt has been very useful for understanding and explaining a shared developmental trajectory in many southern rim states since World War II (Schulman, 1993) and has been particularly valuable in describing high-growth metropolitan areas in those locales (Abbott, 1987; Bernard and Rice, 1983; Findlay, 1992; Perry and Watkins, 1977).[2] And while the notion of the Sunbelt seemed to be falling out of favor among scholars by the mid-1980s (Goldfield and Rabinowitz, 1990), it has experienced a resurgence among demographers (Frey, 2002) and especially historians (Lassiter, 2006; McGirr, 2001; Rothman, 2002).

A distinct set of cultural norms and practices is associated with the evolution of the paradigmatic Sunbelt states during the second half of the twentieth century, resulting from the timing, pattern, and extent of their population growth as well as migration patterns from other jurisdictions. Their development is closely tied to the emergence of new post–World War II economies, such as military base and weapons industries, air transportation, electronics and computer technology, and expanded service industries (Abbott, 2003). These rapidly growing areas have been characterized by the proliferation of large, master-planned suburban-style communities; even major Sunbelt cities like Phoenix and Houston are distinctively low density, lacking large and concentrated core centers, and are functionally similar to the surrounding suburban communities. The metropolitan population in such cities sprawls for miles, and single-family homes in relatively homogeneous housing developments dominate the housing stock in many such urban areas (Nicolaides, 2003).

The growth of the coastal South and the Southwest as population centers meant that places like Arizona in the West and Florida in the South, which were geographically isolated and/or politically uninfluential during the first half of the twentieth century, began to have an effect on national political culture by the 1960s. Population shifts from the Northeast and Midwest to the Sunbelt resulted in a proportional reallocation of congressional seats and electoral college votes to the southern and western growth states, thus increasing the region's influence in Congress and in presidential elections (Trubowitz, 1992). Indeed, by 2030, demographer William Frey (2005) estimates that the Sunbelt will have a 146 electoral college vote advantage over the "Snowbelt"; in 1970 those regions held about an equal share of such votes.

This would not be significant if there were no notable differences in political ideals, cultures, and practices as a function of region, yet it is well documented that in a number of important ways the Sunbelt has developed in opposition to the Northeast rather than in coordination with it (McGirr, 2001). Indeed, several scholars have recently argued—and empirically demonstrated—that the New Right political movement in the United States developed directly out of the suburban Sunbelt areas of the South (Lassiter, 2006) and West (McGirr, 2001), beginning in the 1960s and reaching its peak with the election of Ronald Reagan as president in 1980 (see also Davis, 1986; Salt, 1989). In the earliest days of the movement, which started with the presidential campaign of Arizona Republican Barry Goldwater in 1964, the majority of Americans saw as extreme and even dangerous the politics and values associated with this movement—a sometimes contradictory blend of antitaxation sentiments and a desire for limited government; an allegiance to an unregulated free market economy; attention to "morals" issues concerning family, sexuality, and religion; a retreat from civil rights; and a commitment to law and order and a strong national defense (McGirr, 2001). But by the 1980s, such political values had become hegemonic, especially in the national political arena, and had substantially displaced a social welfarist, liberal political agenda (see, for example, Gaffaney, 1999; Simon, 2007).

Nonetheless, even though the political values of the New Right in many ways were part of the coherence of this geographically dispersed region, notable variations existed within the Sunbelt that were at least partially shaped by more deeply rooted and historically long-standing local political cultures. Thus, places like Arizona and New Mexico tended to have more in common with their western counterparts, in terms of their self-definitions and trajectories of development, while southeastern states shared major historical experiences and cultural traditions that shaped their more contemporary development.

For example, although a significant component of the New Right organizing focus has been around morals issues, such as abortion, obscenity, and countercultural lifestyles, states like Arizona and Nevada, with conservative-libertarian political roots, tend to be liberal, relative to the nation as a whole and especially to the Sunbelt South, on such matters (Norrander and Wilcox, 2005; Rivera and Norrander, 2002). Western states, especially in the Sunbelt West, are also more likely to have adopted and to regularly utilize political structures and processes that limit governmental power through a variety of means, especially direct democracy measures, such as ballot initiatives, referenda, and recall power (Haskell, 2001; Smith, 1998).

The postwar geopolitical transformations in the Sunbelt have clearly contributed to some of the changes in state and federal criminal justice policy and practices as well. Although Sunbelt states collectively had a slightly higher incarceration rate than the national average for state institutions in 1950 (109 per 100,000 versus 99 per 100,000), by 2000, that region's combined average incarceration rate exceeded the national average by nearly 100 (528 per 100,000 versus 432 per 100,000) (Beck and Harrison, 2001; U.S. Department of Commerce, 1954).[3] Five high-growth Sunbelt states—Arizona, Georgia, Nevada, South Carolina, and Texas—were among the top 10 states for incarceration rates by 2000, and most of the others exceeded the national average. Nearly half of all the nation's state-level prisoners were held in institutions of 11 high-growth Sunbelt states in 2000; in 1950, that share was just 27 percent. Given that these states were undergoing significant general population growth relative to the nation as a whole, the fact that they not only absorbed the increased population of inmates relative to that growth, but also on average dramatically increased their *rates* of incarceration significantly above the national average indicates a huge fiscal and ideological commitment to a prison-based strategy in response to crime in the Sunbelt.[4] Additionally, the bulk of the postrehabilitative innovations that increase the severity of institutional conditions have originated in the Sunbelt states and spread to other regions from there (see Chapter 7).

Thus, this close examination of Arizona as an exemplary case of penal transformations in the Sunbelt Southwest aims to illuminate the interplay of regionally specific historical trajectories as shaped by distinct cultural norms and traditions with how such states responded to the "crisis in corrections" (Harris, 1973) that emerged during the late twentieth century.

THE SIGNIFICANCE OF LOCALE IN EXPLAINING PENAL CHANGE

By asserting the claim that local and regional factors are central to understanding late modern penal developments in the United States, this book complicates the widely accepted narrative about the nature of American penality. The standard account of early and mid-twentieth-century U.S. punishment history articulates a developmental process during which the criminal was conceived of as a flawed but fixable individual, and the state's responsibility was to provide the expertise and resources needed to remediate those flaws. Thus, in this account, the penal enterprise defined itself in terms of its role in reforming delinquents, and penal institutions ideally facilitated that process, just as schools were designed to educate youth and asylums were designed to treat and cure the mentally ill. Although the specific measures used to achieve such rehabilitation changed shape over the years, the underlying goals and purposes of penal intervention were broadly accepted and unquestioned. Penal experts tended not to ask whether criminal offenders could be reformed, but rather what were the most successful interventions for achieving rehabilitation. Within prisons, programs that ranged from vocational training and education to intense psychiatric and neuromedical treatments were put to use in order to reach the reformative goals.

This understanding of American punishment, then, assumes that the rehabilitative paradigm was widespread and relatively deeply rooted across states and that its "fall" was more or less equally disruptive in those locales. Indeed, much of the penal change literature implicitly supposes that the demise of rehabilitation left a void for the new forms of penality to fill. These new penal forms are typically characterized as just that—new—and few accounts empirically interrogate the precise mechanics through which they were created and put into action, particularly within states, which is where the bulk of criminal justice business occurs. More generally, the majority of contemporary scholarship on the penal transformations of the late twentieth century has treated the phenomenon as a relatively monolithic national-level, or international-level, process, with less direct consideration of the variations in the quality of practices and growth that have occurred subnationally.[5]

Nonetheless, much important theoretical and empirical scholarship has set the stage for explorations such as this one, in that it has provided insights into the macro-level processes that appear to have reshaped the criminal justice field across a wide domain. One of the more influential theoretical pieces of scholarship of this sort, which has sparked much subsequent research about qualitative changes in penality, is the articulation of a "new penology" by Malcolm Feeley and Jonathan Simon (1992). According to Feeley and Simon, the new penological ethos has shifted the penal focus away from aiming to "fix" individual offenders and now prioritizes efficient management of the criminal class and cost-effective containment/incapacitation measures through the use of actuarial kinds of predictive tools (on this, see also Bottoms, 1983; Cohen, 1985; O'Malley, 1992; Reichman, 1986; Simon, 1993; Simon and Feeley, 1995). In this model, reforming individual criminals is not the primary task for the penal system; rather, cost-efficient control of those deemed to pose a risk of reoffending has become a central goal of the system.

Although this line of theorizing fits well with some elements of penal change, and does seem to account for many of the shifts in operational emphasis from rehabilitation to security maintenance and risk management within many criminal justice institutions, it does not adequately explain why states have invested so heavily in incarceration when that penal policy is quite costly and not particularly efficient. It is even more at odds with the fact that a significant portion of the prison growth has resulted from incarcerating nonviolent drug offenders, who would not seem to pose enough risk as to require the very high level of containment that the prison represents; who would be more inexpensively kept in community settings; and who are generally replaced within the illicit drug market as soon as they are locked up, thereby making incarceration of this population completely inefficient as a means of stemming drug dealing and use. In that the new penology perspective is a more global analytical framework that aims to sketch out broad trends over time, it also does not address the variations in penal practices at the state level.

A number of outstanding treatments of the politics of crime at the national level also have done much to further our understanding of how law-and-order rhetoric ultimately shapes policy. Most notably, Katherine Beckett's (1997) empirical work on the rise of law-and-order politics supports the theory that racialized political rhetoric, rather than crime per se, was largely responsible for at least setting off the tough-on-crime and corollary punishment binge that began during the 1970s. She convincingly illustrates the racial subtext of the tough-on-crime political movement at the federal level by documenting how civil rights issues, and those advocating for broader civil rights, were rhetorically linked to crime as a growing problem, such that demands for equality and justice became reasons, for politicians like Richard Nixon, to call for increased crime control. In the same work, Beckett also illustrates how crime as political capital, particularly during the administrations of Reagan and George H. W. Bush, in concert with media attention to state-shaped crime issues, contributed to the expansion of imprisonment as a primary criminal justice policy, especially at the federal level. Although Beckett's work does not speak to regional and local processes, it has served as a model for empirical examination of the mechanisms by which political rhetoric gets translated into criminal justice policy (see also Melossi, 1993, on this issue).

In an innovative theoretical explication, Jonathan Simon (2007) has described the contemporary thrust of "governing through crime" by the political exploitation of repressive crime control as a primary weapon against widespread social insecurities amid a crisis in governance. He argues that crime, rather than issues such as the environment, employment, or health care, became a focal point on which all insecurities came to rest as the New Deal model of governing began to collapse during the 1960s. Flowing from this, contemporary warehouse-style prisons rose as a major symbol of effective neoliberal governance that rewards responsible citizen behavior and comes down hard on those who do not play by the rules. As crime became a central rhetorical concept around which even noncrime policies were framed—including those regulating governance of families, schools, and the workplace—punitive policies proliferated across a number of venues and catalyzed an increased reliance on harsh punishment in response to crime. Simon's work in particular points to the growing importance of the image and role of the American public prosecutor, both literally and symbolically, as a key component in the governing-through-crime phenomenon, often exemplified at the state level by governors, who increasingly campaigned and governed through crime during the late twentieth century.

A number of scholars have also suggested that the current expansion of imprisonment is a form of racialized social control (Davis, 2003; Donziger, 1996; Mauer, 1999). For instance, Loïc Wacquant (2000) has argued that the contemporary prison is a "surrogate ghetto" that functions to maintain racial boundaries in the wake of desegregation and in response to changes in the labor market.[6] This explanation is bolstered by data that clearly indicate that policy change at the state and federal levels, rather than behavioral change among minority populations, accounts for most of the demographic shift within the nation's prison population, especially as it relates to regulating drug offenders. De Giorgi (2006) similarly provides a comprehensive theoretical account of the contemporary political economy of punishment in light of globalized capital and a much more flexible and exploitable labor market.[7]

Probably the most expansive theoretical treatment of contemporary penal change as a macro-level phenomenon has come from David Garland (2001), who has made a very textured, multifaceted argument that the fall of the rehabilitative ideal, and the consequent changes in the crime-control "field," are really the product of a series of late modern social, economic, and political developments in the United States and Great Britain. His treatment of the myriad crime-control transformations of the late twentieth century pulls together and synthesizes a number of theoretical strands. As starting points for understanding the sociopolitical culture of late modernity, he points to such disparate factors as enduring structural changes in the economy that have permanently displaced a portion of the workforce, transformations in family roles and structures, shifts in demographic and geographic population, and the influence of mass media.

In Garland's view, these changes contributed to a rise in the incidence of crime, a less secure middle class, and consequently a broad disillusionment with a welfarist model of governance, of which penal rehabilitation was a part. Thus the 1980s law-and-order rhetoric and the major prison population explosion that accompanied it reflected a reaction to deeper, more widely felt social change and also served to mask the state's growing inability to provide security to its citizens. Within this broader comprehensive reading of the "culture of control," Garland attempts to explain changes in the scale and style of punishment, but this work functions best as an invitation to the empirical study of these phenomena rather than as the final word. And, as is also reflected in most other accounts of what happened from the 1960s onward, his work implies that "penal welfarism" or "the rehabilitative ideal" was equally pervasive and hegemonic within penal and legal institutions across the United States and Britain, which, at least in the case of Arizona and other subnational U.S. jurisdictions, turns out to be a problematic assumption.

As this discussion suggests, many of these analyses have looked at the incarceration explosion and related penal transformations that began during the 1970s in a monotonic manner, assuming similar processes and effects across state and national jurisdictions. Nonetheless, although all 50 states in the United States have experienced massive growth in their imprisonment rates over this period, those rates vary dramatically from state to state and regionally, as do the qualitative aspects of punishment and the rates of minority overrepresentation relative to the general jurisdictional demographics. More significantly, for this project, attention to on-the-ground local social, cultural, and political processes as well as regionally specific conditions helps illuminate the precise mechanisms that trigger penal change, including how policy innovations flow between locales.

While there is relatively little theoretical and empirical work on the Sunbelt as a region in terms of its role in the broader penal transformations experienced throughout the United States, there is a body of scholarship that highlights the importance of considering subnational processes for understanding penal change. For instance, Frank Zimring and Gordon Hawkins (1991), who were among the first researchers to both systematically document and try to explain the increase in the "scale of imprisonment" across the United States, illustrated how the changes across time told two stories about place. They suggested that the explosion in prison population must be treated as a national phenomenon because every state in the country underwent a significant growth in incarceration; however, at the same time, the considerable variation in the scale of imprisonment from state to state and from region to region indicated that the explanation for the growth cannot be limited to either global or local factors alone. According to Zimring and Hawkins's analysis, economic conditions, rising crime rates, demographic factors, and changes in state-level sentencing policy could not in themselves explain the expansion in imprisonment use. Rather, in the end they suggested that a number of factors at multiple levels, coupled with the structural fact that those jurisdictions sending people to prison (counties) do not assume fiscal responsibility for the costs associated with those sentencing decisions, are responsible for this dramatic change.

More recently, geographer Ruth Gilmore (2007) examined California's prison capacity expansion, using a political economy framework to explain how that state coped with multiple surpluses, including surplus labor, at a time of economic crisis after years of growth, by investing in the largest prison-building effort in history, which began in the 1980s. Among other insights, her project illustrates both how community leaders in economically depressed areas have pushed to get prisons built in their towns as the answer to their economic woes, and the state's willingness to "sell" the prison fix to such communities, even though the new prisons are not the economic panacea that they are purported to be. Thus, her work suggests that prisons have morphed into a form of industry and capital investment, rather than being reformative institutions, and as such have grown as a function of their place in the new economy. She also ties the process of penal growth to very specific jurisdictional and regional conditions that particularly speak to high-population-growth states in the Sunbelt West.

Using a very different approach, Katherine Beckett and Bruce Western (2001) have also empirically demonstrated the link between state-level economic factors and the use of imprisonment. They looked at the relationship between state-level social welfare spending, states' racial characteristics, and reliance on incarceration and found that, beginning in the 1980s, the African American population percentage of states negatively correlates with welfare spending per capita and positively correlates with incarceration rates. Among the nine states with the greatest inverse relationship of welfare spending and incarceration rates are six Sunbelt states: Texas, California, Nevada, Arizona, South Carolina, and Georgia. Although Beckett and Western do not make an explicit argument about local or regional differences, their data suggest the significance of both time and place in predicting the degree to which state governance strategies rely on incarceration as a primary mode of regulating socially marginal populations.

Vanessa Barker's (2006) subnational comparative research, which aims to explain state-level differences in incarceration rates by closely examining three states with very different rates, provides some further insight into variations in penal practices as a function of the structures and styles of state governance. She concludes that (among other things) states with low levels of participation by the citizenry and a decentralized power structure are likely to be driven by populist politics, leading to high rates of incarceration relative to other modes of governance.

Although it does not directly examine local practices, a growing body of cross-national comparative research suggests that attention to regional differences provides for an especially useful route to understanding the social, political, structural, and cultural underpinnings of the contemporary state of punishment. In particular, this line of research demonstrates the complex, temporally and spatially specific nature of penal policymaking. For instance, Savelsberg (1994) compares German and U.S. imprisonment policies and practices and finds that the interplay among the relative influence of public opinion, legislative role and government structure, and prevailing cultural ideologies in each locale accounts for major differences in incarceration rates and policies (see also Morgan, 2000, for another illustration of cross-national variations in penal policymaking).

Recent contributions to this line of inquiry include *Harsh Justice* by James Whitman (2003) and *The Prison and the Gallows* by Marie Gottschalk (2006), both of which take a comparative historical view to explain penal harshness in the United States relative to our European peers. Gottschalk's work in particular provides a close look at how U.S. political developments over the nation's history created the conditions, or capacity, that allowed for our anomalously punitive policies (compared with peer nations), including both the overincarceration of citizens and the continued use of the death penalty. She also compares the political and legal structures, traditions, and norms that have developed in the United States with those in several European countries to demonstrate how fundamental differences in these arenas gave rise to distinct responses to demands for women's rights and victims' rights, for example, which began to be voiced during the 1970s. Thus, this work offers insights into how specificities of locale shape unique trajectories of penal developments and provides a window into how crime concerns and their resultant policies move and get reshaped across jurisdictional boundaries.

THE THEORETICAL AND EMPIRICAL APPROACH OF THIS BOOK

Thus, this project begins with the empirically grounded assumption that there are significant differences regionally and jurisdictionally in crime-control politics, policies, and practices and that these penal patterns result from a complex interplay of social, cultural, and political factors. Stuart Scheingold (1998: 860–61) has suggested that "understandings of crime differ from time to time, from place to place (both within and among states) and among different segments of society. [Therefore] the political and social construction of crime has revealing and unpredictable influences on the choice of crime control policies and vice versa." He goes on to remind us that "insofar as contexts are culturally specific . . . it follows that the linkage between the problems of advanced capitalism and crime control policy is more contingent and attenuated than the theorists of the new political criminology seem to believe" (Scheingold, 1998: 887–88). If the U.S. prison population explosion, and the attendant changes in prisoner demographics and quality of life behind bars, are partly related to underlying social/political/cultural factors, then, following Scheingold, we should expect to find differences in how various jurisdictions have responded to crime and reshaped their penal systems in ways that reflect the particularities of the region or locality in which they are situated. We should also expect to find that penal innovations and policy changes flow from place to place, while taking on unique features to fit within each locale, so this transfer process can reveal how and why penal change can be at once a national and local phenomenon.

In the following chapters, I offer a culturally specific examination of Arizona's transformations in an effort to uncover some of the answers that continue to elude us about how our federal and state governments could make such a massive investment of tax dollars to create the most extensive set of penal systems on the globe in a period of just several decades. I also make the case that the penal trends we have witnessed across the country over the past few decades appear to have roots in places like Arizona, where the punishment practices were not deeply entrenched in the ideals of rehabilitation.

In order to explore the complex interaction of the various contributory forces at work, I took an ideographic empirical approach to understanding the process of penal transformation through the case study of Arizona. I accessed and analyzed primary archival materials and secondary sources related to the development and growth of Arizona's penal system over the past 50 years and conducted in-depth interviews with key participants in Arizona's recent penal history. Using these materials, I then reconstructed much of the history of the Arizona Department of Corrections, including the penal conditions in the state before the department's formation in 1968 and the history of state legislative action on criminal sentencing and legislative changes to other criminal justice policies, including the patterns of penal funding. The materials also provided me with the means to assess levels of legislative, governor, interest group, and popular support for (or opposition to) various criminal justice initiatives and activities over time. In particular, I focus on the language that institutional, political, media-based, and public actors used to narratively construct the problems, crises, and solutions to the state's crime and punishment issues.

I use a conceptual framework that features the notion of local culture to understand both continuity and change over time in how the problems of criminal justice, particularly punishment, are dealt with, by examining the discourse and action of a range of constituencies. My use of culture is shaped by Swidler's (1986: 273) suggestion that culture can be thought of as "a 'toolkit' of symbols, stories, rituals, and worldviews, which people may use in varying configurations to solve different kinds of problems." For Swidler, this toolkit shapes strategies for tackling problems both by constructing the definitional parameters of those strategies and by ordering the plan of action. Culture, then, affects interests and action within the structural bounds of any given setting but does not do so in a monolithic manner. Rather, actors strategically use whatever cultural tools from that large and varied toolkit seem appropriate for a given situation or response-demand.

During periods of social transformation, culturally formed ideologies are more likely to reign, in that they provide "a highly articulated, self-conscious belief and ritual system, aspiring to offer a unified answer to problems of social action" (Swidler, 1986: 279). Ideological systems, then, emerge over contested cultural terrain and seek to dominate members' worldviews and assumptions. In the Arizona case, I reveal how political ideologies arose in response to social, cultural, and economic change, and how those ideologies, which had roots in long-standing historical traditions and cultural norms in the state, reshaped punishment policies and practices to provide a solution to penal "crises" that emerged in the state. The ideologies were articulated and shared by political actors, institutional managers, and the local media and consequently determined the trajectory of state action at several key moments in this history.

In this usage, culture is not simply an extraneous descriptive feature that merely adds a quality of uniqueness to a larger story of social structure, nor does it fully supplant structural explanations for social phenomena. Rather, cultural elements work to provide the frameworks of meaning and contours of acceptability within social and institutional structures, thus shaping the possibilities for action. With respect to punishment, the range of possible practices, including the degree of penal severity, is constrained by the reigning cultural norms and traditions at a given time and place. As David Garland (1990: 199) puts it, "penal practices are shaped by the symbolic grammar of cultural forms as well as by the more instrumental dynamics of social action, so that, in analysing punishment, we should look for patterns of cultural expression as well as logics of material interest or social control."

Although the book proceeds in a rather straight chronological narrative, a series of thematic threads about Arizona's cultural traditions and norms that shape how politics get done in the state weave through the timeline. As I elaborate in Chapter 1, the long-standing and broadly accepted cultural traditions that recur throughout the book include a political and popular distrust of government in general, and the federal government in particular; the valorization of small, fiscally conservative governance; a heightened distinction between "outsiders" and "Arizonans," especially at moments of conflict; and a relatively stable commitment to a philosophy of less eligibility, which holds that prison conditions should be more unpleasant than the living conditions experienced by the least fortunate free members of society.

In addition, the narrative includes recurring themes about how the state's most influential newspaper, the traditionally conservative *Arizona Republic*, shaped political and popular discourse and action on criminal justice issues. The paper became an active player in influencing outcomes of several major policy battles, including, most significantly, one over sentencing reform during the early 1990s. It also played an important cultural role in helping articulate the meanings of various social crises and the state response to them, including providing the linkages to (and reminders about) Arizona cultural traditions that were offered up as "answers" to the crises. For example, as the prison system underwent all kinds of crises and contestations during the 1970s and 1980s, the paper engaged in nostalgic constructions of the past when the prison was run by a stern disciplinarian who understood that punishment ought to be harsh.

Chapter 1 sets the stage for the case study by offering a broad-stroke history of Arizona as a social and political site during the late nineteenth through the mid-twentieth centuries, including its penal history. The state's early development shaped its political culture, which in turn shaped how punishment got, and gets, done in Arizona. In this chapter, I introduce two powerful players in the state's penal system before the Department of Corrections was established: Arizona State Prison Superintendent Frank Eyman, and his counterpart in the juvenile facility, Superintendent Steve Vukcevich. Both men mobilized penal strategies designed to maintain maximum authority and control over those within their institutions. This particular history reveals a penal character that challenges the widely held assumption about the hegemony of rehabilitation and illustrates a regionally specific style of penology that several western states share.

Chapter 2 examines the birth of the state's Department of Corrections, with a focus on how various state actors conceived of its goals and mission and the kinds of resistance to its development that were expressed in the early years. I illustrate how "enlightened" penal policy was imported into the state and how the attendant changes were received—politically, popularly, and institutionally. This chapter illuminates the complexities of such policy importation as the ideals and practices that prevailed in other locales were reshaped, and in some instances resisted, to fit within local cultural norms and expectations.

In Chapter 3, I describe a period of turmoil within the Arizona correctional enterprise when ideas about the nature of what the Department of Corrections should be doing entered into a state of chaos, not unlike what was happening in a number of other states. Relevant state and federal actors—the governor, legislators, criminal justice personnel, and the federal judiciary—all worked to resolve the crises that dominated this period and through such attempts tried to redefine the fundamental values and mission of the state's penal system. I examine these changes within the context of concurrent national turmoil over the meaning and mission of state punishment, and I describe how opening the system to outsiders, as had occurred at the formation of the department, facilitated other kinds of "border crossings" into the state's penal machinery, culminating in legal and political activism among prisoners and their advocates and massive federal intervention into the state's penal operations. I conclude by analyzing the factors that should have impeded the development of mass incarceration in Arizona, as well as those conditions that seemed to be necessary to allow for the imprisonment boom, which began to occur by the middle of the 1970s.

Chapters 4, 5, and 6 detail the rise of stability in the department during the 1980s through the ascension of a new harsh penal regime that continues into the twenty-first century. I explore several key features of this regime in these chapters: first, the regime is one that gave credence to local norms and history, through an explicit rejection of "outsider" expertise and intervention. Here, a model of what can be called tough-and-cheap, western-style penology was implemented throughout the state's correctional institutions and organizational arms. State actors explicitly looked back to their past, to the era of Warden Eyman and Superintendent Vukcevich, to find answers to the penal crisis that gripped the system.

This new ethos also played out in the courts, where the Department of Corrections, with the full support of the governor's office, proactively and successfully battled to dismantle a series of federal protections previously extended to Arizona inmates. Implicit in these chapters is my argument that the "success" of the new punitive period in Arizona that emerged during the mid-1980s, and which in many ways served as a prototype of postrehabilitative penology, is due to a number of local and national contingencies, from the fairly constant congruence over this period between the department administration, the governor, and the majority of the legislature about how punishment should be done in the state, to the massive flux in rationale for punishment that dominated the national penological and political scenes. The department was also able to fully transform itself into a bureaucracy that had no ties to the progressive ideals that had shaped other state penal systems because of its shallow roots as a state institution. The weight of institutional history pressed lightly, if at all, against the swing of the pendulum, and where it did, the lesson was one that espoused harshness and discipline rather than rehabilitation.

In Chapter 7, I both complicate and advance the current theoretical work about how and why the late modern penal transformations occurred in the United States by addressing multiple factors that operate locally, regionally, and nationally. I specifically address the role of state-level political structures and cultures; the role of regionalism in the rise and decline of rehabilitationalism, and the emergence of the new brand of punitiveness that has infused American criminal justice; the contributions and constraints of state and federal law in the transformation; the place of popular culture and local historical precedent; and the more global changes in social structures that appear to have reshaped punishment across the landscape.

I conclude the book by returning to Arizona, where the penal system is currently in a state of flux, brought on in part by partisan state politics and in larger part by unprecedented budget crises the state faces. This examination will be used as a jumping-off point to consider a final question about penal transformation: what are the outer limits to the growth of harsh penal policies and the attendant imprisonment explosion that we have witnessed over the past 35 years?

1 ARIZONA'S POLITICAL AND PENAL ROOTS

ARIZONA, THE 48TH STATE to enter the union, has developed quite recently and rapidly from a sparsely populated, predominantly rural land to one in which the population is now overwhelmingly urban. From 1950 to 2000 it was the second fastest growing state in the nation, trailing only Nevada (Berman, 1998; U.S. Department of Commerce, 2001). The population growth during that period has largely been concentrated in the major metropolitan areas in and around Phoenix and Tucson. The expansion of Phoenix alone, which is also one of the fastest growing cities in the country (*Economist*, 1999), has been phenomenal over the past 50 years. In 1940, the city had about 65,000 residents; in 2000, its population was 20 times larger, with more than 1.3 million residents within the city limits and 6 million in the greater metropolitan area. Phoenix has also developed into one of the core conservative political centers of the nation over that time.

Much of the recent growth is due to the influx of high-tech companies, such as Motorola and Intel, and the general pro-business and pro-growth environment of the city and state (Schmandt, 1995). Not surprisingly, the rate at which growth occurred in this state over the past half century created a number of immediate "crises" related to the rapid social change, including increased concerns about crime and the administration of criminal justice. People move in and out of the state fluidly, so the transient nature of the population has also contributed to the sense of crisis about various social conditions.

Yet although Arizona has undergone its most significant growth and change since the 1950s, its early cultural and political roots continue to influence governance in the state. Arizona began its life as a state after a long and bitter battle to shed its territorial status, which it held for almost 50 years. Much of the federal resistance to granting Arizona statehood had to do with a majority congressional view that the leading Arizona political figures were radicals who seemed to distrust government. Furthermore, the state was strongly conservative Democratic in its early political makeup, a reflection of the influx of Southerners into the territory during the 1800s, whereas Congress was predominantly Republican around the turn of the twentieth century when the quest for statehood heated up.

The legislative attempts at drawing up a state constitution that would satisfy the federal government while also reflecting Arizonans' political values contributed to the problem as well. The territory was wedded to a variety of direct democracy measures—including the availability of the referendum and initiative process and broad electorate recall powers, including of judges— and insisted on structural controls over elected officials, in part through the use of two-year terms for most offices. These provisions in the various drafts of the proposed constitution led some in Washington, D.C., to label Arizonans as anarchists, and President William H. Taft refused to approve statehood until at least the judicial recall provision was removed. By the end of 1911, Arizona voters agreed to that excision in order to obtain statehood, and two months later, in February 1912, President Taft officially proclaimed Arizona the 48th state. Before the year was out, however, in a show of direct democracy aimed at defying the meddling federal government, Arizona voters reinstated the judicial recall provision.

The political culture from the start, then, has been a blend of southern traditionalistic values imported with the territory's early settlers and a frontier perspective that values individualism, self-reliance, and self-governance. According to political scientist David Berman (1998), the state's political system into the 1950s looked like a traditional one-party (Democratic) southern state, complemented by a strong resistance to governmental "meddling" in daily life, especially by the federal government. This orientation in part accounts for the state's second-class treatment of minorities and the poor, in that the traditionalist culture promoted racial and class hierarchies, and the self-sufficient libertarian streak ensured little support for those who might need government assistance.

Latinos, and to a lesser degree Native Americans, have always been significant subpopulations in Arizona, but their ability to benefit politically from the populist government was attenuated, at best, throughout the twentieth century.

African Americans have consistently constituted only about 2 percent to 3 percent of the population from statehood to the present, yet they, too, have been subject to widespread discrimination. English literacy tests were used into the 1960s to suppress voter registration and participation among minority populations; racial segregation in public schools was required by law until 1951 and then made optional until it was constitutionally prohibited in 1954; and segregation in restaurants, pools, and other such private/public spaces was common throughout the state well into the 1960s. Furthermore, the "frontier" outlook favoring individual self-reliance contributed to the development of social policies that did little to aid those in the lower strata, so state social services and welfare spending has consistently been well below the national average. The funding structure of elementary and secondary schools ensured that schools in wealthy districts had the most resources and those in the poorest districts had the fewest until the state supreme court imposed changes during the late 1990s. Labor generally has also been disadvantaged, given the state's 1946 adoption of a "right-to-work" law that outlawed closed union shops and discouraged labor organizing.

The political system began to open up during the 1950s largely because of the postwar inmigration of predominantly Republican Midwesterners who settled in large numbers around Phoenix. Soon after, there was a smaller but significant influx of more liberal Democrats who tended to settle around Tucson. Although the "native," more conservative rural-based Democrats and Republicans agreed on a number of issues related to curtailing labor rights, limiting federal intervention, and generally opposing civil rights and welfare, the new urban Republicans pushed an agenda of economic development and modernization for the state, a move that helped bring about the establishment of the Department of Corrections in 1968, which many rural Democrats opposed. The new liberal Democrats were at odds with both of the other groups on social justice issues, but along with the new Republicans, they supported infrastructural growth, modernization, and governmental reform.

By the 1960s, even though the state and its political systems were undergoing rapid changes, the political ethos had several enduring features that can be called "Arizonan" in character and that persist in the state to this day. First, there has been a consistent overriding sentiment across Arizona's populace of distrusting government, state or federal. This distrust includes a moderate disdain for expansive state bureaucratization and agency building. Second, the values of individualism and self-reliance continue to play out in the political culture such that governmental regulation of the social and economic spheres is viewed skeptically, spending on social welfare is done only begrudgingly, and most importantly, fiscal frugality is the guiding principle for all government endeavors. Although many state governments espouse fiscal temperance as an operational principle, here it is an explicit requirement, so successful appropriations requests are generally framed in language that foremost emphasizes the long-term savings that might be gained through a given expenditure, and at the very least, that demonstrates how the budget is as cost-effective as possible.

Coupled with this is a reluctance of the polity to pay for governmental services through traditional income tax, so the state's budget base disproportionately relies on a regressive sales tax funding scheme that disguises the cost of governing for the taxpayers of the state.[1] Finally, Arizona is a state that, politically speaking, has historically endorsed the concept of less eligibility and stern punishment in dealing with wrongdoers. Thus, criminal offenders have generally garnered no sympathy from legislators or the justice system, and there has been little concern with their welfare.

This political ethos first became widely known at the national level with the rise of Barry Goldwater's political career. Although he first gained success as a Republican during the Democratic reign in the state when he was elected a U.S. senator in 1952, his political philosophy reflected the Arizona blend of traditionalist values and libertarianism. His political visibility skyrocketed in 1964 when he ran for and won the Republican Party nomination for president after a divisive primary battle with the more liberal New York governor Nelson Rockefeller. At the time, Goldwater was considered an extremist who was out of touch with American values by many, even within the Republican Party. Yet his outlook, which was seen as so radical in many parts of the nation, was quite mainstream for Arizona. More importantly, his rise in political power has been credited with catalyzing the New Right that has since reshaped U.S. political life (McGirr, 2001). Among the core messages in Goldwater's unsuccessful presidential campaign was one that lauded law and order, particularly in response to civil unrest. This message stayed alive even after his defeat and was reshaped by Sunbelt politicians such as Richard Nixon and Ronald Reagan during their presidential campaigns (McGirr, 2001).

ARIZONA-STYLE PUNISHMENT

This political culture has clearly shaped a number of governmental functions into the present, including the state's response to crime, criminal offenders, and the problem of justice. Not only do state politics, including state and local partisan politics, directly affect the contours of the penal system, but the underlying political cultural values described above run through the state's penal history.

Up until the creation of the Arizona Department of Corrections in 1968, the few penal functions that existed in the state operated independently of each other and generally with little organizational or bureaucratic oversight. Thus, each institution and organization had considerable autonomy, and internal operations were well insulated from outside scrutiny. Juvenile institutional placements and parole were governed by the Board of Directors of State Institutions for Juveniles, a five-member lay board appointed by the governor; however, each state-run and contracted juvenile institution operated autonomously, creating its own internal rules and determining release dates for its charges. Adult incarceration was the sole purview of the superintendent/warden of the lone state prison in Florence; adult parole release was overseen by a three-person part-time board (the board was increased to five members in the mid-1960s); and parole supervision was a subsidiary operation of that board, inadequately funded to do much supervision of parolees and run by a director who also worked as a parole officer.

Perhaps the most detailed picture of the pre–corrections department, mid-twentieth-century penal "system" in Arizona comes from a 1958 published evaluation titled *Correctional Services in Arizona*, which was commissioned by the Arizona Legislative Council and conducted by the National Probation and Parole Association, the predecessor to the National Council on Crime and Delinquency (National Probation and Parole Association, 1958). The evaluation studied five aspects of Arizona corrections, broadly defined: policing of juveniles at the local level, probation services in the state, the state Industrial School for boys and the largest contracted school for delinquent girls, the adult state prison, and the adult parole system. The evaluation pointed out the disconnection among these services and institutions, rendering the state without a unified system of corrections and without a means for unified planning.

It also determined that several penal options were underutilized, in particular, county-level probation for juveniles and adults and parole release for adult offenders. Many of those in state institutions, the report suggested, should more appropriately be on county-level probation supervision, but the limited number of probation officers, low levels of training and professionalization, and inadequate resources for local supervision needs across the state's counties pushed offenders into state facilities. Once there, according

to the report, disproportionately few (compared with other states) were released on parole before their sentences expired. This created two problems
in the view of the evaluators: it increased the chance for failure upon release
when offenders were not supervised, and it cost the state considerable money
because it is much more expensive to incarcerate rather than provide community supervision. Although judges had broad discretion in sentencing felony
offenders—the state's penal code allowed judges to set any range of minimum
and maximum sentences under the indeterminate sentencing statutes that
had existed since statehood—prison sentences were often handed out in cases
that would otherwise be more suitable for local options because of the limited
resources at the county level.

Again the evaluation pointed out the antiquated structure of parole release
and supervision in the state; inadequate funding of parole, which required
the three parole officers who supervised parolees across the entire state to
manage caseloads nearly three times the recommended load; and the lack of
professionalization and training of the staff, especially in terms of "modern"
correctional techniques. In particular, the evaluators noted the absence of a
rehabilitative edge to the state's community corrections philosophy and practices. Probation, not only underused for nonserious offenders, offered little
support to probationers that would aim to reduce the risk of recidivism. Similarly, the parole supervision services in the state were so inadequate that the
agents refused to do their one "rehabilitative" duty—to help their parolees
find a job—because they felt if they helped one parolee, everyone else on their
caseload would clamor for such assistance. This style of parole supervision
was institutionalized even further when a retired agent of the Federal Bureau
of Investigation, William Drew, was appointed in 1966 as executive director
of the state Board of Pardons and Paroles. Perhaps as a consequence of his
law enforcement background, Drew made parole revocations a priority for
supervision officers and even set quotas for minimum numbers of revocations
per parole officer. Consequently, parole supervision functioned more like law
enforcement, where agents were encouraged to put their parolees under surveillance, to see whether they could be caught violating parole, rather than
helping them adjust to life outside prison.

The sections of the report that dealt with the state's juvenile and adult institutions similarly emphasized how antiquated, underfunded, and unregulated
they were. Furthermore, the report pointedly noted that none of the penal institutions or other correctional agencies effectively engaged in rehabilitation,

and little or no psychological or psychiatric services were available throughout the system. Thus, the evaluators' major recommendation to the legislative council was to form a Board and Department of Corrections to coordinate the state and local correctional activities and to introduce some needed but currently nonexistent services to the state. In the recommenders' words, "a scientific rather than archaic approach is required" by the state to deal with the growing offender population and its attendant challenges (National Probation and Parole Association, 1958: 154).

In its appendix, the evaluation diagrammed a model structure for this board/department, which would directly oversee juvenile and adult state institutions, state-run penal camps, local jails, and juvenile and adult parole supervision services. It would also be responsible for coordinating with the criminal and juvenile courts and with a reorganized, professionalized Board of Pardons and Paroles, which would oversee only release decisions. It would modernize the system and ideally adopt a rehabilitative philosophy in all of its operations. This model became the blueprint for the new department formed a decade later.

JUVENILE "CORRECTIONS," 1912–68

The state Industrial School at Fort Grant, which had been in operation since statehood was achieved, was the only state-run facility for juveniles until 1967 when the Arizona Youth Center opened. The institution, originally named the State Industrial School for Wayward Boys and Girls, opened in 1912, replacing a perennially troubled industrial school at Benson that had been in operation since 1901. The new school's location was established when the federal government turned a shuttered territorial military post, Fort Grant, over to the state in conjunction with granting statehood to Arizona. This site was in a geographically isolated, rural area of eastern Arizona that was nearly a four-hour drive from Phoenix and was accessible only by an unpaved road. Girls were housed in the Fort Grant Industrial School into the 1930s and then briefly moved to another state-run site, but from the late 1930s until 1972, they were sent to private, mainly religious-based contracted facilities such as the Catholic Good Shepherd School for Girls in Phoenix.

Leadership at Fort Grant was, as at the adult prison, the product of political patronage, so the institution underwent numerous superintendent turnovers and a series of scandals during its existence. The institution relied on a generous definition of "reasonable corporal punishment" to maintain order, and it offered very little to the wards in terms of programs and services for rehabilitation. Because of its isolation, and because of the structural limitations of state oversight at the time, internal operations at Fort Grant were functionally unregulated throughout its history, and it quickly developed into a brutal institution where wards were forced to work in physically demanding jobs under inhumane conditions, were severely beaten, were shot at, and were subjected to harsh isolation as punishment. It became known throughout the state as a "desert Devil's Island" for wayward Arizona youths (Fort Grant Centennial, 1972: 31).

By the early 1950s, these conditions made national headlines, and the publicity helped to finally prompt reform at the institution. In 1952, *Time* magazine (*Time*, 1952) picked up a story of several former residents who went to a juvenile judge in Phoenix to tell their experience of the cruelty that they had encountered at Fort Grant. The judge's investigation confirmed that boys were regularly subjected to severe whippings, blackjackings, assaults, and other extreme forms of physical punishment with little provocation. The FBI launched an investigation into the conditions, and in the end, the superintendent in charge at the time was forced out. In 1953, a politically connected rural Democrat from the area, Steve Vukcevich, was appointed superintendent to clean up the operations, and he remained in that position for the next 20 years.

Although Vukcevich got rid of the employees involved in the publicized brutalities, oversaw construction of new educational and vocational facilities, and introduced more programs for the boys, he maintained the corporal punishment policy (but applied it with considerably more restraint). He also had to deal with a rapidly growing resident population, which swelled from 85 boys when he arrived in 1953 to 261 by 1958 and which necessitated an operational emphasis on discipline and control rather than on individualized attention and rehabilitation. To that end, he enforced a paramilitary-style discipline routine that included mandatory participation in drills, a strict uniform and grooming code, and a code of conduct that required residents to respond to superiors with military-style respect. Misbehavior resulted in "swats," the euphemism for whippings administered with a razor strap; fines levied against the boys; and sentences of solitary confinement coupled with a "low-calorie diet" of a bowl of cereal in the morning and a baloney sandwich at night. His changes to the regime, then, really were a matter of added restraint in the use of discipline rather than a wholesale reform of philosophy and practices.

Although Vukcevich increased the level of professionalism among staff, no mental health workers or other clinicians were employed or on contract at the facility until well into the 1960s. Institutional documents from this period make little mention of the concept of rehabilitation when describing the goals of Fort Grant; rather, the focus was primarily on instilling discipline in residents and "retraining" the youth through work, school, mandatory religious training, and military activities. Almost two-thirds of the residents participated in primary or secondary school or vocational training programs; the remaining group either worked at low-level maintenance and service jobs on-site or were hired out as live-in ranch hands to area ranches, for which the school received up to $2.00 a day and the boys received room and board at their assigned ranches in exchange for their labor.

In his "1958–1959 Annual Report to the Board of Directors of State Institutions for Juveniles," Vukcevich highlighted the symbiotic goals of custody and discipline that undergirded the Fort Grant program, suggesting that "custody without discipline would be worthless," yet discipline would be hard to achieve without "firm enforcement of custodial features" (Vukcevich, 1959: 5). So discipline, as articulated by Vukcevich, was a meld of training and obedience enforcement, reinforced when necessary by punishment, which is a component of custody:

> [Discipline] is the training of mind and character; it is a conditioning process necessary for order and obedience. Many of the boys who reach us are sent here because they . . . did not obey their parents, the law, or the conditions of their probation or placement. Discipline should not be construed as punishment as it is a part of the treatment training process. Punishment is related to the custody part of our program as no one likes to be confined no matter how good the service is. Discipline is merely obedience to rules and regulations. (Vukcevich, 1959: 6)

The 1958 evaluation of the Industrial School urged the state to provide funds for psychological and mental health staff, increase the staffing generally, reduce overcrowding, fully eliminate the use of corporal punishment, and either eliminate military disciplinary activities or make them voluntary and limited to certain settings (National Probation and Parole Association, 1958). Despite these recommendations, the corporal punishment policy was maintained until 1969 when the newly formed Department of Corrections, which took over governance of all state juvenile placement and parole services, changed the institutional policy and banned the practice of razor-strap whippings for discipline. The military style of the school also remained until the institution was converted in the early 1970s to an adult facility.

The 1958 evaluation further recommended that the state invest in a facility for girls, rather than contract out those services to the patchwork of private placements. The state had relied on a hodgepodge of private and religious "homes" and "schools" since the girls' school at Randolph was closed in 1938, yet this practice became increasingly problematic as the number and diversity of referred girls grew over time. The evaluators were particularly concerned about the religious nature of the primary placement used by the state—the Good Shepherd School for Girls—in that it did not seem appropriate for non-Catholic girls. These concerns were reiterated in a later report, issued by a 1967 legislative task force—the Joint Study Committee on Juvenile Institutions—which lamented the problem of oversight since girls were placed in all kinds of contracted settings where the board could not ensure consistent care, treatment, and training (Joint Study Committee on Juvenile Institutions, 1968). Nonetheless, the state's interest in investing in girls' facilities was even less than it was in funding and improving the boys' side. Perhaps because of the small number of girls within the system, this problem was not viewed as pressing enough for the building of a state-run facility to be seriously considered until several years after the state established the Department of Corrections, which subsumed the duties and role of the Board of Directors of State Institutions for Juveniles.

THE ADULT SYSTEM, 1876–1968

Before the Department of Corrections was established in 1968, only one adult prison was functioning at any given time in Arizona: first the Yuma Territorial Prison, which opened in 1876 and closed in 1909, and then the state prison, built in Florence in 1908 to replace the Yuma prison. In an important symbolic way, the short-lived Yuma prison set the tone for the ethos that has shaped much of Arizona's penal practices across its history. Built in a desert region of southwestern Arizona where summer temperatures rival those of Death Valley for hottest in the nation, this infamous prison in some ways functions as an historical cartoon. It has been mythologized in western films and novels as a place so harsh that no prisoner ever escaped alive and where misbehaving prisoners were subjected to the ball and chain and to stints of isolation in the notoriously bleak "Snake Den" dungeon, which was a stark, empty hole of a cell that was dug into the stony ground and covered with solid iron doors designed to block light and prevent fresh air from circulating. The Yuma Territorial Prison opened in the same year as Zebulon Brockway oversaw the opening of the revolutionary "reformatory," Elmira, in New York, yet it was wholly untouched by the reformatory movement that was spreading through the Northeast and Midwest. Although the territorial prison operated for only 33 years and was closed before Arizona achieved statehood, more popular and scholarly attention has been focused on it than on the entire subsequent penal history of the state.

The prison's existence appears to have shaped future penal practices in the state in several ways. First, its original construction set a precedent that continues to some degree today in that the prison was entirely built by its intended residents. The 15 territorial prisoners who were the first to be housed in the new facility lived in tents on the site over the five months it took to construct the original cells and administration quarters (Jeffrey, 1969). In fact, the territorial legislature enacted legislation that inmate labor be used whenever feasible for all prison construction projects (Knepper, 1990). This practice of extensively relying on inmates to help build and improve the facilities to which they are to be confined (including the construction and remodeling of the death house where executions take place) has continued to today.

The use of inmate labor for prison construction is not unique and indeed seems to be a regional phenomenon in the Southwest (Johnson, 1997), but the practice has, from the start, been explicitly used in Arizona as a selling point to the tight-fisted legislature and the tax-averse public as a cost-saving method, and as such it clearly communicates the broader political theme of fiscal frugality. Press coverage of construction projects has, over the years, emphasized the cost savings provided by inmate labor, thus communicating an imperative political message that no wasteful spending is going on.

Second, the Yuma prison continues to stand, memorialized by the state parks department, as a literal and figurative landmark of frontier-style justice and is visited by tourists from around the world. The Yuma Territorial Prison even lives on, in part, at the Florence State Prison that succeeded it. The prisoners consigned to build the new prison moved a set of the Yuma prison's heavy iron gates, as well as the cell bars and gallows equipment, across the desert to Florence and installed them within the new facility where they continue to stand.[2] And like its predecessor, the prison that opened at Florence in 1908 was built by inmates who again lived in tents on the grounds during construction. Although the new prison did not have a dungeon, the name of Yuma's dark solitary cell also continued on at Florence. The underground solitary confinement cells there were referred to by prisoners as "Snakes" into the 1960s, when they were replaced by new solitary units (Jeffrey, 1969).

Whereas the Yuma prison set a particular tone for Arizona's punishment style, the Florence prison took on a wider and more enduring role in the state's penal operations. It remained the only adult institution to be built in Arizona until 70 years later when a medium-security facility dedicated to male prisoners aged 18 to 25 opened near Tucson in 1979.[3] The Florence prison housed both men and women—in separate buildings but on the same grounds—until 1962 when a women's division was built across the road from the men's prison (Arizona Advisory Committee, 1974). Up until then, women had been housed in overcrowded, substandard facilities and were offered almost no work or rehabilitative opportunities.

The quality of this institution's practices and policies before the formation of the Department of Corrections also became both a backdrop for and a counterpoint to the department's development. The Florence prison represented, first, exactly what needed to be reformed and modernized through the

Exterior of Arizona State Prison at Florence, 1954. Courtesy of Arizona State Library, Archives and Public Records, History and Archives Division, Phoenix, No. 97-4827.jpg.

Interior of original Arizona State Prison cell block, 1920s. Courtesy of Arizona State Library, Archives and Public Records, History and Archives Division, Phoenix, No. 97-4746.jpg.

creation of the department and subsequent importation of correctional expertise. Later, as the promise of such reformative efforts faded, political actors and local media, heralding local and regional history and norms, nostalgically reconstructed the old Florence prison as an appropriately harsh disciplinary institution that could serve as an exemplary model for postrehabilitative corrections in the state.

The Florence prison was shaped by both the southern and the midwestern influences of the state's general population and political roots, but at the same time, its institutional history has some rather unique Arizonan and regionally specific features. For instance, the emphasis on agricultural production from its inception had much in common with southern states, and by the mid-1950s, the facility began to take on a feel of the Illinois-style "big house" prison (Jacobs, 1977), albeit on a smaller scale.[4] In a symbolic rejection of other states' practices, though, the institution, from the start, eschewed the "penitentiary" label (and the "reformatory" label) that many states, including most southern ones, used to describe their penal institutions and systems. In Arizona, both the territorial and state institutions were called "prisons" and the custodial staff members were "guards"—one explicit signal that there was little philosophical investment in the progressive reformative project of penology.

In many ways, the prison at Florence was a world unto itself all the way into the 1960s, given its relative geographic isolation within the state, the state's relative political and cultural isolation from the rest of the nation, and the lack of bureaucratic oversight within the organizational structure of the state government. During the first seven years of statehood, the prison was nominally overseen by the Board of Control (at least they annually reported on the prison); however, after that the prison was completely autonomous and free of agency oversight, outside of the governor's office. And from territorial times on, the governor appointed the prison superintendent (warden), with no organizational filter to guide the selection process, so the superintendent was functionally the highest level penal administrator in the state, answering to no one but the governor, until the formation of the Department of Corrections in 1968.

At the same time, because of this structure, institutional leadership was very much the product of patronage and was subject to change with every new administration. No warden could count on being in the position long enough to have much effect, and institutional policies, procedures, and even lowest level personnel were constantly in flux, as leadership changed 23 times from its 1908 opening until 1955 when Superintendent Frank Eyman was appointed.

Guards in new uniforms on prison steps, 1950s. Courtesy of Arizona State Library, Archives and Public Records, History and Archives Division, Phoenix, No. 97-4746.jpg.

The instability was exacerbated by the fact that, until 1968, governors were elected every two years in Arizona. The 1958 report conducted by the National Probation and Parole Association characterized the long-term situation at Florence as follows:

> It is well known that the Arizona State Prison has for many years been a football of politics. With each change of Governors, the Warden of the Prison was also subject to change, as well as many employees being dismissed. Employment depended upon political affiliations and no one was able to get a job at the prison unless he knew the right people. As a result, there was no program, no one was concerned about the prison or its inmates to any degree, and it was allowed to sink deeper and deeper into a morass of poor management, brutal treatment, human neglect, and human waste. These past administrations and the general public have cared little about the program, and each new Warden was usually instructed to go down and run the place "just so you don't have trouble." (National Probation and Parole Association, 1958: 115)

Well into the 1950s, the prison had few rehabilitative, vocational, or recreational programs, except for an informal education system that employed no outside teachers and was primarily administered by the inmates themselves. One of the earlier "industries" was the license plate factory, which opened in 1947 and initially employed only 24 inmates. It was touted mainly for its cost-saving benefits, in that it was expected to save $25,000 annually for the cost of plates. The degree and tenor of discipline vacillated over the years between relatively light on rules and restrictions to a strict disciplinary model, depending on who was in charge (Johnson, 1997), but the larger problem was that prisoners were mainly warehoused in overcrowded and rundown facilities with little to do day in and day out, and there was no constituency within the state that cared to make any changes for the better. The prison ran out of room for housing inmates and for other necessary functions within two decades of opening, yet the legislature was generally unwilling to appropriate the funding needed to adequately upgrade and expand the facilities (Johnson, 1997).

Exacerbating the lack of sympathy from the outside, the prison administration was the subject of several major scandals, from superintendents being accused of misappropriating operating funds to running the prison while drunk, and the prison had relatively frequent inmate strikes and riots (Johnson, 1997; Meadows interview, 2002; National Probation and Parole Association, 1958). By 1953, a state committee on health and sanitation evaluated the conditions of the prison and reported to the governor that the severe overcrowding and lack of facility upkeep had created major health hazards at the prison, including serious problems with pest control, sewage, and sanitation (Special Committee on Health and Sanitation, 1953).

In 1955, the situation began to change. When another riot broke out at the prison, then–Pima County sheriff Frank Eyman was called in to deal with the uprising. Sheriff Eyman was a well-known "lawman" in the region who had spent 25 years in law enforcement in Tucson after an earlier military career. He was especially revered, even to his death, for his 1934 capture of infamous bank robber John Dillinger in Tucson. As a result of Eyman's apparent effectiveness in handling the prison riot situation, he was asked to take over as superintendent of the prison by then-governor Ernest McFarland. Before Eyman agreed to take the job, he asked for a six-year contract so that he could be ensured of some longevity in the position even if the governorship changed (National Probation and Parole Association, 1958). Eyman was extended such a contract and in January 1955 began what would become a 17-year career as head of the Arizona State Prison.

At the time of Eyman's arrival, the prison housed around 1,000 inmates, well over its capacity, and no system was in place for classifying or separating inmates by age, seriousness of offense, conduct, or other criteria. Nor were

Arizona State Prison Superintendent Frank Eyman, date not available. Courtesy of the Arizona Department of Corrections.

there adequate facilities to do so: the two barely functioning cell blocks held around 550 inmates, and makeshift dormitories that had been shoddily constructed or converted from storage areas over the years held the overflow. The physical plant was filthy, in disrepair, and, in Eyman's view, another disaster waiting to happen. He responded to the situation on two fronts: by initiating a program of improvement aimed at the physical plant itself and by cleaning up the prison's occupants through a strict disciplinary regime. These two goals were intertwined in his view: both were in dire need of intervention, and both could benefit from an infusion of discipline, cleanliness, and order.

Eyman was successful at transforming both, despite woefully inadequate resources. The legislature was unwilling to make major investments in the prison, and even obtaining small amounts of capital improvement money was work. Nonetheless, the inmate population grew every year, and the buildings showed more and more signs of distress, so Eyman forged ahead with his program of reform. During the first three years of his administration, he was able to stretch small amounts of funding to build a new laundry, post office, warehouse, dairy, barn, and corrals by relying entirely on inmate labor for design and construction and using prison-produced building materials (mainly adobe bricks and concrete blocks). What he considered to be one of his major accomplishments up to this point was the construction of a large recreational field, designed and built by prisoner labor, that he touted in several annual reports as "one of the finest in the nation" and where inmates could participate in the various sports of the "recreational therapy" program (Eyman, 1958, 1960).

In 1958, the legislature finally appropriated just enough funds to begin building a new maximum-security cell block (which the prison did not have at this point), with the requirement that inmates design and build it. This became an issue over which Eyman was willing to fight. In his 1958 annual report to Governor McFarland, he pointed out that the badly needed construction was delayed while awaiting an opinion from the attorney general on whether he could hire an outside architect, and he noted his serious apprehension about having to build the unit with prison labor alone. In the report, he asked "the proper authorities to strongly consider the contracting of any major construction work" on this job (Eyman, 1958: 4) and warned of the high risk of sabotage and vandalism with inmate laborers doing all of the work. He suggested that a proposed dormitory, for which he was also seeking funds, was entirely appropriate as an inmate construction job, then reiterated his concerns regarding the maximum-security unit.

By the early 1960s, Eyman had been able to secure just enough funding from the legislature and marshal a highly efficient inmate workforce to have completely renovated almost all of the facilities within the prison as well as construct a new women's division, including dormitories and corollary facilities; the new maximum-security cell block; new dormitories for trusties and for first-time youthful offenders; a new school building; and a host of other buildings. In 1963, as the prison population (at more than 1,700 inmates) was growing nearly in proportion to the state's rapid growth in general population, Eyman was able to obtain further funding for a fourth cell block that would also contain a new high-security segregation unit. The legislature even allowed him to put this project out to commercial bid, although its appropriation did not even cover the lowest bid received. With some creativity, he stretched that appropriation to pay for demolishing one of the original cell blocks and building the new unit on the site.

As to his program for human improvement within the prison, Eyman immediately implemented his vision of what proper life behind bars should look like, one that emphasized rigid, almost military-style discipline (Meadows interview, 2002). So while many penal institutions across the nation were fully implementing "scientific" therapeutic programs that were optimistically viewed as the solution to individual offenders' root problems (therefore the problem of crime), Eyman adopted a model similar in style to the penal regimen at Stateville Penitentiary in Illinois, as shaped by its authoritarian boss Warden Joseph Ragen (Jacobs, 1977).[5] In Eyman's prison he was boss, his staff were guards rather than correctional officers, and the residents were inmates known by their inmate number rather than their names.

Shortly after he took over at the prison, Eyman wrote and published a detailed "Inmate Rule Book" that each inmate was given on arrival. Inmates were required to hang the rule book inside their cells for quick access during their incarceration. Eyman's disciplinary program began upon an inmate's arrival, where he employed classic status-degrading, identity-eroding indoctrination rituals to introduce inmates to prison life. He reported in his 1960 and 1962 biannual reports how, on arrival, the inmate "is issued a register number which is stamped indelibly on his clothing. From that moment on, and until the date of his release, his number takes precedence over his name and at all times he is referred to as inmate number ____." (Eyman, 1962: 2). Incoming inmates were then given a military-style haircut and handed the rule book, which was to guide their behavior at all times.

According to his secretary, Della Meadows, who had worked at the prison since 1948, Eyman initiated detailed policies on dress and grooming for inmates and employees alike and was the first warden to require a set uniform for officers and inmates in the prison. Meadows said that "he was bound and determined that they were going to follow [his] regulations or be punished." Eyman could not tolerate "sloth" so expected inmates to be well groomed, upright in posture, respectful when speaking to staff, and engaged in wholesome activities, rather than "lounging against a wall or lying around in the grass" (Meadows interview, 2002).

His authoritarian reputation was convincingly solidified in 1958 in response to a major breakout attempt and uprising at the prison during which four guards were taken hostage. Eyman arrived at the prison, gun in hand, and told the inmates, "if you SOBs even so much as scratch my men, I'll kill all of you" (*Arizona Republic*, 1984). In a show of sincerity, he fired four gunshots into the air and instructed the remaining guards to take back the prison. The guards engaged in a gun battle with the inmates involved in the incident and quelled the uprising; one inmate was critically injured, but none of the guards was hurt. Eyman then welded each prisoner into his cell, as the locks had been broken during the riot, where he left them, stripped naked with only a blanket each, for several days. He justified this act to the press by saying that the inmates "had to learn to behave" and needed to realize that as prisoners in his institution, they didn't have any rights (*Arizona Daily Star*, 1958; *Arizona Republic*, 1958).

Eyman's day-to-day disciplinary regime consisted of work for able inmates, remedial education for those who needed it, and an extensive sports and recreational program. Psychiatric and clinical interventions were nowhere to be found in his program plan or within the prison. There was no psychiatrist, psychologist, or other clinical professional on staff or on contract until the late 1960s, and into the mid-1960s, the need for such personnel within the prison did not even appear to be an issue. Indeed, he viewed inmates with psychological problems as an aberrational subgroup that needed to be removed from the prison entirely. In his 1958–60 biannual report submitted to Governor Paul Fannin, he urged the state to build a "Maximum Security Mental Ward" for mentally ill inmates on the grounds of the Arizona State Hospital in Phoenix to "minister to this type of inmate" (Eyman, 1960: 1). In the absence of such a facility, his response was to keep constant surveillance of the mentally ill and the "moral perverts" within his institution, and he used segregated lockdown for this subpopulation as a major means of control.

For the rest of the inmates, Eyman's version of the therapeutic model of corrections, at best, involved what he called "recreational therapy," which appeared to be the program that made him most proud. He dedicated an entire subsection of many of his annual and biannual reports to this endeavor and included numerous photographs to illustrate the activities and benefits of the recreational therapy program. Within this program, the prison fielded sports teams in the "major sports," including football, baseball, basketball, boxing, and wrestling, that successfully competed (always on home turf) with outside community teams. The program also included activities such as softball, shuffleboard, and volleyball for "elderly and nonathletic inmates" (Eyman, 1960: 7). Eyman believed that this program promoted socially acceptable recreation habits, "moral stamina," and good health habits and taught the value of teamwork and good sportsmanship to inmates (Eyman, 1958; Eyman, 1960). He also developed an extensive music program and was particularly proud of his marching band.

On the educational front, following the recommendation of the 1958 National Probation and Parole Association's evaluation, which highlighted the serious need for educational facilities and trained teachers to deal with the

Rehabilitation — Prison Concert and Marching Band

Prison marching band as "rehabilitation," early 1960s. From *Bi-annual Report: Arizona State Prison, July 1, 1960–June 30, 1962.*

large proportion of undereducated and uneducated inmates, Eyman was able to hire an outside teacher in 1962. The elementary school program, for inmates who needed first- through sixth-grade education, began in the fall of that year after the state superintendent of public education branded Arizona's prison educational and rehabilitation program to be at the bottom of the scale nationally. Eyman had a hard time retaining qualified teachers given the position's low pay, so he ended up relying on inmate teachers off and on throughout his tenure. He completed construction on the inmate-built education building in 1964, "at no cost to the state," according to Eyman. This facility also functioned as a dental lab two weeks out of each year, where the state dental board held its licensing exams for new dentists, using inmates who received "dental work at no cost" as their test subjects (Cavanaugh, 1964: 41).

The "industries" program had the broadest impact on inmate life. When Eyman arrived, the majority of inmates, outside of trusties and those who worked in low-status kitchen and janitorial jobs, had no job assignments or other activities to fill their days. But between the cleanup and renovation work, the construction jobs, the stepped-up farm production, and the development and expansion of a set of small industries, by 1962, Eyman boasted to a newspaper reporter that only 14 of the 1,600 or so inmates "loafed" during the day, and those were the inmates held in segregation (Fifer, 1962). Inmates received two-for-one good time credit for working, so the incentive to work was high even without Eyman's authoritarian insistence on participation.

The result of the work program was that the prison operated as an efficient, nearly completely self-contained village where almost everything needed for daily life was created and manufactured within. There were four separate "ranches" on 1,000 acres of prison land that produced all the food used at the prison: the dairy products came from the dairy cows' milk; baked goods were made from the wheat grown and milled on-site; all the livestock feed came from the variety of grains grown; all meat served came from the cattle, hogs, chickens, and turkeys raised on-site; eggs were produced at the poultry farm; and all vegetables and fruits used were grown in the fields. Even the dog food for the prison's search dogs was manufactured from food scraps there. The prison also operated a cannery so that a variety of food products could be preserved for year-round use, with the surplus sold to other state institutions. Cotton was grown in the fields, so all inmate clothing, from underwear to outerwear, was fashioned from that crop, which was processed and woven at the prison's knitting mill.

Inmates walking to work in fields with guard escorts, early 1960s. From *Bi-annual Report: Arizona State Prison, July 1, 1960–June 30, 1962.*

Most construction materials for the numerous building projects were also manufactured on-site, and Eyman created a building materials salvage yard where reusable construction materials recovered from construction demolitions were recycled and stocked for future projects. The printing shop produced all stationery, forms, and other such products used at the institution. An inmate newspaper was also printed there. By the mid-1960s, the prison added a cabinetry shop, upholstery shop, auto body shop, and shoe repair shop. The final industry in which inmates worked was the traditional prison tag plant, where they manufactured street signs and license plates for the state.

Inmates were not paid for their work. One of the few sanctioned ways to make money behind bars was to sell handmade crafts at the prison craft store, so those inmates with the skills to make such goods were able to earn some spending money sporadically. The only other way inmates could legitimately earn money was by participating in the "bleeding program," overseen by the part-time prison doctor, through which inmates were allowed to donate one pint of blood plasma once every six to eight weeks for $5.00, paid by various laboratories that contracted with the prison to collect the plasma. The maximum donation frequency was increased to once weekly in 1966, allowing participants to earn more money. In 1965, Cutter Laboratories, a company that contracted with the prison to buy blood from prisoners, offered to donate a 30-bed hospital addition to the prison in order to institutionalize the relationship, an offer that both Eyman and Governor Samuel Goddard supported (Goddard, 1966a). By 1967, the facility was built, and nearly all eligible prisoners participated in the bleeding program.

The prison physician also oversaw several research programs for which inmates could volunteer as human subjects, but it does not appear they were paid for this. So, for instance, five inmates in 1959 were injected with hepatitis B virus for a study aimed at developing a hepatitis vaccination. In the 1960–62 biannual report, the prison physician reported that all five contracted the disease and, through their "courageous" contribution to medical science, helped the researchers understand the disease. Inmates also volunteered for studies conducted by pharmaceutical companies for experimental treatment of gastric illnesses and sunburn treatments, and during the 1960s and 1970s, dozens of inmates volunteered to be subjects in studies on sun lotion effectiveness sponsored by Harvard University.

During the first five or so years of his tenure, Eyman did not frame the value of these programs in terms of their rehabilitative potential. But by the early

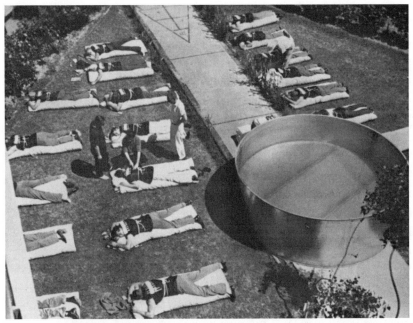

Inmates participating in a Harvard University study on prison lawn, late 1960s. From *Arizona State Prison Annual Report, 1969–70.*

1960s, he began to adopt some quasi-rehabilitative language that almost foreshadows the "self-responsibilization" strategy identified by Garland (1996) and others as emerging during the 1980s. Specifically, he began to refer to the opportunities to work, play sports, or attend school as ways the institution helped "the inmate rehabilitate himself during his stay." In his 1960–62 biannual report, Eyman articulated his philosophy on rehabilitation as a two-way street where "the inmate himself must be willing to accept the opportunity offered to him and be firm in his desire to rectify his life and his thinking in order for rehabilitation to take place. . . . Only a fool would suggest that all of our inmates are capable of rehabilitation. Many, however, show a willingness to acquire a trade, to go to school, and to rehabilitate themselves" (Eyman, 1962: 1).

Eyman expressed this view in various ways for the remainder of his career, seeming to echo the Arizonan ethos of individualism and self-reliance, which expects people to help themselves rather than turn to outside assistance to better their lives. It is also an ethos that ignores psychological elements of the medicalized rehabilitative model that was concurrently in vogue in corrections around the nation. Thus, the vision of human behavior that emerges from the Eyman period is one in which people were seen as simple, rational actors who must decide to make the right choices to better themselves. And indeed, at the time he retired from the prison, Eyman suggested in several interviews that he had not rehabilitated a single person in his prison.

This simple perspective, coupled with Eyman's monarchical style, also shaped how he dealt with discipline. The 1958 evaluation of the prison recommended that the institution develop policies for discipline and form a committee that included noncustodial staff to deal with disciplinary issues. Yet this was an area where Eyman could wield his considerable power, so he was unwilling to cede that control and continued to apply his own judgment about human motivation and behavior to assess inmates. Thus, even after an internal disciplinary committee system that included lay members was established in the 1960s, he maintained the power to set his own punishment, which primarily meant locking inmates up in isolation with restricted meals for up to 15 days, renewable after a brief break. As Eyman told a news reporter about the disciplinary process: "Of course the final word rests with me. I don't care what they (the review board) do. If I think the punishment is too severe, I cut it. If I think it is too little, I up it" (Sweitzer, 1966). He often spoke of how he assessed inmates as being either "good men," therefore deserving of breaks, or incorrigibles who would never change, thus deserving harsh punishment.

Within the first five years of his tenure as warden, Eyman not only had earned the respect of the legislature through his low-cost accomplishments in renovating the prison, he also had learned how to work the appropriations process to get almost enough money to accomplish his goals. First, in 1958, when the various pieces of the correctional enterprise in the state were undergoing the evaluation by the National Probation and Parole Association, Eyman fully cooperated with the evaluators, offering a picture of his operation as one that had done more than what would seem possible with the meager resources provided. Thus, the evaluator noted the "remarkable" improvements Eyman had made, including the recreation field that, borrowing Eyman's words, "is one of the finest in the United States" (National Probation and Parole Association, 1958: 116).

The recommendations put forth in the evaluation included increased custodial and noncustodial staffing, higher salaries and better benefits for staff, major appropriations for construction and renovation, the development of classification and disciplinary criteria and committees, and the creation by the governor of a Board of Corrections, to which the warden would report. In the subsequent annual reports and budget requests, Eyman appeared to adopt the language of this report in pressing for those items on the list that he wanted. He made no mention of the report's recommendations for any of the measures that would disperse the power and control that he and his assistants held, such as the call for a Board of Corrections or even for a disciplinary committee that would include noncustodial members. Nonetheless, his articulation of the need for additional construction projects and personnel, increased salaries, and improved working conditions mimicked the report's recommendations, offering the kind of professional, "modern" penological justifications that he had not previously used.

Second, he used his annual reports to sell his accomplishments as both cost-efficient and successful. For example, after the women's division was constructed, Eyman expressed his pride, both in his cover letter to the governor and in the 1960–62 biannual report, in the accomplishment of installing the "finest [women's prison] in the country," with all the planning and construction completed by prisoners. He pointed out that officials from various other states were amazed and impressed by its quality, and especially its "unbelievably low" cost (Eyman, 1962: 1). His profit-and-loss statements on the farm and industry productions consistently indicated huge net profits and earnings by assessing the market value of the products produced against actual expenses of running the operations. He highlighted the twin values of the work programs in terms of the savings made for the state and how the opportunity to work encouraged the "inmate to rehabilitate himself," which fit well with the broader political culture. Each of his annual reports began with a discussion, generally accompanied by photographs, of the major accomplishments achieved. The reports then articulated the budgetary appropriations and/or legislative changes needed to continue such progress, often illustrating with photographs those areas that needed physical improvement.

Third, Eyman effectively worked the community, especially in Florence, and the regional press in getting out the word of his success in transforming the prison. He regularly spoke to civic groups and reporters and frequently invited citizens' groups and members of the press into the prison for educational tours. During the mid-1960s, he created a slide show illustrating the major improvements he had made in the prison, which he or his assistant warden presented to interested groups around the state. Through this outreach, he shared his penal philosophy and his account of his major accomplishments, which in turn won support from a broad constituency outside of the government.

There were a few detractors—most notably, columnist Orien Fifer Jr., who wrote for Phoenix's major daily newspaper, the *Arizona Republic*, and who, while supportive of Eyman's efforts, frequently criticized the entire penal system, specifically for its lack of state bureaucratic oversight, inadequate parole services, and lack of modern rehabilitation programs within the prison. Fifer shared inmates' and their families' views of the prison experience and painted a picture of an overcrowded, especially violent, dangerous institution that did nothing to rehabilitate its inhabitants. By the early 1960s, several legislators also called upon their peers to modernize the system, while being careful not to denigrate Eyman's efforts.

Additionally, the construction of the women's division in 1962 was partly catalyzed by pressure from a high-powered community group, the Committee for the Improvement of the Women's Division of the Arizona State Prison, that formed during the late 1950s to advocate for improved prison conditions for women. Given the stature of its members, which included at least one wife of a prominent Scottsdale legislator, this group had influence with both the legislature and the governor and so was able to generate political response and media coverage (Buchen, 1959). Again, the group did not criticize Eyman but instead pressured the political side to free up money to allow Eyman to invest in the women's facility. Consequently, Eyman echoed the group's language in making urgent calls on the legislature, also via the press, to appropriate construction funds for the women's division, eventually resulting in the funding. So all in all, Eyman was able to run the prison as he saw fit and was annually rewarded with moderate but increasingly large appropriations from the state legislature to continue his program of improvements in his own vision at least until about a year before the formation of the Department of Corrections.

CONCLUSION

Punishment policy, philosophy, and practices in Arizona from territorial times into the 1960s was largely congruent with the broader sociopolitical culture of the state. Each aspect of the penal system, as it were, functioned under two prevailing tenets: it had to be cheap, and it had to be suitably punitive. These dual objectives were put into practice at Yuma's prison, then at Florence and the Industrial School, and remained a constant operational feature until the formation of the Department of Corrections. In particular, from the 1950s on, both the Industrial School and the prison were led by supervisors who espoused similar philosophies about punishment, which in both cases fit well with the state's political culture. Even the adult parole system, which arguably should, by definition, include elements of rehabilitation in its implementation, did not reflect those reformative ideals that shaped the parole supervision practices of other states. The emphasis on old-fashioned discipline and order, the value of thrift, the unspoken belief in the notion of less eligibility, and the belief that punishment can modify behavior more than rewards were features of both the Eyman and Vukcevich regimes in their respective institutions.

Until the late 1960s, the state's political figures and citizenry seemed generally pleased with this penal model, so apart from the occasional "expert" report suggesting a more progressive model of penality (as in the National Probation and Parole Association evaluation), there was only minor pressure within the state to modernize and bureaucratize. Governor Goddard did occasionally raise private concerns about the conditions of confinement in the Industrial School, particularly about aspects of the solitary confinement regime and its accompanying "low-calorie" diet (Goddard, 1966b; Davies, 1966), but did not suggest or mandate any kind of policy change or other action.

A significant feature of the early to mid-twentieth-century penal scene in Arizona is that it was hardly touched by the penal norms that prevailed in many other states, including neighboring California. The "scientific" approach to rehabilitation was barely a topic of political, institutional, or popular conversation, and up until the mid-1960s, there was virtually no powerful force within the state advocating for this kind of major philosophical reform. As Johnson (1997) has implicitly suggested in her historical work on southwestern penitentiaries, this may well be a regional phenomenon. Prisons in Nevada, New Mexico, and Utah were also slow to adopt the rehabilitative model, which calls into question the degree to which that paradigm really did inform twentieth-century U.S. penology. Such was the case for isolated northwestern states, like Montana, as well (Edgerton, 2004). The geographic isolation and small populations in those states before the 1960s likely contributed to their relative autonomy from trends that flourished in the Northeast, Midwest, and coastal West.[6]

Arizona's lack of interest in rehabilitation was even more pronounced than in its peer states, though, because of several state-specific factors. First, its battle over statehood, which resulted in Arizona being the last of the contiguous states to enter the union, set up a particular cultural relationship with "outsiders" that ensured resistance to attempts at policy importation and outside expertise. Furthermore, because of the geography and climate of the state, the population explosion and heavy migration into Arizona did not begin until the 1950s, when refrigeration and cooling technologies advanced to a level that made it a more habitable place to settle. This impediment to growth kept Arizona both politically insular and geographically isolated for much of its developmental period as a state.

Up until the formation of the Department of Corrections in 1968, Arizona's penal system was also uniquely unbureaucratic compared with those of other states. A number of states formed modern departments of corrections during the 1950s and 1960s, but these departments typically replaced preexisting state institutional structures that oversaw prison and parole operations. So, for example, Florida's penal system fell under the watch of the Department of Agriculture until 1957 (which made sense for a southern U.S. penitentiary system), when its Department of Corrections was formed. States on the coasts and in the Midwest (for example, Michigan, New Jersey, and California) typically formed autonomous governmental bodies devoted to correctional oversight even earlier, with a spate of corrections divisions, boards, and even full departments being established during the 1930s and 1940s. Maryland, which has one of the oldest penal systems in the country, established a Division of Correction in 1912, which expanded to a Department of Correction in 1939;

this organization has been renamed several times, but a continuous, autonomous central organization devoted to corrections has existed there since the early twentieth century. What this meant for Arizona is that the formation of the Department of Corrections occurred on a wholly clean slate—no pre-existing organizational norms had to be reshaped or dealt with at the level of state bureaucracy (see Chapter 2).

Another anomalous characteristic of this penal system was that racial minorities constituted a major proportion of the inmate population at both Florence and Fort Grant. So, for example, in 1959, while the state population was 90 percent white, only 45 percent of the Fort Grant population was white, with the majority composed of those referred to as "Spanish-American" (35 percent), "Negro" (11 percent), and "Indian" (9 percent). In the state prison, the percentage of whites incarcerated varied between 55 percent and 59 percent from 1958 to 1968. African Americans were the most disproportionately overrepresented inside the prison, in that they consistently constituted less than 3 percent of the general state population but accounted for anywhere between 16 percent and 23 percent of the prison population between 1958 and 1968 (see the appendix). This suggests the possibility that Arizona's penal system functioned as a mechanism of racial social control in a way that differed from other states. This kind of extreme overrepresentation of African Americans (measured by the within-state ratio of prison population percentage to general population percentage) is, as noted in the introduction, a later-developing phenomenon generally associated with the postrehabilitation period beginning during the late 1970s.

Latinos have also been overrepresented in the Arizona incarcerated population from territorial times on. The territorial governor who oversaw the authorization of the first prison promoted the idea as a necessity for controlling "Mexican bandits" (he also promoted the benefits of the territory being able to "profit" from inmate labor), thus ideologically setting the stage for the prison to function as an institution of racialized social control. Once the Yuma prison was built, its prisoner population was composed of "Mexican" inmates at rates that ranged from 43 percent to 58 percent of the total population (Knepper, 1990). By the late 1950s, when Eyman began to track the numbers in annual reports, Latinos' relative share of the population was typically around 20 percent, but that share began to increase by the 1990s.

The issue of overrepresentation of minorities in prison was viewed as potentially politically embarrassing even before the Department of Corrections was formed. In 1966, a special assistant to Governor Goddard wrote to Eyman, on the governor's stationery, expressing concern about recording the racial characteristics of the inmates in his monthly reports: "In looking through your monthly report I notice that you include a racial breakdown for each cell block. While you may have good reasons for doing this, I thought I might point out that this kind of thing . . . tends to get us into all kinds of trouble unnecessarily with civil rights organizations" (Starrett, 1966). The assistant went on to assure Eyman that the governor's office was not dictating how Eyman should do his job but just wanted to mention it if it was not a necessary component of the report. The fact that the governor's office felt compelled to write this letter suggests not only an awareness, at the highest level of government, of some of the racial disparity and discrimination problems that existed in the prison, but also a stance that such problems were not worth addressing in a meaningful way, but rather were best hidden so that they did not have to be addressed.

In sum, then, the state of penality in Arizona leading up to the formation of the Department of Corrections differs in several fundamental ways from the prevailing theoretical "narrative" of this period. Most significantly, the hegemony of rehabilitation as the penal ideal was the case for a number of jurisdictions, particularly in the Northeast and industrial Midwest, but it played a significantly weaker role in others. In Arizona, it did not appear to influence punishment practices at all until the 1960s, at which time its paradigmatic dominance elsewhere was, according to many accounts, already slipping.

This meant that progressive reform in Arizona was never fully incorporated and thus did not have to be dismantled (see Chapter 2), which may well help account for the dramatic change of direction and full retreat from modern, rehabilitative ideals that occurred by the 1980s there. Indeed, the early and mid-twentieth-century punishment practices in states like Arizona, Nevada, and other late-developing Sunbelt states where the reformative penal project was not well rooted ultimately may have served as the model for the penality to come after the more global retreat of rehabilitation (see Chapter 7).

2 THE DAWN OF PROGRESS AND
THE MAKING OF A NEW BUREAUCRACY

DESPITE THE RELATIVE CALM that had ensued in Arizona's penal institutions under the leaderships of Vukcevich and Eyman, there was a growing political movement toward bureaucratizing corrections in the state. In many ways, this pressure was part of a larger movement by the politically ascending Republican Party within Arizona to modernize the entire state government. The lack of any state bureaucracy over the penal system became a focal point for these efforts.

The 1958 recommendation of the National Probation and Parole Association to form a Department of Corrections was the impetus for a push, especially by the state Republican Party, to move forward in establishing at least a structure for bureaucratic oversight of the prison. An important component of the 1958 state Republican Party platform was a strategy to create an unpaid lay advisory board to oversee the state prison and parole; this was also a primary agenda item for three-term Republican governor Paul Fannin (1958–64). Following this, Republican legislators, led by Representative Douglas Holsclaw, made several unsuccessful attempts from 1958 through 1963 to pass legislation that would establish a prison oversight board. By 1963, a bill to create a five-member advisory board got as far as passing the Republican-dominated Arizona House of Representatives, but it died in the Senate.

In his frustration over the failure to create such a board, Holsclaw took the issue to the press, complaining to the sympathetic *Arizona Republic* columnist Oriel Fifer Jr. that the state prison was one of only two institutions—the Pioneers' Home for aged and infirm Arizonans being the other—that did not have a supervisory board overseeing its operations. Holsclaw and others characterized the state's penal system as antiquated and out of step with corrections developments in other states, thus linking this proposal to broader efforts to modernize Arizona's government and bring the state in line with its peers.

Much of the opposition to the advisory board idea in both houses of the state legislature came from rural Democrats who argued that Eyman was doing a good job without such interference, that the composition of the board would be the product of political payoffs in the form of member appointments, and that it would create unnecessary bureaucracy. Democratic representative J. J. Glancy characterized the objections in just such terms: "Eyman is doing a terrific job. It is unfair to saddle him with political hacks who might take the job seriously and go down there and try to change things" (Wynn, 1963). Thus the board never became a reality during Fannin's governorship, and the push for modernizing the penal system died down during the two-year term of Fannin's successor, Democratic governor Samuel Goddard.

Despite the failure at bureaucratizing the penal system during Fannin's tenure, just a few years later, a plan for establishing a formal Department of Corrections began to concretely take shape under the leadership of the next Republican governor, Jack Williams. The new momentum came from several sources. In 1966, Holsclaw, now an elected state senator, revived his efforts and wrote directly to the newly elected governor to ask him to consider creating an oversight board for the prison before reappointing Eyman to a third six-year term in 1967. Williams already had criminal justice reform on his agenda, so in 1967, both the new governor and the legislature convened a number of special committees made up of criminal justice experts; local practitioners including lawyers, judges, and probation managers; psychiatrists; and others to study and develop policy recommendations aimed at improving the criminal justice services in the state.

In particular, the legislature convened a special study committee to consider whether Arizona should consolidate its criminal justice activities into a state Department of Corrections. The committee, composed of five criminal justice professionals, considered the 1958 recommendations of the National Probation and Parole Association, as well as the 1966 recommendation from the State of Arizona Town Hall, for creating such a department, and it conducted its own investigation of the issue. The committee recommended to Governor Williams and the legislature that the state should "immediately undertake action to establish a State Department of Corrections" modeled, wherever feasible, after the 1958 National Probation and Parole Association's report (Special Legislative Study Committee, 1967: 3). By the next year, the governor appointed two groups of people to committees devoted to corrections issues: the ad hoc Governor's Advisory Committee on Corrections, which was charged with studying potential courses of action to deal with mentally ill prisoners; and the Criminal Justice Planning Committee, chaired by the state attorney general, which was to explore the coordination of criminal justice operations in the state.

Another ad hoc citizens' advisory committee headed by a Maricopa County judge also reported to the state legislature after developing a set of recommendations for establishing a unified department. Finally, a 1967 ad hoc legislative subcommittee, the Joint Study Committee on Juvenile Institutions, conducted its own investigation of the existing criminal justice operations in the state, with a particular focus on the juvenile system, and concluded that a single Department of Corrections should be formed. This committee's final report proposed a complete structural reorganization of correctional programs, including draft legislation that would establish such a department (Joint Study Committee on Juvenile Institutions, 1968). This draft, which heavily relied on the National Probation and Parole Association report, became the basis of the enacted legislation and was substantially the same by the time it became law the next year.

In a very brief period of time, therefore, the momentum to bureaucratize the penal system in Arizona changed dramatically and had a wide base of support. The proposal for a formal department was not precipitated by any particular crisis in the penal system; rather, it was characterized by those endorsing it as a positive, modernizing development for the state. The various committees and groups that were studying the feasibility and advisability of creating a department framed its value in terms of its ability to bring a "new" centralized model of corrections that would operate from a modern, rehabilitative approach. Thus, if created, it would eliminate the practical problem of the patchwork system that had little coordination, many gaps in service, and some overlap and redundancy while ensuring an overarching philosophy to the correctional task that brought Arizona into the modern age.

The success of this plan, unlike its more modest predecessor, was likely due to the unified support from a range of political actors and constituencies that the proposal had garnered, and it arose in the context of a broader political movement to modernize state government, which was led by the now dominant Republican Party. The penal system was a governmental entity that lagged behind all the others in Arizona, so while the Republicans in power were interested in a number of "modernizing" projects, this one took precedence because of its distinctively backward status of having no bureaucratic structure within the state government. As a result, the 1968 bill to create the Department of Corrections was able to pass both houses of the legislature with little trouble. There was some grumbling by individual legislators, again predominantly rural Democrats who were not keen on creating more state bureaucracy, but their opposition did not even cause a ripple in the process of establishing the department.

Despite its ease in being legislatively established, the new department, as proposed, was going to be a much more extensive and expensive bureaucratic organization than the earlier advisory board proposal that had failed to gain sufficient political support. The department would be staffed by a paid director, deputy directors, and support personnel and would ideally consolidate under one organizational umbrella prison operations, juvenile placements and institutional operations, adult and juvenile parole supervision, and adult and juvenile probation. The department had an establishment date of June 20, 1968, at which time it would immediately begin overseeing the administration of the three state institutions—the state prison at Florence, the Fort Grant Industrial School, and the newly opened Tucson Youth Center—and it was to take over the duty of establishing and maintaining contracts for additional juvenile placements from the board of the State Institutions for Juveniles. The department was also to take over juvenile community supervision immediately and adult parole supervision services for the state by 1969. By 1971, it was to develop a program for uniform statewide probation services to replace the county-by-county system. The legislation extended the state's jurisdiction over juvenile offenders from the age of 18 to the age of 21, thus allowing committed juveniles to be maintained under state control for an additional three years. Finally, it reconfigured the Board of Pardons and Paroles such that the five part-time positions would be replaced by three full-time positions beginning July 1, 1969.

In terms of the players who were directly affected by the creation of the department, the board members of the State Institutions for Juveniles were the most vocal in expressing reservations about the new law. This was the only existing agency that would be eliminated by the department's creation, so its members, somewhat understandably, voiced concern about how juvenile placements and supervision would be handled within this new bureaucracy that would oversee so much, but had yet to even be staffed. One member characterized the move to a newspaper reporter as a step backward from the progress the board had made in the juvenile system, and the board president expressed concern that the extension of departmental jurisdiction over juveniles until they turned 21 would be detrimental to the youth trying to go to college or get jobs, given the stigma of parole status (Taylor, 1968).[1]

The juvenile board's resistance may have resulted largely from the fact that it was left out of the process of determining how juveniles would be handled and indeed was kept relatively uninformed about the bill's implications for the board up until the time it became law. It appears that the board president, Sanford Shoults, learned that the legislation had passed (and consequently realized its implications for the juvenile board) from a story in the newspaper announcing the news. He promptly telegrammed Governor Williams from Tucson to express his displeasure and request reconsideration:

> Dear Sir: Newspaper reports indicate Senate Bill No. 131 creating a new state department of corrections has been passed and is ready for your signature. Information received here indicates this new legislation accomplishes nothing except abolishment of existing state juvenile board until July 1, 1969 [when parole would be subsumed by the department]. After four years of sincere effort to serve with this board on behalf of the less fortunate children of this state, I consider this legislation ill advised, uneconomical and not in the best interests of the children in this state. Also it jeopardizes the care and treatment of more than 700 present wards of the board. I respectfully request an audience for our board with you in your office on March 28 before this bill is signed into law. (Shoults, 1968)

These concerns of the board did not affect the governor, and he signed the bill, as planned, on March 28, 1968. As laid out in the legislation, the board of the State Institutions for Juveniles was indeed dissolved, the existing placement contracts were canceled, and all of its property was transferred to the new Department of Corrections on June 20, 1968.

Both Warden Eyman of the state prison and Superintendent Vukcevich of Fort Grant seemed lukewarm about the establishment of a Department of Corrections, but they ultimately appeared confident that it would not really affect them or their institutional operations. Eyman first revealed his reservations about the potential changes in a 1967 letter to Governor Williams. The precipitating event for his letter was that, as part of the set of studies and investigations that were being conducted about penal operations and future plans for bureaucratization, the governor had appointed a special committee to investigate the problem of homosexuality in the prison. Eyman was not happy to have outside "experts" examining his institution in this instance and expressed in his missive his general displeasure with the whole set of state activities around the penal system, sending the message quite clearly that from his perspective, the prison was best left alone for him to manage: "I don't want to turn my prison into a social organization because I firmly believe that these men have to have discipline. If they had exercised discipline on the outside, many would not now be on the inside" (Eyman, 1967).

Williams responded to Eyman's letter with assurances that they were in complete agreement in terms of penal philosophy. The governor asserted his belief that the system was best based on "just deserts" and scoffed at the "'sound and fury' of the present day reformer" and concluded: "You are so right about the importance of discipline in a society and I hope that we can both proceed with great care to administer our respective jobs so we can have the greatest influence in serving and saving a society that is facing Armageddon" (Williams, 1967). Williams then invited Eyman to become a member of the newly formed Governor's Advisory Committee on Corrections, which Eyman agreed to join. By 1968, when interviewed about the creation of the department, Eyman told an *Arizona Republic* reporter that he did not think that it would change much of how the prison operated.

Vukcevich shared his views with the same reporter, indicating that he felt the department formation was beneficial to the extent that it would take over parole and aftercare duties for his wards, but he was confident that it would not affect Fort Grant institutional operations too much. Thus, for both of these men, who up to this point had each been managing his institution for well over a decade with almost complete autonomy and little outside interference, the idea that their authority would be diminished by the creation of a Department of Corrections just did not seem to be a real concern.

IMPORTING LEADERSHIP: ALLEN COOK'S APPOINTMENT

As soon as the legislation was signed into law, Governor Williams needed to find a director to head the new department. The law required the governor to appoint someone with a master's degree and at least 10 years of experience in the correctional field. Williams's task was made easier by the eventual appointee, Allen Cook, who had retired to Sun City, Arizona, after working 27 years for California's Department of Corrections. Cook actually wrote to the governor's office in 1967 when he first heard that the state was looking into establishing a Department of Corrections and expressed his interest in playing a part in the program's development. Cook followed up with a letter to the governor's assistant about a week after the legislation was signed, reiterating his interest. He indicated his willingness to postpone his summer travel plans to explore the "possibility of my having some part in your new program" (Cook, 1968), and two weeks later, the governor announced Cook's appointment as "state corrections advisor." Cook publicly claimed that he was not interested in the permanent director's job and only wanted to help the state in getting the department successfully set up.

Allen Cook came with "expert" credentials. With a law degree, he met the education requirement, but more significantly, he had spent most of his career in one of the most progressive departments of corrections in the nation (at that time)—the California Department of Corrections—where he had been directly responsible for the development of some of the more progressive programs within that system, including being superintendent of the Deuel Vocational Institution in Tracy, California, which when it opened in 1953 was an exemplar of the rehabilitative model in corrections, specializing in young male offenders who were offered intensive therapy and vocational training. Cook also had previous experience in helping set up a new correctional system: he had worked as a consultant to the state of Hawaii to design and implement its new corrections division in 1961. Governor Williams touted Cook as the ideal man for the advising job, and two months later, he announced that he had persuaded Cook to fully come out of retirement and take on the permanent director position. Cook was easily confirmed by the Senate and began in his new job on schedule.

Cook had an ambitious agenda for the new department. He not only set out to consolidate the disparate corrections operations and develop needed programs to fill in service gaps, but he also began major reform efforts within the existing agencies and institutions. So his task was threefold: to create an administrative structure, including hiring deputy directors and staff, that would subsume oversight of the institutions and agencies that now fell under the department umbrella; to obtain funding to expand correctional services in several areas, most importantly through adding new juvenile and adult institutions and programs to the system; and to rework existing programs to fit with the progressive rehabilitative philosophy that he brought with him from his prior experiences.

Creating a Bureaucracy

The 1968 legislation authorized the director of the Arizona Department of Corrections to establish necessary divisions within the department which he could appoint deputy directors to oversee. The 1967 conceptualization of the department, as laid out in the "Proposed Structural Reorganization" of the Joint Study Committee on Juvenile Institutions (1968), was for there to be no more than five divisions relating to treatment services, custodial services, administrative services, research and training services, and parole and probation services; but the final version of the law provided much more discretion to the director in creating divisions and naming supervisors, which Cook exercised over the first year or so in developing the departmental structure. His first action was to appoint a deputy director, Dr. A. LaMont Smith, a professor of penology from Southern Illinois University, who would be directly below him in the organizational hierarchy. Cook then established, over the next 18 months, six divisions headed by appointed supervisors and an administrative control board to review departmental handling of juvenile cases.

By the end of 1969, Cook reported in his first published progress report that this structure not only had centralized and modernized Arizona's correctional program, it also had provided "reduced unit costs from improved services to the taxpayer and a big step forward in the rehabilitation of men and women, boys and girls" (Arizona Department of Corrections, 1970). Thus, Cook had quickly learned to describe his achievements and his goals in this dual manner that highlighted cost savings to the state first and progressive penology second, in order to politically succeed within this state's governmental and political culture. So although the Department of Corrections made the state's criminal justice costs significantly higher than they had been before its creation, Cook framed the attained and proposed developments as an overall savings when the added value of the improvements made was considered.

His strategy worked during the early years. The legislature appropriated $5.7 million for the department in 1968, $8.7 million in 1969, and more than $11 million in 1970, which included $1 million to begin building a state juvenile facility for girls. Beyond Cook's successes in obtaining generous funding from the legislature, the department also had unprecedented political success in 1970. Cook and Deputy Director Smith came up with a proposal for 22 legislative bills that would affect corrections in a variety of ways and further the goals of the new department. Twenty of these corrections reform bills were passed, authorizing a number of major changes within the system, including allowing the department to have discretion over early parole releases, creating a work furlough program (with rent charged to furlough inmates), providing increased judicial power to seek diagnostic tests of convicts before sentencing, restoring civil rights to offenders after release, and authorizing the department to conduct a research study and draw plans for a training facility for youthful adult offenders. The department deemed this set of bills as crucial to the broader mission of aiding in the transition from a punitive-oriented system to one based on correctional treatment. Although the proposed package of bills came with a hefty price tag, Cook again used rhetoric that blended a theme of long-term cost-effectiveness with that of progressive penology in the written recommendation to the legislature supporting the proposed bills: "Crime in the streets could be reduced by one half if all the knowledge of the available Correctional Treatment programs could be applied. The application [of those programs] will cost money, but it will be more costly not to act now" (Legislative Proposals of the Arizona Department of Corrections, 1970).

Expanding the System and Widening the Net

These early legislative successes allowed the new department to expand its power and reach in a number of ways, resulting in the kind of penal net-widening described by Stanley Cohen (1979, 1985). So although the prison population itself did not grow very much during these early years—indeed, the rate of formal imprisonment in the state consistently declined during Cook's tenure—the number of people under some form of state correctional control did rise. Cook had plans for specialized programs at all levels, which he quickly began to implement. Along with the planned Arizona Girls' School, he proposed to create extensive diagnostic centers where felons would be thoroughly evaluated before judicial sentencing; he planned a young adult training and vocational facility for men aged 18 to 25; he created forestry camps and other such minimum-security facilities; and he constructed halfway houses and community release centers in urban areas for transitional inmates. By 1971, Cook also moved toward taking over county-level probation services (as was authorized by the 1968 establishment bill) and tried to persuade the legislature to give the Department of Corrections oversight authority over county-level jails.

In promoting each of these innovative programs, Cook emphasized the positive therapeutic values inherent in them and the long-term cost savings that would be reaped by minimizing spending on costly and "unproductive" imprisonment. And as he adapted to the fiscal culture of Arizona's government, Cook also learned to stretch his program-building budget in creative and cost-effective ways. In 1969, he successfully negotiated with the federal government to obtain a defunct Job Corps site in rural Alpine, Arizona, at no cost, beating out the Bureau of Indian Affairs, the University of Arizona, Arizona State University, and Apache County for the acquisition. The land and facilities, which were valued at $1.5 million, were offered to the department for free for one year, and if the program was successful, the property would be turned over permanently to it. There, the department created the Alpine Conservation Center, a minimum-security training facility for "better bad boys" (Harrigan, 1970) who were not considered to be serious enough offenders to send to the Industrial School. The youths could get vocational training in the on-site auto repair shop and lumber processing shop, and they all worked in the surrounding forests and lands on various maintenance and conservation projects.

In 1970, Cook obtained another set of federal Job Corps tent/cabin–type facilities for free, which were then moved across the state from Kingman to Safford where the Safford Conservation Center for adult male offenders was established. This facility also offered vocational training and education to its residents and provided soil-conservation and fire-fighting services to the surrounding communities. Cook continued the requisite tradition of relying on inmate labor in constructing new facilities: the conservation center solely used the labor of 12 inmates, dubbed the Dirty Dozen, who were overseen by seven correctional staff members to move the federally donated facilities across the state and reconstruct them on the new site (Arizona Department of Corrections website).

During the same year, the department began construction outside of Phoenix on the first state-run girls' school since the closure of the school at Randolph in 1938. This facility opened in 1971. The first halfway house for adult offenders also opened in Phoenix in 1971, and plans began for three more such conditional release centers in Phoenix and Tucson to serve youth and adult releasees. Cook's pet project, building a training facility for 18- to 25-year-old male offenders, began to take shape as well. After receiving a $35,000 appropriation in 1970 from the legislature to begin planning on the project, Cook applied for and received an additional $100,000 from the federal government to pay for plans and design. This facility aimed to be a model institution worthy of emulation by other jurisdictions and would realize all of the modern correctional goals that Cook had planned for the state. It would be situated within an urban setting and was to include residential and work furlough treatment programs, vocational and educational training, diagnostic services for the courts, and services for probation violators and parole recidivists. As a department spokesman told a reporter in 1971, "Arizona is going to try to establish a new pattern of correctional institutions with this facility by departing from any past traditional type program by design and will try, in part, to create the concept of normal community life" (*Phoenix Gazette*, 1971a).

Reforming Existing Programs

Minor Tinkering at the Prison   Cook was only mildly interventionist with the prison—his more pressing goal was to obtain legislative funding to build new penal facilities and develop alternative programs—but he did impose some changes on Eyman's harsh disciplinary regime. One of his first actions was to take over the investigation that had been under way since 1967 of the "homosexuality problem" in the prison. The investigation had begun when a prisoner filed a complaint with a Cochise County Superior Court judge about rampant sexual assaults at the prison. The judge began the investigation but turned over the task to Cook once the Department of Corrections was established.

This undertaking became an opportunity for Cook to reiterate his goals in reforming the penal system. He quickly appointed an out-of-state expert, Keith Edwards, to look into the charges. Edwards reported back in the fall of 1968, concluding that there was indeed a problem with aggressive inmates who were forcing sex on weaker inmates and that the long-term solution to the problem required constructing new facilities to aid in segregating different levels and age groups of offenders. Edwards praised the staff and administration while condemning the overcrowded and antiquated facilities, which, he suggested, contributed to the chronic nature of the problem. In his recommendations, he suggested the construction of more segregation housing within the prison, called for increased staff salaries, and advocated for the "intermediate" facility for younger inmates that was simultaneously being proposed by Cook, concluding more broadly that "long range planning and adequate funding must be provided in the immediate future" (Edwards, 1968).

Two new inmates entering main gate of prison, 1968. From *Arizona State Prison Annual Report, 1967–68.*

New inmates awaiting classification committee interview at new diagnostic center, 1968. From *Arizona State Prison Annual Report, 1967–68.*

Thus, this first intervention within the prison provided Cook with an opportunity to lobby the governor and legislature for facility expansion funds. The homosexuality issue, which received more than minor media coverage, provided an immediate and specific reason for building new facilities, and Cook used the investigation as a mode to sell that rationale by demonstrating the major problems with the overcrowded and old-style prison. At the same time, he was careful not to step on any toes of the prison management and staff and did not assign blame to those employees for allowing the problem to manifest and persist.

In terms of programmatic changes within the prison, by the fall of 1968, Cook implemented a small vocational training program, which he characterized as "badly needed," to rehabilitate inmates on their way to being paroled. By 1970, he reported that since the foundation of the Department of Corrections, the state prison—which was still the most significant penal institution within the department, housing the bulk of state prisoners—had "launched into developing a realistic, therapeutic program of rehabilitation" (Arizona Department of Corrections, 1970). Although the therapy was still limited to vocational training within the institutional walls because of resource constraints, the goals of imprisonment at the state prison, and the department's aims more generally, were framed in the language of rehabilitation.

Another major component of this programmatic change included the establishment of a "diagnostic receiving and reception center" at the state prison, staffed by a psychologist and three counselors, where incoming inmates lived for 30 days while being tested and evaluated on a number of psychological, educational, and vocational dimensions. After the major corrections legislative successes of 1970, the diagnostic center's operations were expanded to conduct presentencing diagnostic evaluations aimed at determining convicted felons' suitability for prison or probation. These offenders were referred to the department by county-level superior court judges; as a result, the linkage between the state correctional operations and the local court adjudication processes was strengthened, extending the reach of the new department farther into the criminal justice system.

Cook also obtained a technical assistance grant from the federal Law Enforcement Assistance Administration (LEAA) in 1971 to commission a study of the security and custody procedures within the prison "at no cost to the State of Arizona" (Cook, 1972a). He justified this study as a precautionary measure in response to the "insurrections" at Attica, New York, and San

Football game as "recreation therapy" at Arizona State Prison–Florence, 1971. From *Arizona State Prison Annual Report, 1970–71.*

Trophy winners in prison sports program, 1971. From *Arizona State Prison Annual Report, 1970–71.*

Quentin, California, and hired two consultants from the American Justice Institute, who had spent their careers in California's Department of Corrections, to conduct the study. The report made a series of recommendations for increasing security within the facility, all of which converged with Cook's goals for upgrading and decentralizing the adult penal institutional options. Most of the recommendations were for improvements to the physical plant, including the relocation of maintenance shops and the isolation and segregation unit and the installation of new lighting, fencing, metal detectors, and other such hardware in strategic locations.

The report went on to recommend that the department develop a new facility for minors and first-time offenders and that it begin trying to reassign inmates to reduce overcrowding. The consultants leveled no criticism at the prison management or staff, instead framing the issues in terms of needed investments, which was consistent with the previous study that Cook had commissioned. Thus, it appears that Cook utilized these examinations of the prison's operations as a way to bolster the legitimacy of his reform program without risking any political fallout that might be generated by taking on Eyman and his staff.

So in general, Cook left Eyman in charge of operations within the prison and interfered only minimally. According to Eyman's secretary, Della Meadows, Cook would occasionally come through the prison with other corrections administrators or outside visitors (such as during the commissioned studies). Such visits did not please Eyman, but he nonetheless played the host and shuttled the visitors through as quickly yet graciously as he could, showing off those aspects of the prison of which he was most proud (Meadows interview, 2002). In general, Eyman maintained a prison environment that was fairly consistent with his predepartment institution, focusing on keeping inmates involved in the work of maintaining the prison operations and in the various recreation programs he had established.

Several factors likely contributed to Cook's relative hands-off approach to the prison. First, it was possible that he expected that the aging Eyman would retire, at the latest, in 1973 at the end of his third six-year term as warden, so the prison would come under complete control of the new Department of Corrections once Cook could appoint the next warden. The prison was also functioning fairly well given the incredible demands on it, and to fix the problems associated with its aging and overtaxed facilities would likely mean shelving other pet projects. And third, the existing records suggest that Cook's greater vision was to ultimately do away with this old-style facility and make a system that revolutionized corrections. His extensive plans for community corrections centers; small, specialized facilities in urban settings; and variations on incarceration indicate his vision for a new style of penal system that used traditional high-security prisons only for a select, hard-core subpopulation of convicts.

Parole Overhaul   Cook was much more interventionist in the parole supervision division, once it came under department jurisdiction in June 1969. With parole, he did not even try to work with the old regime. Instead, he simply fired the incumbent head of the department, William Drew, whose title had been transformed from executive director of the Arizona Board of Pardons and Paroles to parole director when those operations came under the jurisdiction of the Department of Corrections. Cook terminated Drew three weeks before he had served six months under the new title—at which time he would have earned job tenure—thereby avoiding the need to provide just cause for the firing.

But Drew did not go away quietly, which consequently caused the first major distraction in Cook's reform program and exposed the department to public inquiry, if not criticism, in the process. Cook made few public comments about the firing, leaving the door open to Drew to frame the issues for the local press. After unsuccessfully going through the internal state personnel appeals process, Drew filed a suit in Maricopa County Superior Court claiming that his firing was arbitrary and that the state had erroneously classified him as a probationary employee. Six months after Drew's firing, the judge who heard the case ruled that Drew was not a probationary employee so was to be reinstated in his job with full back pay. Cook had recently filled the position with an experienced community corrections person from California, and this person actually started work on the very day that the ruling was announced. Cook gave his new employee a different title, reinstated Drew, and then immediately suspended him, with pay this time, from the position for cause. Cook also refused to authorize the back pay to Drew unless Drew put up a bond for the total amount until the case was resolved on appeal.

Drew went back to court and asked the judge to hold Cook in contempt if he did not fully comply with the court order. The battle over Drew's status, including the back pay issue, continued to be fought in the courts through the summer of 1970, garnering press coverage that never failed to point out that two people were potentially going to be paid (including exact salary amounts for each) for one position. Although Drew won the initial decision at the trial court level, once the state appealed the decision, the appeals court granted a stay to the state for the duration of the legal process, keeping Drew out of a real job in the department and allowing his back pay to be held in escrow.

Nonetheless, Drew and his attorney took to commenting to reporters on the case and in one instance framed the heart of the issue in terms of insider versus outsider, denigrating Cook's practice of appointing out-of-state people to administrative posts. Drew's lawyer directly linked the department's unwillingness to repay Drew as was ordered by the judge with the appointment of outsiders:

> If they don't have to comply with this judgment . . . any employee could be discharged for one reason or another, and then if the state loses the first round it could turn around and try to dismiss for cause. Meanwhile, they can appoint one of their own little clan of Californians—this is the third little boy from California—and after playing footsy with the court the newcomer would have gained tenure. (Boyles, 1970)

Although this was the first significant public challenge that Cook faced during his tenure, it foreshadowed the coming battles he would have in asserting authority and maintaining legitimacy for himself and his progressive reform programs. Indeed, these struggles culminated over the next major termination that Cook attempted—of Superintendent Steve Vukcevich at the Fort Grant Industrial School.

Disciplinary Reform at Fort Grant Cook had also immediately set out to reform the disciplinary practices that had endured at the Industrial School since its inception. Within six months of the establishment of the Department of Corrections, Cook ordered that the use of the razor strap and all other forms of corporal punishment be eliminated and promoted "the use of a psychological approach to solving disciplinary problems within the school" (*Arizona Republic*, 1968). Superintendent Vukcevich defended the practice of whipping with the strap, describing it as a mild form of corporal punishment administered under strict control to only a small percentage of the students, generally limited to five to 15 "swats on the posterior" (*Arizona Republic*, 1968). Nonetheless, he agreed to comply with Cook's directive and said he would phase out corporal punishment over the next year. By late 1969, corporal punishment as an officially sanctioned disciplinary option was no longer to be available at Fort Grant, although it seems to have continued to be used after that date. Finally, in October 1970, the Department of Corrections forced the elimination of the strap by drafting a formal order that outlawed the use of any corporal punishment in any of the state's facilities.

Cook also pushed for changes to the solitary confinement policy at the school. This practice, euphemistically referred to as "meditation," involved confining boys in a dimly lit room equipped with nothing except a mattress and toilet/sink fixture and reducing meals to two a day. Boys were allowed no visitors, no clothing other than their underwear, no reading materials, and no other recreational gear for the duration of their stay. Cook advocated instead for a system of earned privileges, such as field trips and expanded checkout privileges at the library, which could then be rescinded for bad behavior. By 1971, Cook had successfully banned the diet component of meditation and loosened the restrictions on what materials inmates could have with them in solitary. Boys were allowed books, radios, phonographs, and even roommates in meditation, which in Vukcevich's view meant there were no disciplinary tools left for his staff to wield.

Vukcevich's cooperation with the "enlightened" regime was short lived, as was Cook's tolerance of Vukcevich as superintendent. Vukcevich, whose Democratic political connections ensured that he would have an audience for his displeasure, began to voice a number of issues he had with Cook's program reforms. He complained to local legislators about how Cook was stripping his authority, and the legislators took those complaints as an opening to publicly challenge the entire department and its liberal, spendthrift ways. By early 1971, the complaints began to be aired in the press by both Vukcevich and his allies in the legislature. At first, Vukcevich was subtle in his public criticisms, suggesting to reporters that he and Cook had different views and philosophies about discipline and treatment, but the animosity between Vukcevich and the department administration quickly grew. By February 1971, an all-out war of words was being waged in the local press, with three southeastern Democratic legislators and Vukcevich accusing Cook of ruining the program at Fort Grant and demanding an investigation of the entire department. Cook and his deputy, LaMont Smith, characterized the problems raised by the Vukcevich camp as merely a "fear of change" among Fort Grant staff (*Arizona Republic*, 1971b).

The precipitating event for the showdown between Director Cook and Superintendent Vukcevich was a spate of runaways from the Industrial School. The number of runaways and the period when this problem was said to have cropped up were both in dispute. Vukcevich and his political allies pinpointed the "crisis" as beginning as soon as the ban on corporal punishment was put in effect. Cook countered that runaway numbers had actually dropped from the year preceding the ban to the year after the ban was in effect. Local ranchers took Vukcevich's side, complaining at various meetings and to the press that they were being "victimized" by runaways and that local women didn't feel safe in their homes (*Arizona Republic*, 1971b). They collected signatures on a petition presented to the governor that demanded he investigate the escape problem. Residents also voiced to the press their support for Vukcevich's disciplinary policies, arguing that Cook "was more concerned with the rights of delinquents than for the safety of law-abiding citizens" and that when corporal punishment was used at the school, the fear of punishment had made the boys think twice before running away (*Arizona Republic*, 1971b).

The runaway crisis was clearly more of a symbolic episode representing a clash of penal styles and beliefs, as well as a partisan political fight, than a serious crime wave that truly threatened the community. Fort Grant had always been an open, minimum-security facility with no fencing or barriers to keep the wards inside, and boys had intermittently walked away over the course of its existence. For years under Vukcevich's supervision, a significant number of the boys had even lived with and worked as ranch hands for the very ranchers who were now feeling so "terrorized" by Fort Grant runaways.[2] The press reports of the crisis never specified any actual crimes committed by the escapees but repeatedly referenced the community's fears of crime and violence that could potentially result from the escapes. Even an editorial in the *Arizona Republic* newspaper during the height of this battle reflected the gap between the prevailing rhetoric of pending disorder and any real threat posed by Fort Grant runaways. The editorial, while expressing concerns about the potential for abuse of corporal punishment in such a setting, nonetheless implied that such intervention might be the only way to control the delinquents at the facility:

> It is easy to argue the value of the swat system, or the value of punishment generally. . . . But what about the farm and ranch families in the Ft. Grant area? Surely they are entitled to safety from the terrorism that has beset them in recent months. . . . Why should they have to live in a virtual state of siege, afraid to venture outside lest some delinquent(s) from Ft. Grant terrorize them? Why should their lives be made miserable by roving gangs of escapees? (*Arizona Republic*, 1971b)

In March 1971, Governor Williams ordered an investigation into the escape problem, prompting a secondary fight over who would conduct this investigation. Williams left it to Cook to hire a juvenile corrections expert to conduct the probe, and Cook and the Department of Corrections decided to appoint an out-of-state corrections expert. Vukcevich's legislator supporters blasted this plan on several grounds. Recognizing that the governor supported Cook and concurred with him on the no-swat policy, they drafted a letter to Williams demanding that Cook not be involved in the selection of an investigator. They also called for an independent investigation of the entire department for its mishandling of the state's penal system, which in their view must be done by an in-state person. So, in a fashion similar to the rhetoric generated during the Drew parole firing, the legislators framed the central issue as being about insiders versus outsiders: "We feel that we have people right here in the State of Arizona qualified to conduct such an investigation, and we resent spending tax money to bring an out of state investigator. . . . The problems at Fort Grant have arisen since these men [Allen Cook and LaMont Smith]—both out-of-staters themselves—have taken over the Department of Corrections" (Boyles, 1971).

In the end, two federal representatives from LEAA conducted the investigation, and they submitted their final report in June 1971. The report, not surprisingly, made a series of conclusions with which the Department of Corrections had "no basic disagreement." It cited major lack of communication between Vukcevich and the department as a primary issue, while it downplayed the seriousness of the runaway problem, suggesting that such a thing was to be expected with an open facility like Fort Grant. The investigators endorsed Cook's ban on corporal punishment and recommended that staff members be retrained in alternative methods for dealing with problem behavior. Specifically, the report recommended training in behavior modification techniques, emphasizing the use of positive reinforcement to gain compliance from the wards (*Phoenix Gazette*, 1971b).

Troubles continued to simmer between the department and Vukcevich even after the runaway crisis died down. By the fall of 1972, Cook essentially evicted Vukcevich from Fort Grant, locking him out of his office at the institution. Vukcevich was told that he could take a "promotion" to a newly created position in the central corrections department at equal pay, or resign. Cook expected that Vukcevich would refuse the new job partly because it was located in Phoenix, which was nearly four hours away from Fort Grant. Like Drew before him, however, Vukcevich did not go easily. He accepted the new position and simultaneously filed an appeal with the state Personnel Commission, arguing that the job transfer was actually a demotion. Vukcevich's political forces mobilized and organized a letter-writing campaign among judges from Flagstaff to Nogales, who wrote the governor in support of Vukcevich. The legislature also called a special meeting of the budget committee to investigate the creation of this new job, as there was no budget line item for the position and therefore no appropriated money for the move. Cook was able to demonstrate how he had funded the position, but his explanation did not completely satisfy the committee, or the press. An editorial in the *Phoenix Gazette* characterized the incident as some sort of "cover up" by Cook and called for transparency and honesty from the department about what was going on at Fort Grant (*Phoenix Gazette*, 1972b).

Because Vukcevich did not resign on his own, Cook implemented his backup plan (referred to as the "Monday plan"). On the Monday that Vukcevich reported to his new job, he was given the option of either resigning by noon that day or being fired that afternoon. Vukcevich refused to resign so was presented with a list of 46 dismissal charges and told to vacate the state-owned Fort Grant home that he and his wife occupied. The charges included a range of improprieties—from various forms of theft, including using the state gas pumps for private vehicles, stealing facility-grown hay for use at his privately owned resort ranch, and giving himself an unauthorized pay raise; to charges related to the treatment of boys, including using extreme punishment practices and levying excessive fines against those boys with money in their accounts. Five months later, the Personnel Commission considered Vukcevich's demotion/dismissal appeal, and after a month-long hearing, it found 14 of the 46 allegations to be true and upheld the firing.

Then, in early 1974, one of the judges who had participated in the pro-Vukcevich letter-writing campaign 18 months earlier ordered Vukcevich reinstated to his job with full back pay, ruling that the dismissal charges were "ridiculous" and were clearly simply the product of a personality conflict between Cook and Vukcevich (*Phoenix Gazette*, 1974). By this point, Cook had resigned his position as corrections director, Fort Grant had been converted to an adult facility, and Vukcevich himself was beginning to launch an election campaign in a run for the state legislature. Vukcevich was elected to the House of Representatives later that year, where he served five terms before retiring, so he never returned to the Department of Corrections despite his court victory.

COOK'S FALL FROM GRACE

As with the Drew firing, Cook's effort to reform the Industrial School by dismissing its long-term, politically connected supervisor ultimately made his entire program of change more vulnerable. Both incidents created an opportunity for a long-standing Arizonan political critique to be leveled against Cook—that he was a meddling "outsider." Although the reigning Republicans during this period were not fundamentally opposed to relying on outsiders for expertise, and indeed actively recruited them in some instances, there was no sense in which they were ready to declare those outsiders as somehow superior to true Arizonans. So as soon as Cook earned the label of outsider who did not understand or respect the way things were done in Arizona—largely through these two incidents—it became more difficult for his political supporters to fully and publicly back him. For instance, Governor Williams never publicly turned on Cook, but he did not offer much public defense of him either. And during the last year of Cook's tenure as director, the governor, under some political pressure, appointed a citizens' review committee to study and make recommendations for improving the state's corrections and rehabilitation programs. This, of course, was a clear indication of Cook's falling stature as the state corrections leader and visionary.

Both neutral and opposing factions used this opening to try to tear down Cook and his reform program. For instance, from about 1970 on, the press scrutinized each of Cook's administrative appointments for further evidence that he was building an empire made up of out-of-state appointees. Several local judges also went to the press to complain about Cook's reform program, pointing out that Arizona state laws (at that time) fundamentally required public safety as a penal goal rather than rehabilitation (*Phoenix Gazette*, 1972a). More progressive judges, on the other hand, complained about the poor conditions in the prison, which in their view turned convicts into hardened criminals. These judges articulated a "lack of trust" in the department and refused to send any but the most "hopeless cases" to the state facilities (Warne, 1972a). And as is illustrated by the Vukcevich dismissal and its aftermath, individual, primarily rural Democratic state legislators seized this opportunity to challenge the legitimacy of the entire department and its goals.

The legislature began to punish Cook as well, both in its appropriations and in its legislation. Although 1970 was a watershed year for Cook in that his 1971–72 budget request was fully funded and the bulk of his proposed bills were passed, he faced some serious funding setbacks in his 1971 and 1972 legislative requests. A growing number of legislators noted that the corrections bureau-cracy and budget were ballooning while the problems that the department was supposed to address were not decreasing. Thus Cook's 1971 budget request seeking an additional $30 million to fund his building projects (primarily construction costs for the young adult training facility) was shot down.

This major setback was the result of a convergence of factors. An influen-tial Phoenix engineer who had a private dispute with Cook scrutinized Cook's construction budget numbers on all of his projects and lodged a complaint with the legislature and the governor that Cook's figures were outrageously high for what was being proposed. This critic compared Cook's square-foot costs with significantly lower construction costs of a recent system center built by the Tennessee Valley Authority and argued that if anything, the prison construction costs should be even less. Cook countered with figures that com-pared Arizona's proposed costs with other states' prison construction costs to demonstrate how inexpensive his proposal was, but it was not enough to get the appropriation. While Governor Williams voiced skepticism about the engineer's critique, the state finance department simultaneously issued an analysis that criticized Cook's request for all of the construction money up front. The legislature, as a result, refused to allocate any of the construction funds requested (Bolles, 1971).

Cook's budget troubles continued. In early 1972, the state auditor general issued a critical report of the Department of Corrections' accounting prac-tices, further contributing to the growing public and political perception that Cook was fiscally irresponsible. During the fall of 1972, Cook's more modest request for a $12 million budget hike was also almost completely rebuffed.

At around the same time the legislature convened a "prison reform" in-terim subcommittee that made a series of recommendations for eight different corrections bills. Unlike the earlier corrections bills, these did not originate from Cook or the department, but rather aimed at intervening in the depart-ment's operations. The bills required the department to improve its record-keeping, establish training programs for prison staff, and create an office of ombudsman for prisoners. Although the establishment of this legislative group was largely a response to increasing complaints about and inquiry into the state's prison conditions, it also functioned as a form of second-guessing about Cook's policies and practices. And although this subcommittee was not hostile to Cook or his ideas—early on, this group also espoused an interest in supporting more rehabilitation and recommended adopting a completely indeterminate sentencing scheme, funding for counseling, and reentry services—its very existence functioned to reduce Cook's authority over correctional matters.

The criticism of the Cook regime from within the state, then, was threefold. First, he was an outsider who did not sufficiently respect the way things were done in Arizona. This led to the second and third points, which were that he advocated expensive, oversized, bureaucratic government that wasted taxpayer dollars; and that he was, on one hand, not tough enough on criminals, but on the other, not sufficiently handling problems with poor prison conditions, which were prompting further outside intervention.

CHALLENGES FROM OUTSIDE

Cook opened the state's penal system to the outside world in unprecedented ways. He sought and obtained all kinds of federal funding as well as other federal resources, he received technical assistance from outside state and federal corrections experts, he oversaw investigations and evaluations of the state's penal operations conducted by various outsiders, and he filled his administration with out-of-state practitioners who brought with them different penal styles and philosophies. Clearly, this was part of a deliberate strategy to modernize and impart change, in his own vision, within the state's penal operations.

Yet such exposure and input not only brought the kinds of transformations that Cook sought, it also brought new scrutiny from outside to the state's practices, over which Cook had no control. A telling moment of this transition occurred in 1972 when Ellis MacDougall, a corrections expert who at that time headed Georgia's Department of Offender Rehabilitation,[3] was commissioned by the legislative subcommittee on prison reform to conduct an evaluation of the entire Department of Corrections through the LEAA technical assistance program. This was exactly the kind of outside intervention that Cook had introduced to the state, but before this assessment, he had always been directly involved in seeking such support and shaping the process. This time, though, the legislature acted on its own to assess the department with outside expertise. Cook was not "permitted" to discuss the evaluation or its findings with MacDougall before the report's completion (Cook, 1972c), and he was the third in line, after the legislature and the governor, to even receive a copy of the finished report.

His displeasure with this turn of events was made evident in his letter to Governor Williams in response to the report. He was particularly bothered by

MacDougall's recommendation that the governor, with the legislature's consent, appoint a seven-member board of corrections that would be empowered only to hire and fire the director of corrections. In the report, MacDougall lauded Director Cook and suggested that this recommendation would actually protect Cook from the legislative politics that seemed to be brewing in the state. MacDougall went on to outline a recommended increase in salary for the director position so that the state could hire a top administrator and defined a set of specific educational, personality, and dispositional qualifications required to attract "a man of such caliber" to run the department (MacDougall, 1972).[4]

Cook's letter expressed his thoughts about this and other aspects of the report and illustrates his growing frustration over his relationship with the legislature:

> Like you, I certainly cannot agree with [MacDougall's] Recommendation IX concerning the establishment of a Board of Corrections. I have always felt that the Director should be directly responsible to the Governor in order to create a "two-way street" thru which procedures can be expedited rather than having them delayed by a Board. I have worked in both types of systems and I think ours is more efficient.
>
> It is unfortunate that Mr. MacDougall was not permitted to discuss his observations with us prior to writing his report. Such a conference could have prevented his making some recommendations that are contrary to Arizona law, although laws can be changed. However, for instance, we could have told him that the Legislature has authorized the construction of the Correctional Training Facility which will take these kids out of the prison but they have not provided the construction funds to get the job done. (Cook, 1972c)

Thus, this evaluation, although not critical of Cook or the department and which resulted in a set of recommendations that were for the most part in line with what Cook sought for improving the quality of corrections, represented a challenge to Cook's authority and a dilution of his power within the state. Ultimately, the existence of the legislative subcommittee, which was taking a fairly activist role in the prison system, signified the coming end of Cook's standing as the sole expert who knew how to reform Arizona's penal system to make it more modern and progressive.

The diminution of Cook's role did not mean that the newly introduced philosophy of rehabilitation for penal operations was already on its way out, but it did in many ways point to its fragility in this particular jurisdiction. As noted, the recommendations of the legislative subcommittee were generally progressive and explicitly sought to improve rehabilitation. The critiques of Cook were not even primarily about the rehabilitative reforms he wanted to implement, but the longer standing ethos that required at least a bit of pain and discipline for wrongdoers became salient at least in the partisan political battles being fought around him and his department. Thus, Cook's fall from grace allowed older cultural norms, which he sought to eliminate, to be revived and reasserted in the struggle over defining the purpose and goals of punishment.

CHANGES WITHIN

Cook's reforms also appear to have prompted a series of changes within the state that may have been both slower in coming and less dramatic without such exposure. These internal events led directly to unwanted outside intervention—in the form of legal inquiries and federal lawsuits—that Cook does not appear to have been prepared for at all. Specifically, by virtue of instituting reform throughout the state's penal operations, Cook introduced the possibility for change and reform to the prisoners themselves. Before Cook came, prisoners and confined juveniles had little voice or power in the state. Both state penal institutions were run by highly authoritarian leaders, and any unrest within the facilities was quickly quelled and constructed in the local news media as the product of "problem" convicts, rather than as legitimate protest.

But once the Department of Corrections began, first, to label certain practices and conditions as being detrimental to those confined and, second, to actually institute change, the opportunity for inmates to demand improved conditions arose. Of course, an increasing concern about the rights of criminal defendants and inmates was simultaneously occurring across the nation as federal courts became more involved in prison operations (Feeley and Rubin, 1998), so it is hard to imagine that federal intervention would not have touched Arizona. Yet it might well have hit this state with less force and would likely have triggered less turmoil without the coincidental transformations happening within the state as prompted by Cook's reform regime. Lawsuits over the conditions of confinement quickly came to dominate the way corrections evolved, institutionally and bureaucratically, legally, and politically over the next decade and beyond (see Chapters 3 and 6).

The first indication of a direct legal challenge to Cook, signaling the coming onslaught of challenges, occurred in 1970. The Arizona Civil Rights Commission wrote to Cook to inform him that the agency's director was going to launch an investigation into charges concerning "possible discrimination against minorities at the Arizona State Prison" (Smith, 1970). This investigation was prompted by prisoner complaints made to the commission and to the League of Latin American Citizens, an Arizona nonprofit advocacy group, that white inmates were given preferential treatment within the prison.

As was the historical pattern at the prison, nonwhites were a disproportionate percentage of the population, consistently comprising almost 50 percent of the inmate population while the prison workforce remained predominantly white. Complainants alleged that nonwhite inmates were kept from the best jobs and that whites disproportionately held paying jobs in general (only about one-third of all jobs were paid), especially the highest-paying jobs. White inmates also were disproportionately overrepresented in the vocational programs, which tended to have long waiting lists, and in the educational programs. On the other hand, inmates complained that nonwhites disproportionately bore the brunt of discipline within the state's institutions.

Cook's response to this initial inquiry reveals his relative lack of awareness about potential litigation and its adversarial nature, which he did not significantly face during his earlier California career:

> We will sincerely welcome such an investigation and you may rest assured that Superintendent Frank A. Eyman and his staff will cooperate with you to the fullest extent of this endeavor.
>
> I have every reason to believe that you will find everything in good order at the Prison. Mr. Eyman and I both watch the situation with regard to the minority races very closely and we know of nothing that is out of order. You are aware of the fact, as well as I am, that incarcerated people are never happy with their lot. Therefore, it is not unusual for inmates to make complaints that are unjustified. (Cook, 1970)

Cook went on to lament the overcrowding problem in this letter, specifying that the prison currently held more than 1,700 inmates when it was designed for only 804 and that they were trying to obtain the funds to secure new housing to alleviate this problem. His response, then, almost seemed to be another attempt to use the inquiry to further his goals, by highlighting the problems with overcrowding and lack of funding even though the inquiry was specifically limited to allegations of discrimination against minority inmates.

The investigation did not go anywhere for two years, other than resulting in a report about the severe underrepresentation of racial minorities among correctional staff. In 1972, the Arizona Civil Rights Commission turned over the complaint to the U.S. Civil Rights Commission, which launched a full-scale "study" of the men's and women's divisions at the Arizona State Prison that was actually conducted by a locally appointed committee, the Arizona Advisory Committee to the U.S. Commission of Civil Rights (see Chapters 3 and 6). This inquiry was not only about the original complaint of racial discrimination; it also set out to examine the quality of vocational and educational opportunities, the general treatment of prisoners, and the rehabilitation programs.

The inquiry of the Civil Rights Commission was only the second one launched nationally by that body (a similar one had been conducted in Ohio), so clearly this was a significant event for the Arizona department. Yet Cook still does not seem to have grasped its seriousness. The local advisory committee liaison to the commission pointed out to an *Arizona Republic* reporter that Cook seemed more concerned about "brick and mortar" changes to the prison; in his words, the commission was "all for that too, but the evidence we have now indicates there should be some other kind of changes" (Armstrong, 1972). Cook expressed his dismay over the whole process, telling a reporter that he spent two hours with the commission staff member when she told him about the inquiry, but he did not understand the reason for the inquiry. As he told the reporter, "She did not ask me any civil rights questions." Cook also expressed his frustration over the inquiry, given that the legislature was also working on prison reform. He reported that "all it will do is upset the inmates and make more trouble for us. We'll cooperate and do everything we can, but I don't see the reason for it" (Armstrong, 1972).

The other set of incidents that vexed Cook during his tenure were the spate of lawsuits that inmates filed against the department and the negative news reports that cited inmate complaints about their treatment. It appears that these things, for Cook, crossed the line of authority. Although he was progressive in his penal philosophies, at least by Arizona's standards, he was not too terribly different from Eyman in terms of his conception of the prisoner's role. In his view, he and his administration knew what was best for inmates, and they should be the grateful, or at least willing, recipients of the "correction" and reformation that his program offered. Therefore, he treated their lawsuits and complaints as illegitimate and inappropriate.

For example, in August 1972, Cook asked the legislature to consider enacting a law that would exempt his employees from tort actions, which were increasing in frequency within the state. Many of these claims were, in his words, merely a challenge by inmates to "the idea of incarceration." He described the suits as being a time-consuming distraction and potentially very costly to the department, in that "some jailhouse lawyer may come up with a case that will cost the state or an employee a great deal of money" (Warne, 1972b).

Cook also responded to various news reports about poor prison conditions and abuses, generally labeling these allegations as "lies." He wrote letters to complain about such coverage and tried to rebut in print such allegations. For instance, in 1971, the department was the subject of a critical editorial that detailed complaints by former inmates and others about abuses in the prison. In response, Cook wrote the state attorney general to protest and, it seems, to implicitly encourage some form of legal action:

> Please note the attached copy of an editorial in the Yuma and Tempe papers. . . . The story, of course, is basically a bunch of lies. Furthermore, I have damaging evidence against nearly every one of the storytellers present. It may be too late to accomplish anything constructive with the Legislators. For this reason, I plan to go to the press for the preparation of counteracting stories—if they will publish them. (Cook, 1971)

A final assault on Cook's expertise and authority, from his perspective, was the success of a lawsuit, *Taylor v. Arizona*, filed by inmates over the disciplinary practices within the prison. In a stipulated agreement referred to as the "Copple Order," so named for the federal district judge in the case, the state settled with the plaintiffs and agreed to implement major changes to the disciplinary procedures at Florence (see Chapter 6). The orders of the agreement took effect in December 1972, with minor issues resolved over the following months, and meant continued intervention by the courts in correctional business. That case, along with Cook's knowledge of cases in other states in which directors were being successfully sued for monetary damages, were cited by Cook's protégé, LaMont Smith, as contributing to Cook's decision to resign.

THE CHANGING WORLD OF PENALITY
AND THE FALL OF COOK'S VISION

Ultimately, Cook seemed to be a casualty of the times, in that he represented an older generation of corrections experts who were true believers in the value of rehabilitation and who operated with the kind of paternalistic style that was central to the left and radical critiques of the rehabilitative penal project. Changes and major upheavals that were occurring in penal systems around the country began to emerge within Arizona, and Cook seems to have been ill-equipped to deal with those challenges. Indeed, he was out of sync with the more progressive developments in the penological field that openly questioned some of the longstanding penal "truths" that had guided his career in corrections.

Cook's discomfort with changes in the penal world was reflected in the way he publicly and privately responded to outside events such as the prison uprisings at Attica and San Quentin. These events prompted Cook to seek LEAA assistance for the 1971–72 prison security study. After the San Quentin incident, he told the press that Arizona should learn a lesson from California's experience and not get lax on security and screening procedures, even though the department was "constantly bombarded [by prisoner demands and lawsuits] to let down" (Warne, 1971). He reported that he planned to continue to censor mail and search all visitors to protect against an event like Attica's and expressed hope that the department would not be "forced," presumably by a court order, to change its strict security policies.

Governor Williams was of the same view as Cook (and, for that matter, as Frank Eyman) and in several correspondences sounded the Arizona-style ethos in reaction to prisoner uprisings. For example, after the California and New York disturbances, Governor Williams sent Cook several out-of-state newspaper articles that reported on these incidents, with attached letters of commentary. In one such letter, Williams wrote: "I hope you have assured Frank Eyman that in Arizona the prisoners do not run the prison! Furthermore, that just as they gave no chance for negotiation with their victims they have no right to negotiation as long as they are in prison. They earned their way to prison now let them earn their way out!" (Williams, 1971).

This philosophy was directly tested when, during the following spring, the prisoners at Florence went on "strike." In early May 1972, almost 1,000 of the 1,277 inmates refused to go to their work assignments until the administration addressed their "curriculum for reform," which listed 13 grievances and demands for action. This action within the prison coincided with prisoners' rights activity happening outside: at the same time, a group called the Arizona Citizens' Commission on Prisons was organized by activists, primarily based in Tucson, to highlight the problems in the state prison. Its goal was to expose government officials and members of the public to the specific issues and reforms needed to improve conditions within the facility at Florence. The strike lasted just 16 days and was fairly uneventful, but the department handled the incident as if it had the potential to lead to a major riot or other violent confrontation. The incident also provided an impetus for further action to the citizens' commission, which sponsored hearings in Tucson that summer during which ex-convicts testified about their experiences in the prison. Thus, although Cook and the governor, in essence, tried to maintain an authoritative yet "progressive" stance toward prison reform, forces from within and outside the prison were pushing to change the terms of the state-prisoner relationship by promoting the concepts of prisoners' rights and human autonomy in their demands.

For Eyman, the strike was like old times, and he used it as an opportunity to share with the prisoners and the public, via the press, his long-standing penal philosophy. At the start of the strike, he voiced his opinion that "do-gooders were pressing too hard in the wrong direction," which had emboldened prisoners to strike (*Arizona Republic*, 1972a). He said that the discussion should be centered around inmate reform, not prison reform, to change the "anti-social, militant, drug-oriented problem prisoners" who now populated the prison. Eyman's immediate solution to the trouble in prison was to "lock everyone in his cell," and his longer term solution was to use his "therapeutic" program of physical fitness and athletic competition to teach the value of co-operation and respect for rules and regulation (*Arizona Republic*, 1972a).

A week later, as the strike wore on, Eyman more directly asserted his authority, threatening the inmates that if they resorted to violence, he would "make Attica look like a picnic" (*Arizona Republic*, 1972b). One of the outside prison reform activists proposed that William Kunstler, who had represented the prisoners at Attica in negotiations, be brought in to help resolve the strike and negotiate the prisoners' demands for them, but Eyman insisted that Kunstler "is not coming through the door" of his prison (*Arizona Republic*, 1972b). The Phoenix paper reminded its readers of Eyman's prior commitment to the iron fist approach, when he had welded inmates into their cells for inciting a disturbance. Thus, for Eyman, with the help of a sympathetic press, the unrest provided an opportunity to voice his concerns about the "modernization" project and to remind the public about the value in his old-style disciplinary approach to penology that Cook had weakened.

Later that summer, as the prisoners' rights movement came into full swing around the nation, Cook and Williams had to address a request from the National Alliance on Shaping Safer Cities to adopt their newly drafted Model Act for the Protection of the Rights of Prisoners, which was written by the National Council on Crime and Delinquency. In their personal correspondence about this request, both Williams and Cook expressed disdain for the document and what it represented. Williams asked Cook to draft a response that "we can live with," and in his request, he let Cook know that he "did not want to play into the hands of prison reform folk who will create more problems than they will solve" (Williams, 1972b).

Cook responded by first denigrating the drafters of the document, the national council, by saying that the organization "has gone completely liberal and is activist in nature," adding that he used to be a member but dropped out when it "went off in the other direction from my thinking" (Cook, 1972b). He then reported that he maintained his membership in the American Correctional Association, which he characterized as "conservative in nature, but still progressive" and which did not at that point support the Model Act. He attached a response letter for Williams to send back to the National Alliance on Shaping Safer Cities, which Williams adopted verbatim. That letter ended with the following: "With some temerity, I would like to suggest that, in the interest of safer cities, your organization get the prisoners of our institutions to draft a model act for the protection of the citizens upon whom they prey" (Williams, 1972a).

So as Cook finished his final full year as a correctional administrator—he would resign as director and permanently retire from corrections two months into 1973—his rehabilitative vision was no longer adequately supported within the state, which was most significantly felt in the lack of appropriations by the legislature; it was not appreciated by those it was supposed to help—the prisoners; and it was increasingly out of step with the broader transformations in penology brought by new prisoner demands, court orders, political and community activism, and other such social upheavals.

Because the bureaucratic roots of the Arizona Department of Corrections were so shallow and unentrenched within the state, Cook's reformative efforts were vulnerable to complete and radical overhaul as soon as he lost such support. Certainly, his singular vision, which imagined a new kind of correctional system that would replace traditional prisons and blur the lines between the correctional population and the community, would not be implemented by him or his successors. What that seemed to portend for the department, once Cook was gone, was turmoil that affected everything from the day-to-day operations to the underlying mission of the organization.

3 AN INSTITUTION IN SEARCH OF MEANING

CLEARLY, ARIZONA'S PENAL SYSTEM underwent a number of changes during the 1960s and early 1970s that were a product of social, cultural, legal, and political forces emanating both from within and outside of the state. Contributing to these transformations was the fact that the state itself was in the midst of massive change and growth. Indeed, the Sunbelt states of Nevada and Florida were the only jurisdictions in the nation to exceed the growth levels of Arizona from 1960 to 1970. The population in Arizona grew by 36 percent from 1960 to 1970 and an additional 54 percent between 1970 and 1980 (U.S. Department of Commerce, 2003). The state was also becoming more urbanized as it grew in size, as most of that growth occurred in the two urban counties—Pima and Maricopa—that also produced the bulk of the penal population.

As noted in Chapter 2, Arizona's political landscape also began to change dramatically during the 1960s: the old-style conservative Democrats had lost their hold on the legislature as Republicans wielded more and more power, and the new liberal Democrats, who primarily came from the Tucson area (with a few also representing parts of metropolitan Phoenix), became more activist in their representation. If Allen Cook had needed to contend only with the resistance of the conservative rural Democrats in initiating his penal reforms, he might have been more successful. But the complications of a growing and changing populace and the progressive resistance to his leadership on top of the conservative antipathy, as well as the expected resistance from old-timers and traditionalists, meant that Cook had to fight battles on multiple fronts, with victories in one area often meaning defeat in another.

Arizona's penal turmoil was exacerbated by administrative-level turnover that immediately preceded Cook's resignation. During about a six-month period between late 1972 and early 1973, no component of Arizona's correctional system was left untouched by administrative flux. The parole supervision division was still in disarray after the firing debacle of William Drew. Frank Eyman, who was expected to retire in 1973 when his third six-year contract expired, abruptly resigned his position in August 1972. A month later, Steve Vukcevich was evicted from his position at Fort Grant, beginning a legal (and political) battle that lasted years. Five months later, Cook resigned the directorship. Thus, the future direction of the fledgling Department of Corrections was far from certain, with no continuing leadership in the midst of ongoing growth, issues, and challenges. The potential was present at that point for the state to go in any number of directions: the likely possibilities were that it would abandon its experiment with "progressive penology" and return to its more disciplinary approach to punishment; alternatively, it could continue on Cook's path with the appointment of a like-minded administrator; or, the potential existed for it to move toward a more revolutionary, minimally incarcerative model that academic penologists and criminologists across the nation and beyond were envisioning. Ultimately, it took more than a decade of leadership roulette, accompanied by state attempts to implement a variety of correctional models, before a new penal paradigm emerged that seemed to stabilize the department and its operations, albeit at the expense of the prisoners' rights, privileges, and general well-being.

COOK'S LEGACY AND BEYOND

Cook's five-year tenure as pioneering director of the Arizona Department of Corrections had helped the penal system progress in some important ways from where it had been when the department was created in 1968. He introduced a more conventional model of rehabilitation to the framework under which corrections operated. This was tangibly seen in the introduction of halfway houses for adult offenders and the development of minimum-security camps for youths and adults, comprehensive reception facilities for juveniles and adults, and a state-run "ultramodern" school for girls that aimed to replace the contract placements that housed most of the girls in state custody.

But it was largely a story of dreams and visions unfulfilled. The majority of the population under the control of the department were still housed in the two traditional institutions that had been the subject of so much criticism to begin with: the prison at Florence and the Industrial School at Fort Grant. The proposed institution for youthful adult offenders that was to revolutionize corrections in the state was, at best, just a plan on paper with no funding to bring it to fruition. Even with Vukcevich gone, Fort Grant was still a rural, isolated institution that remained hard to fully reform, given the staffing logistics and its history in that setting. And the state prison was still bursting at the seams with inmates, perpetually run down, prone to security and safety problems, and physically inadequate to handle the state's diverse penal population. Nonetheless, the largely unfulfilled mission that Cook brought to the department did not die with his departure, despite the fact that the department had become reactive to mounting problems and challenges in the penal institutions rather than proactive during the early 1970s.

Cook's resignation does not appear to have been demanded from above; rather, records indicate that he had wanted to step down for some time but was persuaded to stay on by the governor. By early 1973, however, Cook was unequivocally ready to go back to his retirement, which he had deferred for about five years, and Governor Williams was clearly ready for leadership change so did not actively discourage Cook's departure. Given the state of affairs in early 1973, Governor Williams could have opted to abandon the mission as well as the man in replacing Cook, but he did not. Instead, he sought someone who would continue along the same path as Cook in terms of developing and implementing more progressive rehabilitation techniques within the system.

Cook's replacement, John Moran, brought skills and an outlook that were not so different from Cook's. Moran was also an outsider and a career (albeit much younger) correctional professional who had worked in the penal field since 1955 upon receiving his master's degree in social work from Boston College. He came to the Arizona job from Delaware, where he had spent two years as director of adult corrections and two years previous to that directing juvenile corrections for the state. His resignation in Delaware was the result of political fallout—he had been the golden boy of a Republican governor who was unseated by a Democrat—so he was aware of the political nature of the Arizona appointment. Thus, when faced with pointed questions about his approach to corrections during the Arizona Senate confirmation process, he was ready with answers that were vague enough and appropriately moderate to ensure his confirmation.

His confirmation hearing, which ended with unanimous support for his appointment, revealed the wariness of some senators about the increased "permissiveness" in corrections that had, in their view, been occurring in the state. He was asked about his position on capital punishment, his views on uncensored mail for prisoners, and whether he ascribed to a "social worker" approach to corrections. He assured the skeptical senators that he believed in discipline first and that no rehabilitation program could succeed without control in the institutions. He described himself to the press as a "middle of the road" kind of disciplinarian.

Yet Moran's tenure with the Department of Corrections lasted much longer than his political support in the state. He remained in the directorship until late 1977, but by that time, the system was being overseen in large part by a governor-appointed commission, the legislature was barely providing the department with enough revenue to maintain operations, and the courts continued to respond favorably to inmate lawsuits challenging their conditions of confinement, requiring the department to continually operate in crisis management mode.

Moran began with big plans for continued reform within the system and had immediate goals of bringing to fruition much of what Cook had envisioned. His first order of business was to make the case for the changes that he felt were imperative. He went on several highly publicized "inspections" of the prison during his first few months on the job, after which he declared the facility to be the "worst prison [he had] ever seen" (Boyles, 1973). He spoke to reporters, legislators, and civic groups around the state, describing the kinds of problems the prison had and the extent of reform needed. This strategy was successful during his early years. Within three months of taking over, he had obtained legislative approval with accompanying funding to restructure the department's administration by increasing top management from one deputy director to four. The legislature also allocated funds to increase frontline staffing at the prison and conduct major physical renovations throughout the institution; most significantly, the department received an appropriation of $5.1 million to build the long-planned facility for youthful adult offenders near Phoenix.

But Moran was quickly stalled as the prison crises did not disappear and the legislature cut off the flow of funding. As had become the case under Cook's tenure, the prison remained a focal point of the department's energies from day one for Moran, so it was very difficult for him to work at a more systemic level of reform. The few changes he did achieve during his early years included developing several more halfway houses; converting, with the legislature's approval, the long-troubled Fort Grant facility into an adult minimum-security institution; and converting the state-run juvenile girls' facility near Phoenix into a coed juvenile institution to deal with the displaced Fort Grant population.

THE EFFECT OF INTERNAL AND EXTERNAL UNREST

Multiple sources contributed to Moran's fall from grace, most of them emanating from the state prison. The prison was as overcrowded and decrepit as ever, and with Eyman's retirement it had lost almost all sense of order. Eyman's interim successor, former assistant warden A. E. "Bud" Gomes, was deemed a nice man but ineffectual as a warden, and this showed in terms of the level of chaos within the institution. Although many of the problems inside the prison predated both Moran's and Gomes's tenures and were a direct product of the overcrowding that resulted from the legislature's unwillingness to fund construction for new facilities, Moran still took the brunt of the blame.

The level of violence within the prison escalated after Eyman's resignation, and within months of Moran's appointment, it was no longer contained as a matter for the department to handle internally. The last major newsworthy incident under Cook's and Eyman's leadership had been the 1972 inmate strike, which provided Eyman with the opportunity to reassert, through the press, his tough disciplinary values. In contrast, the first major newsworthy incident of Gomes's tenure demonstrated his relative weakness in this regard. In late May 1973, prisoners took four guards hostage for several hours, and Gomes's publicly shared reaction was to label it an "isolated" incident, prompted in part by the inexperience of the guards themselves. He met the demand of the hostage takers' leader (he wanted to talk to his children) in order to ensure the safety of the hostages. Normal prison operations resumed the next day, and Gomes agreed to set up a meeting with a delegation of convicts to discuss their demands. Eyman undoubtedly would have taken a much more aggressive and punitive approach to fully demonstrate his authority.

As it turned out, Gomes's assurance that this was an isolated incident was premature. Three weeks later, inmates took two more guards hostage—one of them had been among the hostages during the previous incident—and murdered them. This event exposed the gravity of the disorder in the prison. Moran brought in more than 100 state police officers to sweep the institution for weapons and contraband. Furthermore, Moran had appointed a new warden, with extensive experience from outside the state, to take over for Gomes, and his start date was moved up several weeks to allow him to come in and clean up the mess.

The six-day sweep uncovered a zip gun factory on the prison grounds, inside the license plate building, and a number of prison-made guns stashed throughout the institution. Officers also found a counterfeit money operation in the print shop and truckloads of other weapons and contraband. In the immediate aftermath, the Department of Corrections was able to use this incident to garner increased staffing and pay raises for institutional frontline staff members in an effort to improve the quality of the prison employees. More than 100 new positions and a 7 percent salary increase were authorized by the State Personnel Commission to deal with the chronic understaffing that most felt contributed to the incident.

Yet the prison remained a problematic institution and impeded the department's forward movement. Moran had responded quickly and decisively to the guard killings and subsequent discovery of so many weapons, but the prison problems began to define the entire departmental function. The Phoenix newspaper recalled with nostalgia the "tough" regime of Frank Eyman, as a counterpoint to the news of continued expansion of prisoners' rights in the midst of the disordered chaos that was ongoing at Florence, implicitly suggesting that Eyman's style of penology should be resurrected.

There was little room for positive system-level reform and change while the prison remained such a troubled place. The formalized court order making permanent the interim Copple Order that had been stipulated to by the department and the plaintiffs in December was issued just two months later, solidifying prisoners' rights in disciplinary hearings. The timing was not great from the department's perspective; several state actors deemed it, somewhat derogatorily, as a "bill of rights" for prisoners that provided the most extensive set of prison rules in the world (Mazurek, 1973), implying that it was a reward for those who had, in their assessment, behaved so horribly in recent months.

Six months later, the U.S. Civil Rights Commission held hearings in Arizona to address prisoner and staff complaints about prison conditions, which some political leaders saw as a pointless exercise that only aimed to provide inmates with (again) a prisoners' bill of rights, which they in no way deserved (Schwartz, 1974). And Moran's efforts to mitigate the problems within the prison by moving forward on the planned young adult facility were also stalled. Citizens' groups in the Phoenix area, where the facility was to be built, successfully kept that from happening. Every time the department came up with a suitable site, opposition groups sprang up to pressure their legislators to prevent the site from being approved. In a press interview, Moran warned the legislature and the public that these battles contributed to the overall prison crisis and pushed the potential cost of the facility higher and higher. Nonetheless, the legislature succumbed to public pressure and eventually this facility's site was moved out of Maricopa County completely.

Just a little more than a year after Moran's appointment, the *Arizona Republic* raised the question of whether the "honeymoon" between Moran and the legislature was over (Sommer, 1974). What that meant for Moran was reduced fiscal support, decreased sponsorship and approval of bills that Moran crafted to aid the department, and increased second-guessing by the legislature for the remainder of his time in Arizona.

Nonetheless, county courts continued to send felons to prison, so the system had to grow in order to meet demand. The imprisonment rate in the state began a slow but steady ascent under Moran's tenure. It had been less than the national average through Cook's last years, but by the end of 1974, Arizona's incarceration rate was back above the national average, where it has stayed ever since. From 1971 to 1975, the incarceration rate in the state jumped nearly 60 percent whereas the national rate increased by less than 20 percent during the same time (U.S. Department of Commerce, 1976). In terms of sheer numbers, the population that Moran had to deal with grew quite large by the mid-1970s, jumping from 1,401 in 1971 to 2,647 in 1975, with no major new facilities added to the system to provide housing. The conversion of Fort Grant and a new halfway house added several hundred low-security beds, but Moran mainly had to find ways to stuff the extra men and women into the already overtaxed facilities at Florence. In the midst of this, the legislature reined in some of the department's discretionary power to use back-end release methods, such as early release for good behavior, as well as county judges' ability to provide alternative sentences. The legislature took its first swipe at judicial sentencing discretion in 1974 when it passed a mandatory minimum sentencing statute for armed robbery. This was followed by more extensive legislation requiring mandatory minimum sentences for a range of felonies, which was passed the following year and went into effect in 1976.

The year 1975 turned out to be a lengthy crisis period in the history of the Department of Corrections. By the end of that year, an unprecedented 2,000 inmates lived in the Florence facility, which was well above its capacity and an acknowledged disaster in the making. Arizona's penal system was ranked second in the nation for level of overcrowding and eighth in the nation for overall imprisonment rate (Evaluation report No. 76-5, 1976). Recognizing the gravity of the situation, the legislature formed a Joint Interim Committee on Corrections to study the problems with the system and devise a set of potential solutions. First among the identified problems was the severe lack of bed space along with the problem of lack of activities and programs available to most inmates. In a note appended to a rough draft of its final report, the committee implored the governor and senate leaders to take immediate action:

> THIS COMMITTEE FINDS THE ABOVE PROBLEMS TO BE SO SEVERE THAT A POTEN-
> TIALLY EXPLOSIVE SITUATION DOES PRESENTLY EXIST AT ARIZONA STATE PRISON
> AND THAT, IF THE STATE OF ARIZONA FAILS TO TAKE ADEQUATE AND APPROPRIATE
> MEASURES, SERIOUS DAMAGE MAY OCCUR TO LIFE AND PROPERTY. BECAUSE OF THE
> SITUATION, WE PETITION THE GOVERNOR OF THE STATE OF ARIZONA TO CALL, IN CO-
> OPERATION WITH THE PRESIDENT OF THE SENATE AND THE SPEAKER OF THE HOUSE,
> FOR A SPECIAL SESSION OF THE 32ND LEGISLATURE ON OR BEFORE JANUARY 7, 1976
> TO IMPLEMENT THE RECOMMENDED ABOVE LEGISLATIVE SOLUTIONS. (Joint Interim
> Committee on Corrections, 1975)

Yet instead of a special session to deal with the situation, the department got another prisoner strike, which began in early January.

This was not the full extent of Moran's problems; a large amount of political discord and blame throwing was going on beginning in late 1975 through the remainder of his tenure. Several left-leaning Democratic legislators became actively involved in prisoners' rights groups on the outside, most notably, the Alliance for Correctional Justice. Lucy Davidson, a state senator from Tucson, led this effort by organizing a series of meetings, making demands on the governor and fellow legislators, and working with legal advocates in an effort to improve conditions at Florence. Her coalition asked that Moran and Warden Harold Cardwell be fired.

The conservative wing of the Democratic legislative body, led by former Fort Grant superintendent Steve Vukcevich, also called for Moran's dismissal but on the grounds of his laxity and lack of tough, decisive leadership. Vukcevich recommended that Moran let Warden Cardwell "run the prison as a prison and go easy on the rehabilitation" (Tragash, 1976: B-3). He even suggested that he himself should take over from Moran, as he was the most qualified person in the state to do the job.

State Supreme Court justice William Holohan, a longtime critic of the department, publicly called for Moran's ouster because of his ineffectiveness as a leader and his inability to get the young adult facility built (Daien, 1975). Even the prisoners asked for the removal of Cardwell and Moran among their strike demands. Governor Raul Castro weighed in, backing Moran as director and blaming the legislature for all of the problems the department faced for not providing the funds needed to improve the prison system.

By this point, Moran's stature and authority within the state, and credibility with the legislature, were irreparably eroded. In short order, various Senate subcommittees directly targeted the department with cutbacks of power and resources. The appropriations committee killed the plan for a medium-security facility in Phoenix. The Senate Government Committee approved legislation cosponsored by Lucy Davidson to create an ombudsman position, appointed by the legislature, to oversee the entire Department of Corrections. Funding was appropriated at a bare minimum to maintain the status quo within the department, despite the steady increase in demands on the system, particularly the institutions. Individual senators and representatives continued their public criticisms of the department and Moran in particular, and in 1977 a select committee on corrections again asked the governor to fire Moran. Although Governor Castro once again voiced support for Moran, he also appointed a Governor's Commission on Corrections to come up with solutions to the mounting problems in the system. Federal civil rights investigators from the U.S. Department of Justice also returned to the state with new allegations of mistreatment and discrimination in the prison. Although Moran dismissed their inquiries as "going over old ground" from the previous probe, they were actually following up on new prisoner complaints (Adams, 1976).

The press was relatively unforgiving of Moran in its coverage. Although the papers had faithfully reported on prison troubles throughout the history of Florence, and across the tenures of several administrators, the local print media seemed to up the ante in creating and perpetuating controversies once an administrator began his descent in terms of legislative support. It happened to Cook, and it happened again to Moran. The 1976 escape of a convicted murderer from the Fort Grant minimum-security facility became the catalyst for continued coverage of the problems within the department.[1] In March 1977, the *Arizona Republic* conducted what it referred to as a study on how the department selected prisoners for minimum security and work furlough and reported that the department had lowered selection standards even further after the 1976 escape.

At Florence, violence continued to be the norm, and prisoner strikes and riots dominated life inside. Within the first five months of 1977, two major riots and a three-month-long prisoner strike resulted in extensive damage to several housing facilities, multiple fatal and nonfatal stabbings, and the shooting of a prisoner by a staff member. The legislature finally appropriated money to add new cell blocks within Florence, but instead of giving the funds to the Department of Corrections, it gave the money to the Department of Administration, which was directed to oversee the construction project. This unprecedented funding scheme was articulated by those on the Appropriations Committee as a deliberate, direct slap at Moran's authority. They acknowledged the critical need for more bed space, especially in light of massive changes in the criminal code that would take effect in 1978, but they did not trust Moran's ability to control or manage the funding.

Prisoners also regularly petitioned the federal courts for relief on a range of alleged constitutional violations. The climax of the legal challenges of this period was a lawsuit sponsored by the National Prison Project of the American Civil Liberties Union (ACLU) that sought an injunction to halt new admissions to the Florence prison because of the extreme overcrowding in the facility. In September 1977, U.S. District Court Judge Carl Muecke agreed with the plaintiffs in this case and granted an injunction in *Harris v. Cardwell* ordering the prison at Florence to reduce its population to 1,750 by the new year (see Chapter 6).

The court order added an immediate sense of urgency to the prison problems and necessitated significant involvement by a wide range of stakeholders at the state and local levels. Although the primary concern within the department, the executive branch, and the legislature was to figure out how to comply with the order, some of the political reaction within the state clearly foreshadowed the penal ethos of the next decade. Several legislators grumbled about the federal government's intrusion into state business and asked the attorney general's office to investigate whether a federal judge really had the power to let people out of prison if the state did not comply with the population caps.

SENTENCE REFORM

Despite the thorough lack of fiscal and moral support for the department at this point and the new sense of urgency brought on by Judge Muecke's order in *Harris v. Cardwell*, the legislature nonetheless simultaneously passed legislation that would necessitate rapid, continued expansion of the penal system. In 1977, the entire criminal code was overhauled to dramatically decrease judicial discretion in sentencing, increase mandated sentence lengths for many felonies, and close the loopholes on discretionary release at the back end. The new "presumptive determinate" sentencing code (Arizona Department of Corrections, 1992) also made it explicit that prison terms were for the purpose of punishment rather than rehabilitation.[2] The new code also mandated prison sentences for some offenses that had previously been eligible for probation or other alternative sanctions, so its effect was that more convicted felons were sent to prison for longer average sentences, with fewer options for early release. The feature of the new code that really drove up sentence lengths, though, was a section mandating long enhancements for prior felony convictions.

What is so striking about this reform is that the Department of Corrections provided detailed analyses to the legislative and executive branches about what it would mean in terms of the demand for bed space and costs to meet that demand, thus making it clear that the code change would necessitate a massive investment in corrections. At the same time, of course, the state legislators were aware that the system was operating under court order not to take additional prisoners without building new facilities and that the state was already facing difficulties in even complying with the court mandate. Nonetheless, the legislature, with little resistance, went ahead with the code change anyway. Although this sentencing reform was in step with broader national trends—at about the same time, California, for instance, also underwent a major code overhaul to return to determinate sentencing—it was out of character for this "pay-as-you-go" state to so deliberately ignore the fiscal ramifications of its actions.

Nothing at the time indicated that the legislators were willing to take the political risks necessary to fund the inevitable consequences of the sentencing reform—it would require diverting a considerable share of state funds from other governmental services, potentially raising taxes, and stepping on constituents' toes when siting the new facilities—but at the same time the federal courts had the state in the position that it could no longer continue to pack prisoners into its decrepit existing facilities. Yet the legislature knew the numbers. In his 1977 annual report and budget request, Moran presented the projections through 1981 for inmate populations, and their associated costs, using several different scenarios under consideration. He calculated predictions for growth, assuming no change to the existing criminal code and assuming the various possibilities under the proposed code change. The results were frighteningly stark. With no significant change to the code, the expected inmate population growth was 50 percent over five years; under the code change conditions that the legislature preferred, that growth was predicted to be 85 percent over the same period.

Given the history of inadequate funding for new construction, coupled with the legislature's tendency to punish department directors by withholding funding, it was hard to imagine how the system would be able to function at all in the immediate future, even without the projected increases in the inmate population. In the midst of planning for the code change, the state was also scrambling to comply with the court order to *reduce* the population in Florence. So simultaneously, Arizona legislators, administrators, and other political actors were carrying on in a frenzied pace to try to appease the federal court by reducing the number of inmates in the system, to plan for enormous increases in inmate numbers with no discernible funding stream to do so, and to contend with the potentiality of the new law that would severely exacerbate this problem in the near future.

In the short term, the Joint Legislative Budget Committee decided to hold an emergency session to consider appropriating funds in order to comply with the Muecke court order. For its part, the Governor's Commission on Corrections, appointed in March 1977, took on making the compliance happen as its primary business. The Department of Corrections, in conjunction with the commission and the attorney general, came up with a creative plan to comply: it contracted with three other states to house some Arizona prisoners, it sent all prisoners with concurrent sentences in other states to those locales to complete their sentences; it released some lower level offenders who were Mexican nationals to the Immigration and Naturalization Service for deportation; it moved a number of inmates into lower custody settings, such as the training camps and community centers; and it negotiated with local jails to house state prisoners. However, it still could not achieve the kind of population reduction at Florence that was ordered, given the existing facilities, staffing, and limits on release options.

In the midst of the scrambling to meet the court's demands, the legislature ended up passing the most extreme version of the proposed code changes, which would, when enacted, most significantly increase the state's prison population. This moment seemed to signal a change in the politics of crime and punishment in the state. The message itself was not particularly new:

harsh sanctions had a long-standing place in this state's justice system. What was different was the willingness to shelve the practical considerations of the policy change for the political payoff that was expected to be gained by the adoption of a toughened-up determinate sentencing code.

Previously, the legislature had quietly allowed the prison to function as almost a hydraulic valve so that when it got too crowded, release mechanisms were available to the department to maintain at least a modicum of stasis. The prison was always close to the breaking point, but the population was generally held in check by allowing for back-door release measures. The new code almost completely closed off these avenues for future sentenced offenders. Thus, this appears to be the first significant incidence in which the symbolic politics trumped the practical in criminal justice policymaking to such an extreme degree within the state.

State lawmakers at the time articulated their values and goals in terms of the criminal justice system as, ideally, ensuring punishment and incapacitation for recidivists while maintaining fiscal conservatism as the guiding principle for corrections expenditures. The new code provided for mandatory minimum sentences for a broad range of felonies that increased significantly for repeat offenders. The legislature was still willing to fund and promote first-offender diversion programs for some lower level felonies as a cost-saving measure, and it grudgingly committed to providing humane treatment to comply with the various consent decrees now in place. But the larger message by this point was one that heralded harsh and certain punishment of felons.

Furthermore, the legislature's lukewarm commitment to "constitutional" punishment had its detractors. The seeds of what would become a major thrust of the state's penal philosophy (see Chapter 6) were planted by several influential legislators over the very issue of whether a federal judge—in this case, Carl Muecke—had the authority to tell them how to run their prison system. Thus, the discontent with federal meddling—again a deeply rooted political value in the state—began to be voiced, setting off a course of resistance that would become central to the punitive revolution of the 1980s.

DEPARTMENT DIRECTOR ROULETTE

In the end, John Moran would not have to tackle the seemingly insurmountable problem of housing the new influx of prisoners projected to pour in as a result of the code change while simultaneously decreasing the population at Florence. For better or worse, he was relieved of his duties in late 1977, a month after Secretary of State Wesley Bolin was appointed to take over as governor from Raul Castro, whom President Jimmy Carter had appointed to be the ambassador to Argentina.

In Bolin's press release announcing Moran's firing, he blamed the director for all of the problems in the prison. He echoed some legislators' views that the federal courts should have no say in the state's corrections business but said that it was Moran's fault for letting the situation get that far. Nonetheless, to the surprise of some of his allies, he concluded his statement by announcing his decision to bring in another out-of-state director to solve the prison problems. He said that he was seeking the help of the governor of Texas in finding a suitable candidate from that state because "Texas has the finest prison system in the nation" (Bolin, 1977). In the meantime, Bolin appointed one of his staff members (someone with public utility experience but little correctional experience) as interim director until he could appoint the right Texan.

His Texan of choice, Ronald Taylor, turned out not to be the silver bullet envisioned. Indeed, his botched appointment highlighted the rashness of Governor Bolin's decision to fire Moran in the midst of continuing turmoil. Taylor's administrative experience in corrections was fairly limited—he was a former rodeo director for the Texas prisons and had most recently been a public affairs officer for the corrections department. More importantly, he did not meet the minimum requirements for the position, so his permanent appointment was impossible without legislative action. He had just six years of total experience in corrections, and the position statutorily required a minimum of 10.[3]

Ultimately, the legislature was willing, albeit reluctantly, to change the law so as not to require a specified amount of corrections administrative experience, and on an emergency basis, to make the change effective immediately. But by the time the legislature voted on it, just two months into Taylor's tenure as acting director, Taylor decided to turn down the opportunity to become permanent director and instead returned to his position in Texas. At that point, it was fairly clear to Taylor and many others that, even with the change in qualifications, he would not be able to get the support in the Senate to be confirmed for the permanent position. With this setback, Governor Bolin appointed a longtime corrections figure within the state, John McFarland, as the next acting director and hastily assembled a search committee for a permanent director. This debacle incurred significant criticism of Bolin by a number of legislators as well as among newspaper columnists. Just weeks later, in

March 1978, before much work had been done on the search, Governor Bolin unexpectedly died and then–attorney general Bruce Babbitt was appointed governor.

Babbitt made the corrections search a top priority. His search committee received applications from more than 40 candidates, including eight from within the state. Nonetheless, Babbitt went outside in naming his candidate: University of South Carolina criminal justice professor Ellis MacDougall, who had served as the state's consultant during Cook's directorship (see Chapter 2). MacDougall had extensive administrative experience, heading the corrections departments in South Carolina, Georgia, Connecticut, and for a brief time, Mississippi. MacDougall was the fifth person to be in charge of the still-troubled agency in seven months.

Like Moran's and Cook's before him, MacDougall's tenure lasted longer than his political support within the state, so although he brought some stability to the department, his reforms generated less and less excitement within the legislature over his four and a half years in Arizona. He was the darling of that body during his first two to three years and so was rewarded with relatively generous appropriations, but by the time of his resignation in December 1982, he had become reactive and defensive in his negotiations for resources and legislative reforms.

MACDOUGALL'S VISION

MacDougall joined the Department of Corrections in June 1978 while it was still in the midst of dealing with Judge Muecke's overcrowding order and just as it was preparing to deal with the effects of the code change in criminal sentencing that was to go into effect on October 1. His penal philosophy was decidedly more progressive than his predecessors' and than the legislature as a whole, but he was successful at selling his proposals, which included alternatives to prison, in decisive, practical, fiscally conservative terms that the state could accept. For instance, about seven months into the position, he told a reporter for the *Arizona Republic*, "I don't think the Arizona taxpayers will be able to afford it [the growing cost of corrections] unless they adopt alternatives to incarceration, or sacrifice budget priorities like mental health and higher education" (O'Brien, 1979: B-2). He went on to point out that the average inmate was serving five years for stealing something worth less than $200 at a cost to the taxpayer of about $100,000. Thus, he played right to a core political value in the state, fiscal frugality, when advocating what would otherwise be unpalatable to many lawmakers and voters. This message was repeated in varied forms throughout his tenure in Arizona.

The medium-security young adult facility finally opened in Tucson in early 1978—10 years after Allen Cook had conceived of it—which gave Mac-Dougall much more flexibility in housing inmates. The institution had been fully transformed from the time of its conception to its concrete realization nearly a decade later. The metamorphosis symbolically reflects the change in priorities over those years and is indicative of the movement toward a mass incarceration state that was larger and more structural in nature than the top correctional administrator's vision. In other words, even though MacDougall was in many ways the most "left" in his penal perspective of all the directors who had served in Arizona, the forces at work within the state had morphed what was to be a "revolutionary" institution into, simply, just additional bed space for housing the growing influx of prisoners.

This facility had been originally conceived of as exclusively for young adult inmates, aged 18 to 25, who would receive extensive training and education and would have the benefit of being in an urban setting for the progressive process of reimmersion into the community while being shielded from the damaging influence of older and wiser convicts in the system. Under Moran's tenure, as the facility made it out of the planning stages, it was still seen as designed for the youthful offender; however, that youthful offender had lost some of his innocence in the department's rhetorical construction. By late 1973, under Moran's directorship, in a document that reported on the department's rationale for the institution, the targeted offender was still described as needing training and other rehabilitative intervention away from the "contaminating" influence of older prisoners, but he also was constructed as an "aggressive, dangerous, acting out, disturbed young man who needs controls and security so he can be most effectively treated" (Preliminary Plan, 1973). By the time the facility opened in 1978, its name—the Arizona Correctional Training Facility—was the strongest representation of its original vision; in practice, it was another place, like Fort Grant and all other department-run facilities outside of the Florence main cell blocks, to divert prisoners in the state's effort to comply with the Muecke order. And although it was, in its early years, used only for young adults who were 25 years old or younger and for juveniles convicted as adults, over a matter of just a few years, it offered little to differentiate it from any other medium-security prison.

Even with this institution's opening, there still was not enough space for maximum-security inmates, so MacDougall used creative classification changes to move enough men out of the units under court order to nearly achieve the population ceilings imposed by Judge Muecke. At the same time, MacDougall began to implement some of his own progressive reforms within the system. It is these reforms that later represented the antithesis of the harsh philosophy that prevailed during the 1980s under Director Samuel Lewis. Indeed, MacDougall's philosophy was an academically informed one that very much emulated the nascent community corrections trend that was competing with the emerging "tough-on-crime" model around the nation (and beyond).

Given the criminal justice ethos within the state, as exemplified by the change in the criminal code that now defined its purpose as aiming to "proscribe conduct that unjustifiably and inexcusably causes or threatens substantial harm to individual or public interests, . . . insure the public safety by preventing the commission of offenses through the deterrent influence of the sentences authorized; [and] impose just and deserved punishment on those whose conduct threatens the public peace" (Arizona Revised Statutes, 1978: 1–2), MacDougall's success would depend on how well he could continue to recast his views in politically acceptable language. His agenda was fairly ambitious and was composed of several key initiatives that he began to implement in 1979.

Urban Institutions

MacDougall and Governor Babbitt were resolved to build the next few institutions in urban settings—specifically in or near Phoenix as Tucson had ended up with the first planned urban facility. MacDougall's view (in line with that of his predecessors) was that it was essential for the rehabilitation of inmates who would eventually be released into the community to be housed near their homes, and the majority of the penal population came from the Phoenix area. MacDougall also saw the goal of diversifying staff as much more difficult when facilities were sited in remote, rural areas. Yet in promoting this position, he emphasized the cost benefits of centrally locating institutions, in terms of hiring and maintaining staff. During his first year, he and Babbitt pushed hard to get two medium-security facilities approved to be built in Litchfield Park in West Phoenix. The alternative proposal brought by several legislators was to build all future prisons in Florence, as that town's residents were used to having a prison in their community. MacDougall suggested that such a plan would cost up to $6 million more over time because of Florence's distance from urban centers. Ultimately, the Phoenix plan earned majority legislative support, although there were some vocal detractors.

The planning was held up, however, by Litchfield Park residents who organized and sued to prevent the facilities from being built. This effort was perhaps the most organized and forceful group activism to have ever occurred in the state around prison issues. The residents were not opposed to building more prisons, or to the harsh policies that would ensure the need for more facilities; they were simply well-organized and vocal NIMBYs who did not want to see their property values decline and their sense of safety erode with a prison in their midst. Petitions signed by thousands of residents were sent to Governor Babbitt, state legislators from the Litchfield Park area became major advocates for keeping the prisons out, local political figures aided in the effort, and the activists worked the local press to keep the story in the news.

This battle slowed down the construction program over the next few years, as the challenges worked their way through local courts. Unlike previous incidents of urban residents' protests against building prisons in their vicinity, however, in this case, the Department of Corrections forged ahead with its plans, determined to break ground even while engaged in fights on several fronts about the site. The department got a win in August 1979 when a Maricopa County judge dismissed the two lawsuits filed in an effort to prevent the prisons from being built. The plaintiffs appealed, but the preparations for construction moved ahead. The department and the residents eventually reached a settlement whereby the department agreed to strict limits on population numbers and density. Thus, the new 1,200-bed men's and women's prison, named the Arizona Training Facility at Perryville, was under construction by 1980, with an opening date set for the first units in 1981.

As part of his larger plan to enhance the quality of the system, MacDougall also established the Alhambra Reception and Treatment Center within the Arizona State Hospital in Phoenix. Here, new male arrivals to the system underwent an intensive weeklong intake process. During intake, staff administered a battery of psychological and cognitive tests to assess programming needs, conducted medical exams, took a full "social and criminal" history of each inmate, and then determined proper classification level and placement (MacDougall, 1980: 21). Psychotic inmates were also housed here for treatment.

In another controversial move in 1979, MacDougall moved the women's division into a converted motel in central Phoenix that the department leased from a private businessman. MacDougall justified the move on ideological grounds as well as practical ones. The new facility, the Arizona Center for Women, was to be an interim facility until the women's unit at Perryville (Litchfield Park) was opened. The women had been temporarily housed in space leased in the Maricopa County Jail when their unit at Florence had been taken over for the use of male prisoners in an effort to comply with the Muecke population reduction order. Maricopa County needed the jail space back to accommodate a growing number of county inmates, so the department had nowhere to house its 160 female inmates. The motel was the right size, with more than 200 rooms, and it had the benefit of facilitating community-based corrections for that population. In his annual report, MacDougall cited the advantage of the location and design of this facility in that it "not only allows some of the women to go outside the institution but brings the community into the institution" (MacDougall, 1980: 34). He urged the state to buy the building outright because it was not only a bargain, but it had potential for innovative community programs along the lines of his vision for corrections.

Area business owners, along with Phoenix city officials, tried to keep the conversion from happening, appealing to individual legislators and the governor and ultimately seeking an injunction from the Maricopa County court. Nonetheless, as with the Perryville facilities, the department proceeded quickly to complete the necessary construction, moving trusty prisoners on-site to do the work while the legal fight played out in court. After a two-week court trial, the judge ruled in favor of the department, and within a few months, the inmates were relocated to the newly converted facility.

From "Inmates" to "Residents"

MacDougall's philosophy on inmate identity was in direct contrast to Warden Eyman's perspective, which had been institutionalized in the system more than 20 years earlier. As MacDougall told a reporter in early 1979: "I try to give inmates a sense of identity. For instance, I let them grow mustaches and have long hair. Without some sort of identity, they lose self-esteem" (O'Brien, 1979: B-2). In keeping with that philosophy, MacDougall recast "inmates" as "residents" and revamped the "Inmate Rule Book" into a "Resident Orientation" handbook (individualized for each unit). Although this handbook did delineate rules and procedures, it read more like something that would be given to college dormitory residents than to prison inmates. It was devised by an orientation committee that was composed of equal numbers of staff and "residents," and it touted the many programs and activities available to residents. The procedural sections emphasized the benefit of courtesy and cooperation in going about one's daily business, rather than making demands for strict compliance and threatening disciplinary action.[4]

MacDougall also loosened the clothing restrictions to maximize a sense of individuality, making it possible for residents throughout the system to wear their own street clothes if they obtained them through gifts or purchase. Residents were also allowed a huge array of personal property, limited only by the capacity of their cell space and their access to goods, including, for the first time, privately owned televisions in their cells.

He relaxed rules about movement within each institution as well, so inmates no longer marched en masse at specified times from one location to the next; each resident could earn the privilege of moving about the entire unit on his own schedule. There were, of course, those who were under disciplinary restrictions who did not earn such privileges, but the general mode of each institution dramatically changed shape under MacDougall such that residents were given much more autonomy and sense of identity than they had ever had.

He added a number of programs within the prisons that were somewhat revolutionary, at least in Arizona. Perhaps the most progressive was the "Resident-Operated Business Enterprises," under which residents could run their own businesses from inside, including the production and sales of various crafts, inventions, and intellectual properties (primarily manuscripts). He also established the prison industries program, dubbed ARCOR Enterprises, and oversaw the 1981 construction of a warehouse at Florence exclusively devoted to that program. He developed a grievance procedure within the prisons that allowed residents to seek relief without going through the courts as a first step, and he invited a number of community groups to come into the institutions and establish chapters and programs.

Deinstitutionalization

MacDougall strongly supported alternative programs to traditional incarceration and worked with the legislature to provide for more flexibility in seeking such alternatives for felons under the jurisdiction of the department. He had several successes on this front. He continued to expand the capacity of the community treatment centers (halfway houses) for adults and juveniles. He closed the remote Alpine Conservation Center and in its place opened the

Desert Valley Learning Center in Phoenix, which he described as follows: "[The Learning Center] will provide a unique experience for juveniles. This facility will provide an 'alternative to incarceration,' on an economic yet effective basis. The Center, a community-based non-residential facility, will offer highly structured activities. Students will be required to attend 10 hours daily" (MacDougall, 1980: 45).

His major effect on deinstitutionalization, though, came through the expansion of the furlough program and increased powers he was able to achieve through legislation to use back-end release mechanisms as needed. In 1979, the legislature approved MacDougall's less stringent policy that allowed inmates to be furloughed directly from prison institutions for work, education, or vocational training as long as they were within a year of their release date. Before MacDougall's tenure, only residents at the halfway houses were eligible for the furlough programs, which meant that the number on furlough at any time was quite small—in the dozens rather than the hundreds. The eligibility criteria were loosened even further over the next two years to allow inmates who were up to two and a half years away from their release date to be eligible for furlough. This change dramatically increased the number of people eligible to be out in the community for significant portions of their sentences, and MacDougall's tendency was to apply the new policy broadly and generously.

Second, through a provision of the old criminal code, the director had discretion to release inmates who had been sentenced under that code 180 days before their scheduled release date if he deemed they warranted such treatment. This policy was a holdover from the days when the department was given more discretion to manage populations; MacDougall used this provision liberally as well, referring each person eligible for the earlier release to the parole board. MacDougall also used it in conjunction with another, newer statutory requirement that all inmates be released 180 days before sentence completion to be on a term of community supervision, and he allowed generous calculations of good time credits to release some inmates as early as three years before their maximum sentence date and to discharge them from parole before their maximum release date.

In 1979, the state's attorney general, Bob Corbin, who was not particularly fond of MacDougall's style of penology, put a stop to what he interpreted as excessively early release dates, claiming that the department was misapplying the statute in such a way that inmates were getting out three to six months too soon. By that point, MacDougall had used the provision to release almost

600 inmates early, and only 12 had been returned for violations. MacDougall decried the attorney general's ruling in the press, pointing out the low recidivism rate for those so released and the negative effects of the changes the attorney general demanded, namely, that it would cost an additional $3 million and result in a surplus of 400 inmates in six months. Nonetheless, the attorney general's interpretation stood, and in the process, one of MacDougall's most effective tools for population control was rendered much less potent.

In his later years with the Department of Corrections, MacDougall went to the press to publicly push for alternatives to incarceration for a wider range of first-time offenders, such as "restitution centers" for property offenders (which he had developed in Georgia) and decriminalization of narcotics use, advocating for drug-treatment programs instead of incarceration. His success on this deinstitutionalization front, however, tapered off beginning around 1980, and by MacDougall's last year in Arizona, the legislature was pushing to roll back the powers that it had earlier granted him—especially in terms of the furlough program.

WAREHOUSING BEGINS

Despite MacDougall's philosophical bent, and his resolve to transform the penal practices in Arizona, and despite Governor Babbitt's full support of MacDougall in these efforts, the number of sentenced felons that arrived from county courts, especially with the new criminal code operating in full force, quickly overwhelmed the system and forced a model of confinement that literally involved warehousing in the state. It becomes clear at this point that leadership philosophy, in terms of both the agency itself and the executive branch, was not powerful enough to stave off mass incarceration. Under MacDougall's leadership, the state correctional population began to explode, and most committed offenders ended up in traditional prison institutions. When MacDougall started with the department in 1978, about 3,200 inmates were confined to the state's prisons; by the time he left at the end of 1982, that number had swollen to nearly 5,800. The annual net growth rate of the institutional population jumped in one year between 1981 and 1982 from around 250 to 1,350, a trend that would escalate in the coming years.

Even with the opening of the first units at Perryville in 1981, the department never had surplus beds. Rather, the population influx so outstripped capacity that MacDougall, like his predecessors, spent much of his time dealing with the nonstop scramble for places to put inmates, as the department was forced to make room for inmate beds wherever it could. Thus, the new ARCOR Enterprises warehouse built exclusively for the young prison industries program was immediately converted into an inmate warehouse—100 "residents" were housed in the sweltering building for most of 1982 because there was no more space for them in more conventional housing throughout the system.

And that was not the only makeshift housing: at the Tucson training facility and Safford Conservation Center, the first Arizona "tent cities" were erected in early 1982 to house inmates.[5] Also in early 1982, Senator Barry Goldwater acquired 136 old Quonset huts from the U.S. military that had been in storage for more than 30 years in Georgia. They were allocated to the Department of Corrections as "do-it-yourself" prisons and arrived via train that summer for inmates to place on prison property. They were quickly dubbed the "tin cans" by the inmates who were to move into them from the warehouse (Ariav, 1982). Nonetheless, they went up at Florence and at other prison-owned sites that year, where they continue to be used for housing into the twenty-first century. And in all of the facilities across the state, available recreational spaces, such as lounges, TV rooms, and gyms, were converted into dormitories for the overflow population.

The irony of the MacDougall directorship was that he was the most explicitly oriented toward deinstitutionalization and alternatives to incarceration in the history of the Department of Corrections, yet he oversaw the beginning of the state's move to mass incarceration. Because he was so successful at getting funding from the legislature (correctional colleagues referred to him as a "master" at working with legislatures; see Hait, 1981), that body was generous in funding new construction during his tenure. His line to the legislature was generally that it would be cheaper and more effective not to invest in more prisons but to fund alternatives to prison; however, since lawmakers wanted the long sentences mandated by the new criminal code, he needed the money from them to accommodate the growing number of committed offenders.

As a result, during MacDougall's four years as director, the first Tucson facility fully opened; the motel in Phoenix was converted into a women's facility and opened; the men's and women's units at Perryville, adding 1,200 beds to the system, were approved, built, and opened; a new men's unit that added nearly 400 beds at the Tucson facility was approved, built, and opened; a 140-bed "release center" for nonviolent offenders nearing sentence completion was opened in a leased facility in Tucson; and two new cell blocks, totaling 500 additional beds, were approved, built, and opened at Florence, including an early supermax-style unit, Cell Block 6 (CB-6). Thus, in just over four years with MacDougall at the helm of the Department of Corrections, adult prison capacity in Arizona grew from about 3,000 to more than 5,300, with more construction in the planning stages. His annual operating budget (excluding construction allocations) had tripled during the same period, from $30 million to $90 million.

The CB-6 unit was part of the transformation brought on by the explosion in the number of inmates, but it also represented the onset of the transformation of prison life. It was opened in 1979 and was referred to by MacDougall and his staff as a supermax unit where inmates would be in solitary confinement for 23 hours a day (Boyles, 1979). It was designed to isolate problem inmates as a control technique, which contrasted with the way the use of such confinement was generally framed in the modernist, rehabilitative era. Isolation, or solitary confinement, has been a penal technique since the first U.S. penitentiaries. Traditionally, it was used as a tool to reshape the offender by giving him time alone for penitence or moral cleansing, as a specific or general deterrent, or as a deserved punishment for the confined offender. The supermax concept is associated with a more actuarial, new penological rationale, in that it is used as a management tool to maintain order and efficiency in the system rather than as an individualized intervention. MacDougall argued for this unit and framed its value in terms of its utility as a management tool rather than in terms of its utility to change individual offenders, thus pioneering one of the hallmarks of the postrehabilitative prison (see Chapter 4).

In all of this expansion, MacDougall, like his predecessors and successors, touted the cost savings of using inmate labor wherever feasible. Gone were the days that inmates actually built full-fledged cell blocks, as they had in Eyman's time before the department was established, but inmates did supply a significant amount of labor in all of the construction and retrofitting projects. And MacDougall knew enough about the state's politics to be sure to mention this fact in several press interviews and before the legislature.

MACDOUGALL'S DEMISE

MacDougall's popularity with some members of the legislature had begun to wane over the battle to build the Perryville prisons in Litchfield Park. The division over prison siting was significant in itself and also became an issue around which partisan politics began to play out. By this time, both chambers of the legislature were controlled by Republicans, and within that group, a

growing number had moved farther to the right politically. Less than two decades earlier, the Republican legislators had been the more moderate members
of that body compared with the traditional Democrats, favoring expanded
government when necessary and "enlightened" social and legal policies; but
by 1980, there was a powerful movement within the Republican Party away
from such a moderate philosophy. It was noticeably emerging around issues
of crime and punishment, and the "soft-on-crime" accusation began to be
hurled at Democrats whenever the opportunity arose.

Thus, MacDougall and Governor Babbitt, a Democrat, were lumped together as arrogant and inflexible and out of sync with the state's citizenry
by some vocal Republicans in the legislature and the party as the battle for
Perryville came to a head. For instance, the chair of the Arizona Republican Party distributed prepared remarks to the press in March 1980 that were
aimed primarily at Babbitt, taking him to task for going forward with building Perryville while the case was being litigated and for the arrogance of forcing the prison on a community that did not want it, especially when Florence
was willing to take it. The statement shaded the issue such that the move
to build the prison was rhetorically constructed as almost a soft-on-crime
measure, in that it would make the residents of Litchfield Park "prisoners of
fear!" and that it violated "the most fundamental rights of the people . . . to
safety and security of life and liberty" (Pappas, 1980: 1–2).

MacDougall also had a pesky foe in Attorney General Bob Corbin, a Republican, who put significant energy into impeding MacDougall's more liberal
reforms. Corbin prided himself on his law-and-order credentials; he was the
proud former county attorney who originally prosecuted Ernest Miranda, of
the landmark case *Miranda v. Arizona* (1966), and he was an active member
of the National Rifle Association and served as vice president and president of
that organization. As noted above, Corbin had done the analysis and issued the
directive that cut back MacDougall's discretion in releasing inmates sentenced
under the old code, and he was a major figure in stirring up the trouble around
the work furlough program. He alleged, in accusations made through the press,
that nearly half of all furloughed prisoners who had serious or violent felony
convictions were rearrested while out on furlough. The department challenged
his statistics with their own, which indicated a much lower arrest rate and an
even lower conviction rate on new criminal charges among furloughed inmates.
Many of the failures were technical violations of the program rules (such as
being consistently late to work or refusing a drug test), but once the accusation

was made so publicly, the program and its champion—Ellis MacDougall—were forced into a defensive position.

By early 1982, enough Republican legislators were convinced that the furlough program was a problem that a House Judiciary Committee investigative hearing was scheduled to determine its fate. The attorney general's office and a number of Republican lawmakers viewed the work furlough program as being used by MacDougall to get around the mandatory sentences required under the new code. Although MacDougall defended the program on its intrinsic benefits from a correctional standpoint, he also made it clear that it was a necessity for dealing with the overcrowding because there were no beds in the system. "If [the lawmakers] want to end it, that's fine," he told a reporter. "I'll just have to ask them for $30 million to build another prison" (Taylor, 1982: B-2). The hearing got quite contentious during MacDougall's testimony, when his main adversary on the committee, Republican Pete Dunn, continually interrupted him and spoke over him. Dunn seemed to be pushing for abolishing the entire furlough program, but in the end, the legislature agreed to make major modifications that placed more stringent limits on eligibility, in terms of both commitment offense and percentage of sentence served.

MacDougall resigned the directorship at the end of 1982 before he was rendered completely impotent in the role, saying he wanted to go back to his position at the University of South Carolina, from which he planned to retire in several years. He suggested that he might lose his chance to return as the university might not extend his leave of absence. It was clear that he was also frustrated by the modifications that the legislature was going to make to the furlough program, not only because it reduced his autonomy and discretion, but also because it clearly signaled the end of the potential for a progressive approach to the state's penal system. His last few interviews with the press were quite direct on that point. He advocated for policies that he knew would not be adopted, such as decriminalization of drug offenses, and he subtly chided the legislature for its shortsightedness when it came to criminal justice legislation, both fiscally and in terms of making a commitment to sound policy.

CONCLUSION: PLANTING THE SEEDS OF
THE POSTREHABILITATIVE PRISON

In many ways, Arizona should have been a state that resisted the move to mass incarceration, although it did seem to have the requisites for the qualitative shift to the harsh postrehabilitative style of imprisonment that characterizes many contemporary U.S. prisons. What the decade of turmoil that followed Cook's departure reveals is the clash between the seeming impediments to huge penal expansion and the developing catalysts that pushed toward the imprisonment growth that was about to explode. This period also exposes the fragility and fleeting quality of the rehabilitative ideal in a place that had no historical attachment to such a philosophy. Thus, Arizona, as a case study of the late modern penal transformation, is at once predictable and surprising. It is predictable in that its political leaders and penal administrators ascribed to a model of corrections, before outsiders came in to reform it, that looked very much like the model that replaced rehabilitation in numerous jurisdictions across the country. It is surprising in that one of the strongest held political and cultural values—fiscal frugality, and its corollary, small government—had to be compromised in order to feed the imprisonment boom. What happened during the 1970s to overcome that countervailing force and open the door to the explosion in the prison population?

The seeming impediments to the prison explosion in Arizona were many. First, the state had resisted making the heavy up-front investment in new penal facilities for its entire history. The prison at Florence had been built during territorial days, and it took until 1978 for another bona fide concrete prison facility to come into existence. Before the founding of the Department of Corrections in 1968, there was not a single real advocate for such a massive construction project, given that the primary penal authority was the warden at Florence, Frank Eyman. He pitched for funds to build and renovate within his facility but not to construct a new one. Even during the early years of the department, Director Allen Cook advocated for modern new facilities to replace Florence, not to supplement it, given that his philosophy of corrections saw incarceration as just one of many approaches in a graded rehabilitative system. He viewed the old prison at Florence as relatively inhospitable to a rehabilitative program and therefore useful for only a small subpopulation of hardcore inmates who needed maximum-security confinement. Part of the way that this state, like many other jurisdictions, managed to keep expansion in check was through providing a variety of back-door release mechanisms for penal administrators to use as needed to relieve overcrowding.

Arizona's initial move toward capacity expansion was also delayed by community resistance to the proposed plans. The Tucson facility would have come on line at least several years earlier and the Perryville facility would have been built sooner and with more capacity had it not been for local opposition. This

conflict could have been resolved through another route. Because the philosophy of the department from 1968 through the early 1980s dictated that facilities
needed to be in or near urban centers, the community resistance could have
pushed toward smaller, alternative institutions that would have fit better with
the "community corrections" movement and would have generated less opposition. Such a path was consistent with an emerging vision of corrections
that was taking shape much more broadly and that was facilitated in Arizona
by the importation of leadership from other jurisdictions.

Furthermore, although Arizona did experience a crime bump during the
1960s and 1970s, the state had experienced a relatively high crime rate throughout its history (especially theft-related crime), so it was not a new concern
within the polity. Arizona also experienced a population bump over the same
period, so even to maintain the same *rate* of incarceration that had hovered
around 100 per 100,000 citizens in the 1960s and early 1970s, the capacity of the
system would still have had to increase. This should have pushed the outer
limits of the legislature's fiscal generosity. On top of that, the involvement of
the federal court in regulating the population at Florence beginning in the
1970s could easily have pushed the legislature to come up with politically acceptable alternatives, at least for some low-level offenders, just to escape federal intervention.

And, again, the biggest factor that should have impeded the kind of massive growth that we see beginning during this period was the strong cultural
and political value that demanded fiscal tightfistedness and minimized governmental regulation and bureaucratization. This philosophy is regional in
nature—featured in many western and southwestern states—yet it is particularly strong in Arizona, as exemplified in its earliest struggles to gain statehood. This value was most actively pursued by the traditional Democrats in
the state, but it also was adopted by all successful Arizona politicians and
became more fully associated with the Republican agenda, most famously
exemplified by Barry Goldwater. So although there was little sympathy for
criminals in the state throughout its history, there was a coexisting pressure
not to create a huge bureaucracy to deal with that population.

But Arizona started down the other fork in the road—toward mass imprisonment and mega-bureaucracy—as did almost every other state in the nation
by the late 1970s. In Arizona, the turnaround was particularly dramatic. The
state went from being a relatively moderate incarceration jurisdiction to being
a top-10 incarcerator over a few short years. There were a number of prob-

able and definite catalysts to this unexpected development. First, the mere creation of the Department of Corrections ensured that the system would be larger and more bureaucratic than it had been in its unregulated, fragmented state. There was now an advocate to push for funding a number of initiatives, including building new facilities and investing in all kinds of programs, where there had been no such advocate before. This resulted in a dramatic increase in per capita (penal population) funding allocated to corrections almost immediately, a trend that was sustained for decades.

The creation of the department also opened up Arizona's criminal justice system to outside influences. Its leadership was imported from other state systems: these outside corrections "professionals" came with expertise that they used for reform and progressive development. They obtained federal funding and other forms of outside intervention that exposed the system to scrutiny in unprecedented ways. Under the leadership of such experts, the department placed itself in the larger community of other state corrections departments, seeking to compare favorably as a model system on various dimensions. If nothing else, this opening of the system increased expectations within the state, including among inmates themselves, for a higher standard of care and level of professionalism among staff. Thus, the penal system was more susceptible to the influence of broader trends and movements and was no longer isolated and encapsulated within Arizona.

Another catalyst for the move toward mass imprisonment and megabureaucracy had to do with changes in the state itself. The rapid population growth, and the attendant demographic shifts in population—the state was becoming more urban and youthful, and a progressive political element was developing in those urban settings—contributed to a sense of crisis among older residents and some long-standing political players. Both popularly and politically, a characterization of the delinquent criminal as an undisciplined, overindulged substance-abuser emerged in narratives about the problem of crime and punishment in the state.

Punishment policy also became more politicized in Arizona, and three-way battles among old conservative Democrats, progressive new Democrats, and increasingly right-leaning Republicans were waged in the legislature over the crises that the system faced. From 1975 on, Republicans were in majority control of both houses of the legislature, while the governor was a relatively progressive Democrat,[6] which contributed to a move from practical, collaborative lawmaking to symbolic, partisan-based legislating on a number of

issues, especially crime and punishment. This was probably the single largest contributor to the inception of the penal explosion, primarily through
changes in sentencing laws.

Not only did the legislature completely overhaul the criminal code in a
way that guaranteed a huge increase in prison admissions, it simultaneously
cut off most of the back-end release mechanisms that could have mitigated the
effect of the sentencing change. This trend in toughening criminal sentences
began with some limited mandatory minimums that first took effect in 1975,
which meant that county judges were no longer given discretion to sentence
targeted felons to local options such as probation and/or local jail time but
instead had to refer them to the state Department of Corrections to serve a
specified sentence. The 1978 code multiplied this effect by pushing a much
larger number of convicted felons away from local sentencing options to the
state-level penal system. In 1982, the legislature did it again, by mandating that
third-time drunk drivers serve a minimum of six months in *state prison* (not
local jail), legislation that they celebrated as the toughest drunk-driving law
in the nation. This change resulted in 600 unanticipated new prisoners, for
whom there were no beds, entering the Department of Corrections during the
first six months of the law's enactment.

Despite the crisis over bed space in the system, the majority of the state's
lawmakers were unwilling to consider even small modifications to these new
sentencing statutes, nor would they consider the possibility of returning some
back-end discretionary release power to the Department of Corrections. The
federal court had also forced the hand of the state in terms of needing to spend
and build. The consent decree entered into in *Harris v. Cardwell* required,
among many other things,[7] that prisoners at Florence be provided a minimum of 60 square feet of living space in dormitory settings and that they not
be double-bunked in dormitories or double-celled in traditional cell blocks.
Given all of these factors, the only alternative for managing this dilemma was
to figure out how to fund corrections at the accelerated rate that all of these
factors demanded.

4 THE NEW-OLD PENAL REGIME

TWO THINGS WERE EVIDENT once the imprisonment boom started in Arizona. First, the "vision" of corrections in the state remained fragmented and not particularly visionary at all. By the time the glow wore off of Ellis MacDougall, there was a stronger vision of what state corrections should *not* be in the state than what it should be. Clearly, the 1970s were characterized by the reactive crisis management mode that stunted the development of a unified and holistic approach to punishment, but by 1982, when MacDougall left, there was a significant void in mission and leadership that was waiting to be filled. At that point, the frontline staff in the Department of Corrections, the legislature, and the attorney general's office, among other factions, had all identified MacDougall as being too "liberal" in his correctional philosophy and not punitive enough in practice, so it is not surprising that the push would come to move the department back to its disciplinary roots. That move began to be realized by 1985.

Second, it is also strikingly clear that in the case of Arizona, the push toward mass incarceration was not a bottom-up process. The catalysts for growth were primarily intragovernmental at the state level and did not appear to be prompted by significant populist constituent pressure, by local law enforcement pressure, or even by any careful legislative analysis of the crime problem in the state. Rather, state legislators increasingly adopted an inflexibly harsh posture on crime while demonstrating a decreased trust in penal administrators on one end of the system, and in local judges on the other, to exercise discretion in regulating sentencing and punishment. Thus, the legislature became more proactive in passing tougher sentencing legislation that increased sentence lengths and decreased autonomy and discretion at both ends of the system. And, for the first time in the state's history, the legislative majority became more willing to invest significant amounts of money in the penal hardware needed to comply with the newly enacted tough-on-crime legislation.

Arizona's legislative body became less and less pragmatic in its approach to crime and punishment and more and more symbolically punitive in response to the seemingly unfixable problems facing the criminal justice system. The governor's office during Babbitt's terms also moved from a practical, problem-solving stance on criminal justice to one that, if not rabidly law and order, was not willing to challenge that rhetoric. That branch of government went on to join the law-and-order chorus (and indeed became a band leader by the 1990s) after Babbitt was out of office (see Chapter 5). It was this congruence in governance that ultimately moved Arizona toward the head of the pack in the postrehabilitative penal innovation and excess.

THE FINAL STOPGAP BEFORE THE NEW ERA

Governor Babbitt had to move quickly to find a replacement for MacDougall and again searched outside of Arizona for expertise. He found James Ricketts, another highly educated, career corrections administrator, in Colorado where he was director of that state's correctional system. Ricketts had previously worked with MacDougall in Georgia's system, but he was more moderate in terms of his penal philosophy and in his assertive power. Indeed, Ricketts was ultimately viewed as a fairly ineffectual leader, which may have been the unfortunate consequence of following MacDougall, who was an extremely forceful personality.

Ricketts arrived in early 1983, but in many ways, he was on the sidelines for most of the battles that corrections faced during his tenure, at least in terms of dealing with the legislature. He appeared before the legislature on occasion with figures indicating the massive growth in prison population, with the system showing a net gain of about 100 prisoners a month in 1983 and 1984, and asking for appropriations to help deal with it. Other than that, he ran the flooding ship from behind the scenes, in part by tinkering with the administrative structure of the Department of Corrections in an effort to instill some order in the out-of-control system.

In a change of practice, the politics surrounding funding new prisons and their operation, revising legislation to stem the population crunch, and even intrainstitutional construction, such as allowing for double bunking, were directly fought between Democratic Governor Babbitt and the Republican-controlled legislature. Because of this new configuration, corrections became a more political, and politically partisan, issue than ever during Ricketts's tenure.

Despite all the new facilities that opened during MacDougall's time as director, the bed shortage persisted, so the correctional focus in the state remained on how to fund the construction and operation of even more prison facilities. The prison population had more than doubled, from 3,200 to more than 6,600 in the five years since 1978, and all projections pointed to continued growth of that magnitude through the 1980s. The legislature had always fully funded its projects, which functioned to some degree as a check on runaway growth. By the early 1980s, though, the "pay-as-you-go" model that relied on the existing stream of revenues was no longer fully feasible, given the amount of penal expansion needed to keep up with the committed population influx and the associated costs of building and running the new facilities. In late 1982, Governor Babbitt raised the possibility of issuing revenue bonds as an alternative for funding new prisons, and the legislature expressed its openness to exploring that and other alternative funding strategies. The governor's office and the legislature came up with several proposals that would raise some revenue, including increasing traffic fines for violators, for new prison bonds (although not nearly enough to fully pay for the needed expansion), but those bills failed to pass.

The 1983 state budget planning process was somewhat dismal. The economy was not strong and revenues were down in the state, and Babbitt had already asked each department and agency to come up with a 6 percent cut from its previous year's allocation. There was certainly no surplus to fund prison expansion, but once again the flow of inmates into the system was even larger than projected. All involved—the governor's office, the legislature, and the Department of Corrections—vowed to look at any and every option to deal with the continuing crisis, although it quickly became clear that the majority of legislators would not seriously consider any proposals that would shorten sentences currently being served, provide alternatives to incarceration, or alter future sentencing through code changes.

Babbitt first proposed revising the mandatory provisions of the criminal code, among other alternatives, to help stem the flow of inmates, but he received no legislative support. So as not to be accused of being soft on crime, he suggested that changes could be made that would decrease sentences for lower level offenders while still retaining the "punitive, deterrent quality" of the statute. In response, the Republican chairman of the House Judiciary Committee, Jim Skelly, argued, "We need more people in prison, not less" (Nilsson, 1983b). Babbitt also suggested that the legislature consider expanding the work furlough program, again to give more flexibility to the Department of Corrections to manage the population and to help avert another court order on overcrowding, yet this proposal, too, met with resistance. It was clear that for the legislature, the perceived "value" of being tough on crime outweighed the practical considerations of maintaining a financially prudent criminal justice system.

By the fall of 1983, the situation was untenable, and Babbitt called for a special legislative session to deal with the "crisis in corrections," as the department called it. By this point, Babbitt had retreated from his earlier suggestion that the criminal code be modified in any way, telling the press, "we are committed to the mandatory-sentencing provisions in the criminal code" (Sowers, 1983). He was also relatively silent on other proposals for alternatives, other than to suggest the development of restitution centers and work release centers as less expensive ways to add bed space to the system. Democratic legislators, who were in the minority, still pressed for some alternatives, but theirs was a losing battle from day one.

The single overriding goal of the special session was to come up with a plan to add enough bed space to the penal system to manage the growing population through the next few years. This meant figuring out where to add space, at what security level, and most importantly, how the state would fund it. Legislators and the governor worked out a two-step plan for the special session to respond to the crisis. The first step was to approve and fund a package of $10 million to $20 million in emergency funds to immediately deal with the housing shortage, and the second was a multiyear plan that would address the space needs into the late 1980s.

The special session went on for an unprecedented four months during late 1983 and early 1984, with parts of it running concurrent to the regular legislative session. The first step was approved at the start of the session, with an appropriation of $16 million to add 1,650 emergency beds by 1985. These beds were generally low-budget additions, including adding dozens more Quonset hut and tent housing units on existing property, buying more motels around the state to be converted into minimum-security facilities, buying an airport hangar at a small rural airport to convert into a prison facility, and double-bunking wherever legally feasible within existing facilities.[1] The battle was over the more expensive long-range plan, which had to include building higher security facilities from scratch.

After almost three months of work, right before Christmas, the Republican leaders from both legislative houses agreed on a plan to add 2,237 permanent beds in six facilities over three years at a projected cost of $82 million. The package of bills was pushed through on straight-party-line votes in both the House and Senate. Babbitt had threatened to veto the bills if they did not come with concrete funding plans, which had the effect of uniting the normally bickering Republican legislators. They were angry at Babbitt's threat, which he fulfilled by Christmas Eve, since they had worked so long and had come up with a plan for emergency first-year funding. This collective anger, however, brought a new sense of unified purpose when they returned to work on the issue in January.

By late January, the Republican senators and representatives had developed a funding scheme for the expansion plan, which turned out to be a bit more ambitious than the one Babbitt had vetoed. The new bills, again approved along party lines in both houses, authorized the addition of more than 4,000 adult beds to the system, including the previously approved and funded emergency beds, as well as 300 juvenile beds. They proposed to finance it through a somewhat regressive series of tax boosts and budget cuts that would raise $163 million over four years. The bills authorized raising taxes on liquor and cigarettes, adding sales tax on private sales of vehicles, and cutting the state's contribution to the state employee pension fund.

In a move that harkened back to the Eyman days (and even to territorial days), they also passed legislation that required all of the prison construction projects to be completed "predominantly through the employment of inmate labor" (Ricketts, n.d.: 4) as a cost-savings measure. Although Director Ricketts expressed his concern to the legislature about the cost-efficiency of this policy, once it was mandated, the department's official stance on it was one of pride: "In undertaking the largest construction project in the history of the Department of Corrections we are mobilizing the largest inmate labor force in Arizona history in support of this project. The inmate labor force as a taxpayer resource will ultimately save millions of dollars" (Ricketts, n.d.: 3).

Thus, the crisis in corrections, and the special session that was called to deal with it, catalyzed two important developments in the move to mass incarceration. First, it solidified, with dollars, the state's commitment to an incarceration strategy and its explicit rejection of alternate paths for dealing with the problem of crime. State legislative actors not only had to voice the tough-on-crime rhetoric that was becoming a political necessity here and elsewhere, but they had to compromise the core political value in Arizona of fiscal frugality when Babbitt forced them to put money where their mouths were. Raising taxes, even if they were predominantly "sin" taxes, was extremely risky politics in Arizona, yet the Republican members of the legislature were willing to do it in order to build more prisons.

The Republican accomplishment in committing to incarceration during this special session was not limited to funding the additional beds. Republicans also successfully shot down almost every single proposal Democrats made, including the Democratic governor's, to include some alternatives to prison in the strategy for dealing with the lack of bed space. The criminal code was deemed untouchable unless it was amended to *increase* sentence lengths, and proposals to revitalize the work furlough program and shorten sentences of nonviolent offenders failed to go anywhere in the legislative process. There were only two token prizes to the Democrats in the entire package. First was a commitment to build an experimental 50-inmate residential restitution center in Tucson that would allow offenders to work in the community during the day to pay back victims and sleep on-site at night, and second was a commitment of funding to hire 25 more probation officers throughout the state to try an intensive probation program to be administered at the county level.

The second significant effect of the special session was to solidify partisan politics in the state and unify elected Republican leaders around the issue of crime and punishment. The 1960s and 1970s had experienced quite a bit of flux around party politics at the state level in Arizona—Republicans were relatively progressive in some areas, moderate in others, and conservative in still others while Democrats were truly a bipolar group, including some of the most conservative and some of the most liberal politicians in the state. Although this no doubt added to the sense of intraparty fissure and division, it did have the effect of minimizing the partisan use of symbolic politics and in some ways contributed to a more pragmatic form of governance in the state.

As Republicans, who held the majority in the legislature, came to unite during the late 1970s and early 1980s around their stance on criminal justice, and Democrats began to join together in opposition to the Republican approach, clear lines were drawn that would feed into the highly partisan politics that dominated the 1980s and 1990s at state and national levels. The straight-party-line voting on all of the proposals that emerged from this session was a testament to that process. And indeed, the Phoenix newspaper and several Republican legislators themselves credited Governor Babbitt's threatened (and carried out) veto of the initial bills that emerged from the special session with bringing them together as a more cohesive group than ever before in their shared anger at the governor (Willey, 1983: A1). Governor Babbitt's subsequent ratification of the Republican bills was a major disappointment to his Democratic peers in the legislature but was no doubt the politically savvy move to make at that time and place.

THE RISE OF SYMBOLIC PUNITIVENESS

This period also brought with it an emerging trend of novel and recycled legislative proposals that were on their face symbolically rich "get-tough" measures. For example, in early 1983, as legislators were grappling with where to put additional beds, the Senate Judiciary Committee approved a proposal to allow double-bunking in cells that were originally designed as singles. The plan was framed for the press as a way to get tough on offenders, rather than merely as a pragmatic strategy to quickly add beds. The bill's sponsor, Republican senator Hal Runyan, argued to his committee members that the state could no longer afford country club–style living by prisoners, as "they are bad people. They were put there [in prison] because they committed crimes. It's time we got back to basics" (Nilsson, 1983a). This theme of cushy living by prisoners was picked up by an *Arizona Republic* columnist later in the year, who opined that the "plush state prison [at Perryville] takes the Constitution a step too far" (Wynn, 1983). He cited Attorney General Bob Corbin as his legal authority for making such a claim, as Corbin had advised him that prisons only need be a secure and clean place of daily labor. The columnist criticized the prison for still maintaining day rooms that could be converted to dorm halls to add bed space and for the investments made in an expensive dishwasher and bread-making machine in the kitchen.

In another attack on the "good life" that state prisoners experienced behind bars, Attorney General Corbin joined frontline prison guards and their union in early 1984 to complain about the community college programs that were offered to inmates at no cost, while law-abiding citizens in the state had to pay for higher education. Several Republican legislators voiced concurring outrage over this, but the college educational program was able to survive a few more years before it was eviscerated. The following year, the House Appropriations Committee chairwoman pushed to cut most of the funding for prison chaplains, complaining that she supported religion in prison but didn't think the state should pay for it. Her example of the "excesses" brought by state-funded chaplains was the fact that there was a push to hire two "Indian shamans" earlier that year, leading her to the conclusion that the entire system should rely on volunteers (Thompson, 1985).

Furthermore, in March 1983, the Senate Judiciary Committee unanimously approved a bill that would require inmates to do 40 hours of "hard labor" while incarcerated, including doing public works jobs such as road cleaning and repair. The Department of Corrections pointed out the added expense of this requirement for maximum-security inmates as the plan would require intensive staffing for those inmates while on the job. Yet the legislators did not seem to mind this weakness of the plan; it became law that year. Again, the legislature added the proviso to the prison expansion bill that construction be carried out by prisoners themselves, which both harkened back to the state's tougher old disciplinary days and was congruent with the new get-tough mantra that was emerging here and elsewhere.

A few months later, concurrent with the special session, just as legislators were trying to figure out how to pay for the expansion needed to deal with the huge number of inmates coming into the system, three Republican legislators drafted a bill that would require 25-year sentences for all felons on their third felony conviction, anticipating the kind of three-strikes bills that were the national trend a decade later. This move, of course, would only add to the state's crisis in corrections, yet the Republicans roundly supported it. Over the next few years, the legislature continued to ratchet up mandatory minimum sentences for specified offenses, including increased sentences for second-degree murder and a whole range of sex offenses, which also had a notable effect on prison population numbers and rates for years to come.

THE DEMISE OF RICKETTS AND BACK TO THE FUTURE

Unlike his predecessors, corrections director James Ricketts was mainly a background player in all of this penal policymaking. Although called upon to provide information (and chastised by legislators for not doing a good job of supplying it), he was not influential in shaping the debate surrounding the special session. Indeed, the entire Ricketts period was distinctive for how political leaders deliberately sidestepped departmental expertise on corrections matters. Neither the legislators nor the governor called upon Ricketts or his staff to lead the discussion about how to resolve the crisis in corrections. He was relegated to being a mere administrator of a troubled bureaucracy and was generally brought into discussions to be interrogated or upbraided about the failures of the department. Furthermore, individual legislators went out of their way to interfere in the minutiae of Ricketts's responsibilities.

For instance, the Republican chair of the legislative Prison Oversight Committee, Bob Denny, not only took Ricketts to task for resisting the use of inmate labor for major construction jobs, but also insisted that the new facilities be built in the traditional Auburn style of stack-tiered cell blocks rather than in the more modern single-level circular design that Ricketts favored. Denny wrote to the governor, complaining that his committee's mission was to figure out ways "to build and operate prisons cheaper" but that Ricketts was not cooperating with the plans they had devised. The committee wanted to follow the model of the economical construction projects in Texas and so implored the governor to pressure Ricketts to be a "team player" or else fire him (Denny, 1984). Ultimately, Denny and his committee got their way on the design and the labor issues but then complained publicly when the construction fell behind schedule as a result.

Ricketts's marginalized role was both deepened and solidified when Governor Babbitt reassigned three people from other state agencies, including one from the governor's own staff, to top positions in the Department of Corrections in the fall of 1984. The alleged catalysts for the moves were the late-summer escape of nine inmates from the reception center in Phoenix and the slow pace at which the prison building campaign was moving. Ricketts's high-level aides, who were replaced during this shakeup, were functionally demoted by being moved to "temporary" new positions. At about the same time, the Department of Administration was again assigned the task of managing the prison construction projects along with the funds earmarked for those projects (pending approval of legislation that would effect the change), which was another challenge to Ricketts's authority. The reassignment of personnel was publicly presented in a joint press release as Ricketts's own move to improve security and speed up the construction process, but it became quickly evident that the change had been imposed from the governor's office.

Two of the new managers came from the Department of Public Safety— the state police agency that had primary responsibility for highway patrol. One of those men, Colonel Sam Lewis, was appointed as the chief deputy director of the department, which was the second highest position in the agency.

Colonel Lewis (his preferred self-reference) quickly became the favored leader of the department, at least from the governor's perspective, and usurped Ricketts's authority almost immediately. In an attempt at impression management, the media relations officer of the department controlled access to the two men, making sure that no reporter talked to Lewis after Ricketts had given an interview so that Lewis would not directly contradict his "superior" and let it be known publicly who really had authority in the department (Lopez, 1985).

Five months into the new arrangement, the lid was off and the local press reported extensively about Ricketts's troubles as department head. Several of the governor's close aides, various legislators, and some on the department staff spoke to reporters about the situation, relating that Governor Babbitt had lost faith in Ricketts's abilities during the special session and sharing the extent of control that Lewis exerted within the department. Indeed, several sources suggested that the only reason Ricketts had not been fired was that Babbitt's future plans were in flux and it would be hard to recruit a quality director if he was a lame duck governor. And according to one legislative staff source, Lewis and one of the governor's aides "make all the major decisions," so keeping Ricketts around, although "overpriced" for his contributions, was a workable solution from the perspective of many (Lopez, 1985).

But not for Ricketts. Despite publicly stating in mid-February that he would continue to serve at the governor's pleasure as long as he was needed, he resigned a month later, announcing that he had been "abandoned" by the governor and "betrayed" by the legislature (LaJeunesse, 1985). In an interview, Ricketts expressed his frustration: "When I came here, I thought I was working for the governor. How wrong I was" (LaJeunesse, 1985). At some point in the weeks leading up to Ricketts's resignation, Lewis had changed his story about his interest in staying on in corrections. He was officially on loan for a year from the Department of Public Safety, and he had consistently told colleagues that he could not wait to go back, even as late as a month before Ricketts's resignation. But by the time Ricketts resigned, Lewis agreed to be considered as a candidate for the director post, which culminated in his appointment just two weeks later.

THE NEW-OLD REGIME

For its entire 17-year existence, the Arizona Department of Corrections had been headed by an outsider who was recruited to the job on the basis of his experience and expertise in running the correctional systems of other states.

That streak ended with the appointment of Sam Lewis as director in April 1985. Lewis had been born in Yuma, had played football at Arizona State University (although he completed his undergraduate education in Michigan while in the military), and had returned to his home state in 1970 after a 28-year career in the U.S. Army, from which he retired as a colonel. He went into local law enforcement upon his return and then moved to the state police department, where he advanced rapidly to the position of deputy director. By the time he was appointed as the director of the Department of Corrections, he did have six months of experience running the department, albeit from behind the scenes, but he was hardly a penal expert or career corrections manager.

In many ways, Lewis's appointment had nostalgic resonance with the appointment 30 years earlier of Frank Eyman as superintendent of Florence. Both were brought in as troubleshooting "lawmen" at the request of the governor to reform the seemingly out-of-control penal system. Both had deep roots in Arizona and came straight from Arizona law enforcement agencies, and both men's managerial style was significantly influenced by their military training. Their philosophies about how to run a prison (or a prison system, in the case of Lewis) heralded old-fashioned discipline and respect, and both believed that institutional life should be appropriately uncomfortable as a deterrent. Each of them also clearly and explicitly followed through in implementing this philosophy throughout the institutional operations.

Yet Lewis was operating in a transformed environment in 1985, compared with the world Eyman had entered in 1955. Lewis was dealing with a different magnitude of prison population, and he had much more fiscal support from the legislature to expand and reform the department than Eyman ever did. Both men could command legislative attention, but by 1985, the Republican-controlled legislature was also committed to spending if it meant appropriately harsh imprisonment for the convicted felon population. In addition, the tough-on-crime mantra that had by this point become the normative philosophy in the political, policy, and populist realms at the national level opened the possibility for an even harsher system than could have been imagined during the Eyman period.

During the 1950s and 1960s, when Eyman was at the helm of the prison "system," the basic humanity of the prisoner was generally perceived to be intact. Although different approaches were taken to reform or dissuade the criminal actor (as the Arizona case aptly illustrates), it was generally accepted that he or she was both capable of being returned to the broader community and in most cases deserved to have the opportunity upon reformation (Lynch, 2008a; Sloop, 1996). By the 1980s, however, that basic recognition was no longer broadly accepted. As numerous commentators have noted, the serious offender had become an entirely unsympathetic "other" who deserved no second chances in many cases (see, for example, Garland, 2001; Haney, 1998, 2006). Thus the standards for the treatment of criminal offenders spiraled down to a new low over the last two decades of the twentieth century, after having consistently risen during the earlier decades of that century, and most people seemed to care little about it (and in many cases encouraged such devolution; see Haney, 1998).[2]

Consequently, when Lewis took over the directorship, Arizona was poised to become a leader in the harsh, no-frills mass imprisonment movement that was rising to hegemony. His philosophy fit well with that broader narrative; he did not have the managerial experience in corrections to temper such an approach with the practical benefits of maintaining at least a moderately humane and rehabilitatively oriented penal system; and he was a decisive (some might say bull-headed), persistent, and influential advocate for his goals.

Sam Lewis knew exactly how to market his appropriations requests before the legislature, and he maintained that power for most of his tenure as director. He oversaw the massive expansion of the state's prison system over the next decade, at a rate unprecedented to this time. During his directorship, the annual budget for adult corrections services and facilities went from approximately $113 million to manage an average adult prison population of 7,477 with an additional 3,600 offenders in community-based supervision during the 1984–85 fiscal year, to $354 million to manage an average adult population of 19,542 plus about 5,500 offenders on community supervision during the 1994–95 fiscal year.[3] Equally important, he changed the nature of incarceration in the state and led the Department of Corrections to become a national innovator of harsh penal practices that are emblematic of the postrehabilitative period. He successfully crafted legislation that found sponsorship and ultimately majority support in the legislature that expanded the department's coercive and disciplinary power and decreased inmates' autonomy and rights.

This is not to say that Lewis's tenure was all smooth sailing. He met with resistance from a variety of sources as he instituted change and had a particularly rough period with Governor Evan Mecham, who succeeded Babbitt in 1987. Although both Lewis and Mecham were politically conservative,[4] Mecham was alleged to have drawn up termination papers for Lewis at least three times during his 16 months in office, in part over Lewis's refusal to hire one of Mecham's major campaign fundraisers in the department. Mecham's own legal troubles, however, which eventually resulted in his impeachment for obstruction of justice and misuse of state funds, sidetracked him from carrying out his threat to replace Lewis (and many others who headed state agencies). In an ironic twist, Lewis testified as a prosecution witness at the Senate impeachment trial (at which Mecham was convicted), dropping a "bombshell" of testimony that helped seal Mecham's fate (*Phoenix Gazette*, 1988).

As would be expected, Lewis's most vocal critics included a number of Democratic legislators, prisoners themselves, and prisoner advocates in the state, including the ACLU and prisoner activist Donna Leone Hamm, who headed Middle Ground, which would become the most enduring prison legislative reform group in Arizona (see Chapter 6). He also experienced some pushback within the agency from various staff and administrative personnel.

Lewis managed conflict and resistance within the department by cleaning house, in part by pushing out several highly placed administrators. Within six months of becoming director, he had seriously disciplined 20 management-level employees, 12 of whom were fired or forced to resign. Among those were three wardens, including the wardens at Florence and Fort Grant; a deputy warden; and several administrators in the central department. Thus, by his second year as director, Lewis had transformed the internal workings of the department administration, and the prison operations, through the replacement of key players throughout the system, with the support of the governor and legislature. Ultimately, Lewis was a driven, forceful administrator who, for most of his years as director, had the loyal support of the Republican majority in the legislature, so was able to institute dramatic penal changes in the state.

THE RETURN TO PRISONS

Lewis's first major, though largely symbolic, move was to rename all of the institutions in the system as "prisons" or "prison complexes" rather than "correctional facilities," as had been the convention since the department's inception. In the first issue of *Directions*—the department's internal newsletter—that was published after his appointment, Lewis announced that "the names of the Department's institutions have been changed so that the public will have a better understanding of what they really are—prisons" (*Directions*, 1985). The column's title was "A Prison Is a Prison," which in many ways forecasted the changes to come. Lewis also wanted to change the department's name to the

Department of Prisons but ultimately did not pursue that wish, both because it would have to be done legislatively and because the expense of changing stationery and other identifying materials would be too great (Lewis interview, 2004). Along with the institutional name changes, the prisoners once again became known as "inmates," as Lewis reversed MacDougall's innovation, which Ricketts had continued, of calling them "residents."

Shades of Eyman's Disciplinary Model

Following these nominal changes, life inside the department's facilities also changed radically under Lewis's leadership. In a manner reminiscent of Eyman's disciplinary approach, within three years of taking over, Lewis had completely reformed standards of personal grooming and appearance for both the inmates and the correctional officers. Inmates lost the privilege of being allowed to wear their own clothes and were put back into uniforms, and long hair and facial hair were banned. Some inmates challenged this latter policy as a violation of their religious freedom, yet the department prevailed in enforcing the standard across the board.

The amount and type of personal property that inmates could keep in their cells was restricted as well. Over the first couple of years as director, Lewis cut back on the near limitless allowances that had existed under the previous two administrations, so by 1988, prisoners were allowed only what would fit within one duffel bag, with limits on the number of books, pads of paper, packs of cigarettes, and personal appliances. This policy change was also challenged, ultimately unsuccessfully, by inmates and their advocates.

Correctional officers and other department personnel were held to stricter standards in grooming and appearance as well. In the summer of 1987, a new internal policy was codified and implemented that required nonuniformed employees to wear "appropriate" and "contemporary" business attire on the job. Uniformed officers were to wear properly fitting uniforms "without undue bagginess or tightness in the trousers or shirt." Buttons were to be buttoned, with "no unsightly bulging of buttonholes," and footwear had to be kept shined. Supervisors were responsible for regularly monitoring the "dress and grooming practices of employees" to ensure compliance (Lewis, 1990b).

Like Eyman, Lewis strove to clean up the physical appearance of the institutions within the department, reporting in his first annual report that "a special emphasis was placed on the appearance of each prison" during his first year as director (Lewis, 1985a: 11). Dissatisfied with the hodge podge finishes on the exterior of the prisons, he decided to paint all prison buildings a uniform color scheme—naval ship gray with blue trim. The paint was donated, and he used all inmate labor for the job. Nonetheless, one legislator called him to task for doing this job in the middle of a budget crisis, since it was not a vital improvement and it still cost the state in staff supervision time. He stopped the painting in the middle of the job, but as soon as the new fiscal year came around, he had it finished (Hamm interview, 2004). During his first year, Lewis also secured a number of plant and shrub donations and initiated landscaping improvement projects throughout the prison complexes at Florence and Perryville. Inmates were put to work at all of the facilities to complete deferred maintenance and repair projects, and permanent inmate jobs were created to maintain the improvements (Lewis, 1985c). Lewis also oversaw the improvement of the exercise facilities at Florence and established structured two-hour exercise programs for prisoners.

As did Eyman, Lewis believed that all able-bodied inmates who were not locked down for disciplinary reasons should work or be active. He strongly supported the requirement that construction projects use inmate labor, and in 1990 he helped push a stronger version of that law, which was passed and enacted. In addition to working on the prison construction projects around the state (the facilities that had been approved to be built during the 1984 special session) and the maintenance and beautification projects at existing facilities, more prisoners were placed in public-private partnership and prison industries jobs, which earned them minimum wage, 30 percent of which was paid back to the state for "room and board" in the prison (Lewis, 1985a: 11). This, of course, was touted as an added bonus to the work program. The industries division garnered a contract with the state Department of Transportation to have inmate work crews provide cleanup and maintenance for Arizona's roads and highways, as well as several contracts with cities to provide such maintenance. By the end of his second year on the job, Lewis boasted that inmate labor saved the taxpayers more than $1 million annually on various work projects (Lewis, 1986).

Under Lewis's direction, the farming industries at the prisons, run almost entirely by inmate labor, were also intensified so as to make the system more self-sufficient and cost-effective. By 1989, three of the prison complexes had farming operations that either grew crops or raised farm animals (beef cattle, hogs, and poultry) for food. A food-processing plant was utilized to flash-freeze vegetables for later use; excess farm products were sold for cash.

Again like Eyman, Lewis was also willing to give up control over problem populations to simplify and philosophically streamline his institutional
operations. For instance, during the late 1980s, he pushed the possibility of
breaking off the juvenile division of the department so that it could become
an independent agency. Because juveniles required more services and programs, and rehabilitation was still considered at least one important aim in
dealing with that population, this branch of the department was more cost-
and labor-intensive than the adult division, and it was philosophically at odds
with Lewis's views. Indeed, he seemed to be utterly uninterested in the juvenile population that was under the control of the department. He rarely
referred to it in his public dealings with the legislature, in the press, or in his
communications within the department, instead touting his measures aimed
at the adult population.

Strategically, part of his hands-off approach to the more difficult populations was through privatization. In a reversal of the trend started with Cook
from the inception of the Department of Corrections, by the late 1980s, the
department increasingly contracted out for juvenile placements, including
awarding in 1986 a bid for a for-profit secure housing unit for the more serious female juvenile offenders. After the legislature enacted in 1987 a law
allowing for the privatization of adult facilities (juvenile wards could always
be sent to private facilities), the department conducted a feasibility study to
determine whether privatization would be cost-effective and if so for which
populations. According to the report, the department director (Lewis) prioritized the subpopulations that would be, from the department's perspective, best to be subject to contracting out to private facilities. They were,
in rank order, the mentally ill, the developmentally disabled, "chronically
ill/handicapped" inmates, and inmates in protective custody. Thus, like
Eyman, as a manager, Lewis seemingly preferred to deal only with those
inmates who did not have special needs for programming or services and
whose treatment within his harsh disciplinary model of corrections could
be justified.[5]

The push to decouple the juvenile division from the department was realized in 1990 after the legislature authorized the creation of the Arizona Department of Juvenile Corrections as an independent new state agency. The
final impetus came from a three-day-long Symposium on Corrections, organized by Governor Rose Mofford in 1988 as a way to deal with the "precipitous
rise in inmate population and the attendant costs" that Arizona faced (Lewis,

1989b). This move was also catalyzed by a major lawsuit against Lewis over the conditions of confinement to which juveniles were subjected (see Chapter 6). The split-off was one of five major recommendations that emerged from the corrections symposium and uncontroversially became law during the next legislative session.

Fortification and Security Take Precedence

From the start of his tenure, Lewis implemented a number of new policies and incorporated all kinds of new hardware to increase security within the system. Indicative of his primary concern with control and security was the department's new mission statement, conceived within months of his taking over as director, which he reported in a letter to Governor Babbitt: "The Mission of the Arizona Department of Corrections is to receive, care, control, and maintain custodial responsibility of persons committed to the State's prisons and juvenile institutions" (Lewis, 1985b). The following year, the mission statement was modified and expanded, as follows:

> The mission of the Arizona Department of Corrections is to serve and protect the people of the State by imprisoning those offenders legally committed to the Department. The Department will accomplish this by:
>
> - Maintaining effective custody and control over offenders
> - Maintaining a healthy, safe, and secure environment for staff and offenders
> - Providing quality programs to the offenders so they will have opportunities to learn more responsible behaviors and increase their chances of returning into society as law-abiding citizens. (Lewis, 1986: 3)

This was a sharp contrast to the philosophy statement that existed under Ricketts just a year or two earlier, which read: "The Arizona Department of Corrections is statutorily charged with the responsibility of protecting society from the offender. In order to live up to that responsibility, the Arizona Department of Corrections provides safe, just, and humane options for improvement for each offender committed to our jurisdiction with the belief that people have the capacity to change for the better" (Ricketts, 1984: 3). This earlier statement then elaborates upon the department's commitment to community reintegration and to providing opportunities for offenders to facilitate a successful return to the community.

Although both missions claim the same purpose—to protect the people of the state from offenders—their priorities in reaching those goals are significantly different. The mission under Ricketts had a decidedly rehabilitative tone and held the department at least equally responsible for effecting positive change in offenders as the offenders themselves. Lewis's mission gave primacy to the job of containment and as its last goal saw the department's role as merely providing programs that offenders could avail themselves of for self-improvement. Over the course of Lewis's tenure and beyond, this foreshadowing of priorities played out in the realization of policies and practices. "Program" opportunities shrank, as did their relative share of funding, while investments in security measures expanded across the system.

The fortification began as a relatively low-tech endeavor, with the installation of razor wire fencing around all the facilities at Florence and at the downtown Alhambra Reception and Treatment Center; the construction and installation of additional security walls, gun towers, security fencing, steel windows, and security screens; and increased lighting around the Florence facilities. An immediate investment was also made in new surveillance technology that was installed at several of the medium-security facilities, including new video surveillance systems, closed-circuit cameras, and motion detector "perimeter" systems, as well as upgrades to communications systems and the purchase of new and additional portable radios for officer use (Lewis, 1985c). Security measures in CB-6, the existing supermax segregation lockdown facility, were improved in part to comply with the stipulated agreement stemming from a lawsuit over the conditions in this unit (*Black v. Ricketts*, 1984; see Chapter 6).

Lewis also instituted a controversial program, Operation Shutdown, that increased the invasiveness of visitor searches for the purposes of "restricting the flow of contraband into the prison" (Lewis, 1985c: 4). Under this policy, visitors had to sign a consent form saying they were willing to be subjected to a strip search in order to be allowed to visit prisoners in the state facilities. In 1987, an inmate's family sued the department after the prisoner's wife and their two-year-old granddaughter were strip-searched at the prison in Tucson. Corrections officials claimed to have had a tip that the family was smuggling in drugs for the inmate, but no drugs were found during the search. This incident also brought demands from several groups and individuals, including a Democratic legislator, an inmate family support group, and Middle Ground, that Lewis be fired for this and his other draconian policies.

Along the same lines, in 1989, Lewis instituted a policy of tape recording all inmate phone calls, which he justified as part of the broader effort to control contraband. He got the idea after seeing the federal prison system's call-recording program in 1987. In keeping with the fiscally prudent ethos of Arizona, the department contracted with a local pay phone company, which passed the total costs of the program on to the inmates and their relatives through added collect-call fees (all inmate calls had to be collect calls). Thus, the program was "free" to the state (Van Der Werf, 1989). This new policy also generated complaints and threatened legal challenges from Middle Ground and the ACLU but became an ongoing practice anyway.

Unprecedented Restrictions on Inmates

Especially under the previous two administrations, residents who were not in disciplinary lockdown had quite a bit of freedom of movement at all of the facilities, whether minimum security or maximum security. Inmates could move between their cells, the yard, jobs, classes, and recreational activities throughout the day on their own schedules; meals were the most regimented activities in the system. But that all changed with Lewis's appointment. First, the concept and practice of an open yard was curtailed at the Florence maximum-security facility (Lewis, 1985c). Inmates were put on program schedules to control the movement flow of the population. Throughout the system's facilities, inmates' schedules became more regimented, and free time in the yard or other recreational areas was restricted.

The most far-reaching system-wide mechanism of restriction came with Lewis's newly devised classification system. Instituted in the fall of 1986, it added an additional "level" of classification that meant that once reclassified, a percentage of the population would move to a more restrictive level than had been the case under the old system, and virtually no one would move down in level toward less restriction. The new system gave greater weight to original offense and deemphasized program needs of the inmates, and it was designed so that it was relatively easy for classification levels to rise (that is, toward maximum security) but difficult for levels to decrease, even after inmates had maintained long periods without any disciplinary actions.

The new system hit the long-termers and lifers the hardest. These inmates were statistically the more stable, trouble-free subgroup of the inmate population, and many had earned minimum-security and trustee status over the years. Overnight, with the implementation of Lewis's classification system, many of these inmates' security levels were elevated back to maximum security. This meant the loss of jobs that required a higher level of trust, new housing assignments in higher security facilities, and many more restrictions of movement for some of the most trustworthy inmates in the system. In addition, across the system, the higher security level facilities became even more overcrowded and the minimum-security institutions became underpopulated.

The new classification system generated broad and sustained criticism from both within and outside the prisons. Citizens' groups (mainly Democratic ones) complained to Lewis, their legislators, and the governor. Middle Ground tried to fight it through political and legal channels. And the inmates initiated a letter-writing campaign to the governor, the news media, and other elected officials warning of the potential unrest that could result from the change and seeking intervention. There were system-wide disturbances within months of its implementation, causing Lewis to tighten the screws even further.

The general unhappiness with the revised classification system was amplified by the fact that newly constructed prison facilities opened at around the same time, resulting in mass transfers of inmates to these more remote facilities. Although some of the transfers were coupled with classification changes, others were simply redistribution moves to spread the population throughout the institutions. Such moves meant that many inmates' families had to travel farther to visit, which decreased the frequency of visits and increased the frustration of inmates and their relatives. Lewis also drastically cut access to the "compassionate leave" programs that allowed inmates to spend part of their time outside of prison for family reasons. Between tightened eligibility rules and the new higher security classification level of so many inmates, many of those who had previously been able to partake in such opportunities found themselves barred from participation.

In addition, in early 1987, the Department of Corrections under Lewis's guidance threatened to close down all of the urban halfway houses in Phoenix and Tucson as a cost-saving measure if the department did not get its requested allocation for the next fiscal year. Because state law at the time required that the department provide six months of prerelease services that allowed inmates to seek jobs, pursue educational opportunities, and other preparatory activities during the day, Lewis still had to nominally provide a facility for this purpose. To comply with the law, he threatened to move the release centers from the urban houses that were distinct from the prison institutions to two very isolated rural prison institutions in Safford and Picacho, far from the population centers and where very few job and school opportunities existed.

Not only did this proposed change pervert the notion of release centers, in that the proposed release facilities were in fact prisons, but it undermined the overriding goal of such centers—that soon-to-be-paroled inmates could set up their work, school, and living arrangements in or near their home communities in order to facilitate success on the outside. The legislature, though, recognized the absurdity of this plan and upon making its allocation to the department, ordered it to fund the urban release centers through the next year. Nonetheless, the release centers, at least for the male population, were ultimately doomed. By 1992, the Phoenix center was closed as a consequence of legislative action, and the Tucson release center for men was converted to a women's release center.

The First True State Supermax Is Born

Just as Lewis was threatening to shut down halfway houses, he oversaw the final construction and opening of the most expensive facility the state had ever seen, the 768-bed Security Management Unit (SMU I) at Florence (*Arizona Republic*, 1987). This unit was the first state-level new construction supermax of its kind and stood as a national model for the coming trend.

The state had already put a very high security 200-bed unit into service in 1980 when CB-6 was opened at Florence. That unit also had been dubbed a supermax by then-director Ellis MacDougall and was used in ways that presaged the use of the supermax from the late 1980s onward. CB-6 was initially designed to be used only as an administrative segregation unit, but within months of its opening, it was reevaluated and reconfigured to be used as a long-term general-population facility. So rather than being used exclusively as a short-term segregation facility that was a punitive but transient experience for most inmates sent there for disciplinary reasons,[6] CB-6 quickly became used as a high security level housing unit as well as a disciplinary unit. Because they were classified at the highest security level, many death row inmates were housed as a matter of policy in CB-6.

This predecessor unit also physically and structurally exemplified what would become the defining features of the supermax. By design, physical contact between staff and inmates was minimal compared with the older maximum-security units in the system. Staff members were secured within control booths and walkways that were situated slightly above and away from the cells. After a number of serious disturbances following the opening of CB-6, the cell doors were retrofitted with Plexiglas coating that further isolated the cell occupants from staff and each other. Guards operated cell doors from the locked control booth and thus could direct inmate movement between individual cells and the showers without getting near the inmates. However, CB-6 had some serious design flaws that rendered some cells unviewable from the guard areas and made movement of inmates to visiting areas and the yard a logistical headache. Thus CB-6, although advanced conceptually, was problematic operationally, conducive to a high level of violence and requiring fairly high staffing ratios.

Life in this predecessor unit showed the signs of serious dysfunction that we now see in supermax units across the nation (see, for example, Haney, 2003; Rhodes, 2004) and that were replicated in the successor units in Arizona, SMU I and SMU II (Lynch, 2005). Each inmate was single-celled and kept in lockdown for everything but periodic showers, visitors, and brief court-mandated periods of "yard" in a small exercise pen, so there was much frustration among the population. Violence levels were high, and staff responded to inmate violence and threats with retaliatory violence and neglect (Goldsmith interview, 2002). As has occurred in contemporary supermax facilities, the ante on punishment was raised as conditions deteriorated. Management built and put into use a "worst-of-the-worst" dungeon cell within the unit, which was covered by a metal door with just a few holes for ventilation (Goldsmith interview, 2002). As added punishment at CB-6, the prison administration instituted a "meatloaf" diet, which consisted of three servings a day of an unpalatable protein loaf made of ground-up vegetables, meat, and grains. When contraband was smuggled into the unit after contact visits, rectal searches became the routine for all inmates who returned from seeing visitors. Conditions in this unit were the basis of a successful lawsuit that forced some reforms of these practices (see Chapter 6).

But the lesson learned from the CB-6 experience was not one of tempered punitiveness; rather, CB-6's failures in some ways catalyzed its "state-of-the-art" successor, SMU I. Ironically, it does not appear from any sources available that this unit was meant to be anything but another, better designed maximum-security housing unit.[7] The department did not lobby for something revolutionary when seeking its funding—the SMU was simply categorized as the maximum-security beds planned (and eventually built). During the construction stage, there was also no mention in any department materials, government papers, or press accounts that this unit was anything more than a maximum-security prison. Officials within the department did not tout its construction efforts as being pioneering at all; it was not until after it was completed that its status as a new and innovative form of penal institution was emphasized.

Among the earliest indicators of its avant-garde nature was an April 1987 article published by one of the architects from Haver, Nunn, and Collamer (HNC), the Phoenix architectural firm that designed the SMU, in the national trade magazine for correctional professionals *Corrections Today*. The two-page article promoted the unique, highly secure yet cost-efficient design of the SMU, specifying the savings offered by making the entire unit windowless and by creating small pods that allowed for lower staffing needs for surveillance (Arrington, 1987).

That article was followed by an ad campaign in the same periodical launched by HNC and another company, Stewart-Decatur, involved in its construction. In a July 1988 HNC print ad that aimed to drum up more supermax contracts, the copy reads, in part:

> *First in Arizona. Soon in California.* An Astonishing, New Dimension in Special Management Units . . . Safety, Security, and Cost-Effectiveness. The future is here and now. Arizona's new 768-bed Security Housing Unit in Florence and California's soon to be built [unit] . . . are living examples of how tomorrow's maximum security prisons will be designed. (*Corrections Today*, 1988a)

The ad goes on to describe how this revolutionary new design allows for "unique" new levels of efficiency, thus requiring lower staffing-to-inmate ratios without sacrificing maximum inmate observation and control. It also elaborates on the cost-saving features of eliminating windows and using the perforated metal cell fronts to provide light from the sky lighted "day spaces."

Stewart-Decatur, the manufacturer of those perforated metal walls, doors, and "unique food pass" devices designed to allow cuffing and uncuffing of prisoners while they are still locked inside, also advertised its accomplishments in *Corrections Today*. In its ad, a photograph of an inmate standing behind the perforated steel wall in a bare cell with his hands in his pockets is used with a quotation from an unnamed Arizona administrator: "New approaches gave us the toughest security" (*Corrections Today*, 1988b; Lynch, 2002).

Very quickly, the SMU took its place on the correctional landscape. Penal administrators from states all over the country wanted to see the new unit. California was the first state to follow in Arizona's footsteps—it hired the same architect and commissioned a similar design for its now more famous (and infamous) Pelican Bay Security Housing Unit. Indeed, the front-page story of the Arizona Department of Corrections' internal monthly newsletter announcing the opening of the SMU pointed out that the "California Department of Corrections was so impressed with Arizona's SMU that they have hired the SMU architects . . . to design a similar facility" (Hack, 1987: 1).[8]

Soon after its opening in 1987, the SMU was filled to capacity with high-security inmates and became the place where "management problems" were sent from throughout the system (Hack, 1987). Given the SMU's "success," the legislature immediately approved funding for a 192-bed addition, which was completed in mid-1988. It was not long after that before the department lobbied for another such unit (SMU II), which was approved, funded, and constructed in the mid-1990s. CB-6 was maintained for death-row inmates, although the more trouble-prone of those were sent to the SMU. CB-6 also was used as a punitive segregation unit in which disciplined inmates cycled in and out, while SMU became, for many of its residents, a long-term housing assignment for inmates classified as level 5, the highest security level in the system, and for "disruptive prisoners," from which it was difficult to be transferred once assigned there.

INCREASING THE DIRECTOR'S POWER

Partly as a consequence of MacDougall's fall from grace, followed by Ricketts's weak position with the legislature, and partly resulting from the changes to the state's criminal sentencing statutes, the power and authority of the role of the Department of Corrections' director had diminished over its relatively short history. Lewis, however, successfully worked to restore the legislature's faith in the director's role, thus allowing him to reclaim some of those lost discretionary powers. In contrast to previous long-term directors such as Cook and MacDougall, Lewis did not appear to seek discretionary power in order to more easily achieve some overriding penological goals. Rather, he seemed more interested in acquiring that power for its own sake. In other words, the accretion of control was an end in itself rather than a means to a penological end. Indeed, Lewis's punishment philosophy—which valued harsh punishment, isolation, and control—would seem to be a contradiction to some of the powers he sought, earned, and wielded during his first five or so years as director.

The first major change that he helped shepherd through the legislative process affected release dates for inmates. In 1985, when he took over as director, the law mandated that all prisoners be released 180 days before their sentence end date to be supervised on parole in the community. Lewis urged the legislature to make the early release date provisional upon the department's recommendation, and by late 1985, that body complied with such a law change. He justified this change on public safety grounds, arguing that many inmates were unsuitable for release because of the nature of their original offense and/ or their behavior in prison. Once the law was changed, Lewis was able to use 180-day early release recommendations as a way of managing populations and as a punitive or coercive measure against selected inmates.

In 1986, again at Lewis's urging, the department was afforded more discretion in recommending first-time offenders convicted of nonviolent crimes for even earlier release to the community to fulfill their sentences on work furlough. The Board of Pardons and Paroles had the final say in granting such releases, but Lewis also used this tool to regulate the inmate population as needed, rather than as a way to aid rehabilitation or community integration. Subsequent to that change, he pushed for a bill that allowed the department to release specified felons for the remainder of their sentences to "home arrest," which meant that they were subject to electronic monitoring at their own expense. The law was enacted in 1988, so he also had this back-end mechanism to control the daily incarcerated population count as needed. In contrast to MacDougall's practices, which reflected his commitment to community corrections and offender reintegration, Lewis recommended far fewer inmates than the total number eligible for both of these programs and would rely on them only when bed shortages reached a crisis point.

Thus, he was clearly agnostic (at best) in his faith in the underlying penological value of early release; he treated these programs merely as strategic tools for maintaining some control over the population, in terms of sustaining manageable numbers, and as a psychological tool, in that he could use early release as both a carrot and a stick when managing inmates. He never publicly framed his endorsement of such strategies as valuable for rehabilitative purposes or any other larger penal goal, and as soon as he did not need to rely on these back-end population management tools, he would stop using them. Such an approach pleased the conservatives in the legislature because it did not reward inmates with shorter sentences unless absolutely necessary for fiscal or other pragmatic reasons; however, it created a sense of inconsistency and unfairness within inmate populations.

Lewis's other major gain in power occurred a little more than a year after he took over the department. From the time he became director, he instituted major policy changes, which affected inmates and their families, in an auto-cratic manner that did not comply with state law. Under the Administrative Procedure Act, the Department of Corrections, like all state agencies, was re-quired to give notice to the secretary of state and hold public hearings on all major proposed changes in rules and policies. When Lewis took over, though, he simply instituted changes without formal notice or public input. When he changed the visitation policy in 1985 to allow strip searches of visitors, Middle Ground sought an injunction to stop the practice because the policy had been made in violation of the Administrative Procedure Act.

In the meantime, though, a clause that exempted only the Department of Corrections from compliance with the Administrative Procedure Act was attached to an unrelated house bill that ultimately passed into law. The bill's author denied knowing how the clause made it into the bill and even indi-cated that he would have opposed it had he been aware of it. The department's spokesperson said that the department did not lobby for the change and sug-gested that it originated in a draft of model legislation written years earlier (Torrey, 1986). Nonetheless, Lewis and the department were the beneficiaries of the law change and became, as of the start of 1987, fully exempt from the rule-making procedures to which all other state agencies were subjected. This change allowed Lewis and his successors much more discretion and freedom in transforming policies and practices within the various penal institutions and in some ways contributed to the acceleration of the flagrant punitiveness that occurred behind Arizona prison bars over the remainder of the twentieth century.

THE PRIMACY OF "COST-CONSCIOUSNESS"

Lewis also fully resurrected the Eyman-esque rhetoric about cost savings and fiscal frugality in all the measures he promoted. He articulated this theme when he addressed everything from the macro-level state penal policy through the micro-level institutional daily business, and it was carried on through the tenure of his protégé, Terry Stewart, as both deputy director and then succes-sor director.

Ironically, among the larger scale policy changes that Lewis initially pub-licly supported, on fiscal grounds, was revision of the penal code to help stem the flow of inmates into the system. His line on this issue was much like Mac-Dougall's, who in most other ways was the opposite of Lewis. Lewis told legis-lators, community groups, reporters, and others that either the state had to be willing to change the code in order to rein in the prison population growth or it needed to continue to invest in building prisons over the long term.

Early in his tenure, Lewis also advocated exploring the possibility of privatizing at least a portion of the system as a cost-saving measure and as a way to avoid building more cells at the state's expense. As already noted, he envisioned using this option as a way to deal with service-intensive special populations, such as mentally ill and developmentally disabled prisoners. Once privatization became a reality in the early 1990s, though, he had to settle for sending the less troublesome inmates, such as the felony drunk-driving offenders, to private facilities because most contracted prisons were not equipped to manage or inclined to accept the most service-intensive inmates.

He created (and publicized) several institutional policies that served the dual purpose of appearing both appropriately tough and harsh on prisoners and fiscally prudent. Lewis was taken with the new "boot camp" trend and advocated for such a program in Arizona after a team from the department visited Georgia's new boot camp program in action. The Arizona program, authorized by the legislature in 1988 under the moniker "shock incarceration," was lauded for promoting "discipline" and physical fitness for first-time youthful offenders while providing cost savings to the state. The program was a 120-day paramilitary, highly structured boot camp–like experience; even the Quonset hut housing units devoted to it were "remodeled" to resemble military barracks. Shock incarceration was axed by legislative action as soon as Lewis retired, however, and the housing was converted back to general inmate beds, partly because it was not the cost-efficient program it was billed to be. As with many "alternative" or "intermediate" sanctions, net-widening occurred with the addition of this program because judges, primarily from rural counties, sent offenders to the program who otherwise would have been maintained on local probation. Also, even though its duration was short for individual offenders, it was expensive to operate and difficult to staff.

At the institutional level, the department pinched pennies in every arena. As noted above, one of Lewis's earliest initiatives was to expand the farming operations, partly as a way to cut institutional food costs and to make "the prison system more self-sufficient" (Lewis, 1987: 9). In later years, the department took to buying food products that were "seconds," including leftover commodities from the Desert Storm military operation overseas and slightly damaged stock from food wholesalers. Emphasis was placed on making the correctional industries program at least self-sufficient if not profitable—a goal that was achieved for the first time in the department's history in 1992. As was tradition in the state, the department also regularly boasted about the cost savings in the institutional construction and maintenance programs that resulted from heavy reliance on inmate labor. Even the conversion of the Death House to accommodate lethal injection was conducted by inmate labor, and the savings generated by this were proudly shared with the press (Leonard, 1993). In 1987, Lewis experimented with an idea to cut off electricity in the cell blocks during the day at the Perryville prisons as a cost-saving measure, as the majority of inmates were out of their cells for much of the day. Policies were also put into place to lower the temperature of hot water within the facilities and reduce the use of heat in the winter and air conditioning in the summer.

Lewis also pushed to pass on more expenses to inmates wherever he could. Those who worked at contracted jobs in which the pay was higher than the standard prison pay (which ranged from 10 to 50 cents an hour as of 1996) were already, by law, charged for room and board at the prison. As noted above, the cost of the telephone surveillance program was the sole burden of inmates' families and associates, who paid for the collect calls inmates made from the institutions' pay phones. The phone company with which the department contracted even provided kickbacks to the department from the collect-call profits, which were used for inmate recreation (Lewis, 1989a; 1990a). Beginning in the early 1990s, the department urged legislation that would allow inmates to be charged "reasonable" fees for electricity if they used any personal items that required electricity in their cell. By 1995, such a law was passed, and the department charged inmates $2.00 a month in utility fees for powering their personal appliances. In 1993, the department pushed successful legislation that required working inmates to earn and save their own "gate" money—the $50 given to each prisoner upon release. In 1994, two more bills were proposed by the department, and ultimately passed into law, that went after inmates' meager earnings. First, the department was authorized to charge "reasonable fees, not to exceed $5.00" to inmates for medical visits (with exemptions for juvenile inmates in adult facilities, pregnant inmates, and mentally and chronically ill inmates) and authorizing the deduction of costs from inmate accounts from those inmates who caused injuries to themselves or others (Lewis, 1995a: 13). Second, the department was authorized to tap inmate accounts for unpaid court costs as well as expenses for damage inmates caused to institutional facilities.

Each annual report issued by the department included a daily per capita cost to the state for prisoners, release center residents, and parolees, and from 1993 to 1995, the report added a section that compared those figures with other states' per capita costs as a way of demonstrating the relative thriftiness of the Arizona Department of Corrections. Thus, from the first year of the reporting in 1993 to the next year, 1994, the department's per capita costs dropped in actual dollars from $68.26 per day per inmate for fiscal year 1991 to $46.08 for fiscal year 1992, and the state ranking dropped from 16th to 36th in expenditure per inmate. In the June 1993 issue of the internal newsletter *Directions*, celebrating the 25th anniversary of the department, the unnamed newsletter writer reported that under Director Lewis's leadership, "real expenditures per inmate decreased by more than $3,300 from FY 1981 to FY 1988, according to the Arizona Joint Select Committee on State Revenues and Expenditures . . . [and the] downward trend has continued since FY 1988" (*Directions*, 1993: 3).

CONCLUSION

In terms of timing, Arizona began the buildup of its prison population just slightly ahead of most other states in the country and thus can be seen as falling in line with national trends. Yet Arizona did it with a vengeance. After a long history of maintaining incarceration rates close to the national average, Arizona leap-frogged over many other states and became a top-10 incarcerator (by per capita rate) by 1984, a standing that it has maintained through the early twenty-first century.

During the early 1980s, two core Arizona values—fiscal frugality and harsh punishment—faced off within the legislature. In 1983, after seven decades of statehood during which fiscal frugality always won, thus keeping prison expansion in relative check, the tide turned and a majority of legislators became fully committed to investing in prisons rather than lessening sentences, even for nonviolent offenders. Thus Arizona's rigid and harsh sentencing scheme was maintained, and made even more stringent for some offenses, despite the direct consequences for the state's prison population. Consequently, Arizona became a national leader in imprisonment rate and rate of growth during this decade.

Equally significant, by the 1980s, Arizona became something of a trendsetter in terms of the punitive, nonrehabilitative approach it adopted within penal facilities, primarily under the leadership of director Sam Lewis, with the support and encouragement of the state legislature. Yet for this jurisdiction, the "new punitiveness" (Pratt, Brown, Hallsworth, Brown, and Morrison, 2005) was at least in part a resurgence of the old. Lewis's harsh, fiscally frugal, disciplinary approach to institutional management had significant parallels to the management style that had prevailed up until the late 1960s in the state. Indeed, the importation of a more rehabilitative management approach, from Cook's tenure through MacDougall's and even Ricketts's, might best be seen as an aberration from the norm in Arizona rather than as the hegemonic model over the state's history.

Ironically, as Lewis's administration transformed the institutional experience into one that was more restrictive, more security oriented, and less rehabilitative in nature, the inmate population in the state was becoming less serious over time, in terms of commitment offense. To illustrate, while Arizona's growth in incarceration rate began to consistently exceed the national average beginning in 1981, the state's rate for those sentenced to prison for serious felonies stayed close to the national rate throughout the 1980s (Arizona Department of Corrections, 1990). This meant that the incarceration of less serious offenders was a significant driving force in Arizona's rise to the top 10 incarcerating states in the nation. As a result, the ratio of violent offenders to nonviolent offenders among the incarcerated population in the state steadily dropped: half of the population inside the state's prisons were violent offenders at fiscal year-end 1980; by fiscal year-end 1993, only 33 percent of the incarcerated population were there for violence convictions. Thus, a larger proportion of less serious offenders were increasingly treated more like high-risk, irredeemable, dangerous offenders under the Lewis regime, and few voices in the state seemed to object.

Yet the penal transformation under Lewis's directorship is not simply a matter of a forceful, charismatic leader whose drive and vision singularly produced the changes. Most of the elements for the imprisonment growth and for the shift (or shift back) to the punitive were already in place before Lewis took over. Furthermore, corrections administrators have only a limited effect on prison population numbers. For the most part, prison institutions are mere recipients of their population and must accept all those sentenced from the state's courts, where sentences are largely determined by a combination of statutory requirements, judicial and prosecutorial discretion, and local sentencing norms. Where administrators may have influence over population size is in their discretionary use of any back-door release mechanisms, to the extent that they exist in a given jurisdiction. In Arizona's case, the legislature had finally begun to demonstrate its willingness to fiscally commit to incarceration as a primary response to the problem of crime by the early 1980s and had, over the years, limited the availability of custodial release measures to ensure that inmates served longer sentences. The governor's office had retreated from voicing opposition to the incarceration strategy even when it seemed deeply problematic, fiscally, if not morally, as the larger political arena had changed around the problems of crime and punishment.

In terms of the changes in the quality of institutional punishment in Arizona, the state as a whole had its own history as a precedent model when the rehabilitative approach seemed to be a failure. Abandoning a more humane and less restrictive penal approach was not a rejection of a centuries-old penal project as it would have been in a number of northeastern and midwestern industrial states; rather, it was merely a case of pulling out of a failed experiment. Still, the appointment of Lewis ensured that Arizona would not simply flounder and follow other states as they underwent transformations in penality.

His appointment in many ways was the catalyst that ensured that Arizona would become a leader in postrehabilitative trends. Because he was not a career penal administrator, Lewis devised policies that were, at the time, well outside the norms and expectations for corrections and that someone with more professional experience, history, and expertise probably would not have conceived. Rather, he was a "lawman" with deep roots in the state and with a philosophy that meshed with core Arizona values, so he gained legitimacy among state actors for qualities wholly unrelated to penal expertise. Thus, as he devised new strategies that would seem to be counter to prevailing correctional norms, inmates complained, but he was resolute in holding out until he got his way, a stubbornness that held even in the face of litigation (see Chapter 6). Unlike his predecessors, the threat or actuality of lawsuits did not cause him to compromise—he was happy to do battle in that arena as well in order to prevail. Ultimately, the political actors who could have intervened to avert legal challenges ended up following Lewis's lead into the courtroom.

5 THE POSTREHABILITATIVE PROTOTYPE IS REALIZED

ARIZONA CONTINUED ITS PATH as a trailblazer in penal harshness through the 1990s, and by the middle of that decade, the state's penal system could legitimately be considered exemplary of the postrehabilitative, warehouse-style prison system that had begun to dominate corrections in the United States. A congruence around issues related to crime and punishment among the governor's office, the legislature, and the Department of Corrections facilitated a proactive strategy that sought to make the prison experience more punitive inside while decreasing outside scrutiny of Arizona prison life. There were two steps to this process: first was a much publicized and media-influenced escalation in the politicizing of crime and punishment, beginning in the early 1990s. Elected officials increasingly used the local news media to compete with the more outrageous tough-on-crime proposals, and the Department of Corrections, in this instance, became an active player in these politics. Local criminal justice and media actors, especially from the large and influential Maricopa County, also became more significant players in this process during the 1990s, contributing to a chorus on crime and justice issues within the state. Second, a corollary "states' rights" rhetoric also became more politically salient during this period, and the task of getting federal courts out of state business became an executive branch priority for Governor Fife Symington, who was elected in 1990. The primary site for this action was in the management of the state prisons, which had been subject to a number of court orders and consent decrees since the early 1970s (see Chapter 6).

It becomes clear that the ultimate transformation of Arizona's correctional system into a fully postrehabilitative model was not just the work of individual politicians and administrators. Sam Lewis, for example, can be "credited" with moving the department farther toward a largely punitive system than a more experienced (thus tempered) director might have done, and Governor Symington adopted a stance on crime and punishment that appeared to fall on the extreme side of the continuum of governors' approaches during the 1990s. Yet as already demonstrated, the conditions for the transformation of prisons in Arizona were already ripe before either of these men took on their roles, and the punitiveness continued to escalate after both were gone.

THE SECOND FORK IN THE ROAD: THE POTENTIAL FOR SCALING BACK THE INCARCERATION EXPLOSION

Ironically, as the 1990s opened, there were signs that the trajectory of punishment in Arizona could change. In the March 1990 Republican primaries, the battle for the gubernatorial nomination was very much right wing versus more right wing, as millionaire developer and state party insider Fife Symington beat competitor Evan Mecham, the previously impeached and convicted governor,[1] to earn the right to run in the general election. Yet the prevailing issue that drove that race, as well as the general race that followed, was the state's dismal economy and which candidate would be the most likely to turn it around.

Symington campaigned on a "government as business" platform, suggesting that his experience as a developer made him the most qualified for the job. In the general election, using a similar campaign strategy, Symington defeated the Democratic candidate (Sam "Terry" Goddard III, son of former governor Sam Goddard) in a runoff election after they virtually tied in the general election. Symington did not fully highlight law and order until after taking office, although he quickly became publicly vocal about getting tough on criminals (except white-collar criminals, whom he felt the courts treated too harshly).

In the Republican primary for attorney general, former public defender and judge pro tem Grant Woods ran as a moderate alternative to Assistant Attorney General Steve Twist, who was the handpicked successor candidate backed by then–attorney general Bob Corbin. Corbin's office was staunchly and proactively law and order, to the exclusion of many other issues it could have tackled, and Twist was among the most fervent on these issues within the office. Woods ended up defeating Twist in the primary and winning the office in the general election, which seemed to foreshadow a change in tenor on crime and punishment issues, at least in that office. The electorate also voted in a Democratic majority to the state Senate, which had the strong potential to at least slow the tide of tough-on-crime legislation. Although short-lived—Republicans regained the majority two years later—this had been the only time in 40 years that either house of the Arizona legislature had a Democratic majority.

This is not to say that crime and punishment had fallen off the radar. In the same general election, 57 percent of the state's voters supported a ballot proposition authorizing a state constitutional amendment providing for victims' rights. Arizona was thus among the earlier jurisdictions to authorize a formal victims' bill of rights, and it was the first significant crime-related ballot measure to pass since 1916 when an initiative to abolish capital punishment was approved (the death penalty was, however, reinstated by ballot proposition two years later). Nonetheless, although this proposition garnered majority support, just two years earlier, the state's voters had rejected a similar referendum, so it was not a deeply rooted or overwhelmingly popular mandate. And in both instances, the push for the victims' bill of rights was more top-down than ground-up. Twist had been the primary architect of the bill while he was working under Corbin in the attorney general's office. Indeed, Twist was a fervent and vocal supporter of the victims' rights movement,[2] so the bill's inception and political viability were largely the product of a state-level political office, rather than of a grassroots movement in the state.

Primarily because of the Democrat-controlled Senate, legislative and executive branch attempts to escalate punitive policies during 1991 and 1992 had little success. If anything, there was movement to scale back on the use of incarceration in the state. In the summer of 1991, an independent study of the state's sentencing policies by the Institute for Rational Public Policy, which the legislature had commissioned in 1989, was completed, and its findings were outlined in a 151-page report (Institute for Rational Public Policy, 1991). The report, whose primary author was former U.S. Sentencing Commission director Kay Knapp, concluded that the 1978 criminal code was largely the cause of the severe prison overcrowding experienced in the state and the proportionally growing share of the budget that had to be allocated to corrections. By the time the report was complete, Arizona's prisons held nearly 15,000 adult inmates, and the state had the fourth highest incarceration rate in the nation.

The so-called Knapp Report also damned the state's sentencing scheme as being ineffective in terms of deterrence and incapacitation—it showed no measurable effect on crime rates—while in practice it had resulted in hugely disparate sentence outcomes for similar offenders because it afforded prosecutors so much discretion in charging (Yozwiak, 1991). Of particular concern to the researchers, as well as to other critics of Arizona's sentencing practices, was how prosecutors could and did use prior convictions to greatly enhance sentence lengths. The report did not condemn the concept of mandatory sentencing schemes; rather, it found fault with Arizona's implementation of such a scheme, particularly in terms of how prosecutors applied it.

The Democrats in the Senate used the Knapp Report to push for a special session to deal with the prison overcrowding problem, with an eye toward sentencing reform. Both the governor's office and the Department of Corrections were quite reserved in their response to the report; neither opposed it in public, but neither jumped on the reform bandwagon either. Republicans in the legislature also remained relatively quiet in the months following the report's distribution.

MANUFACTURING CONTROVERSY IN THE MEDIA

The local news media, however, did not stay silent. The *Arizona Republic*, which was still (and continues to be) by far the largest and most influential newspaper in the state, and its afternoon counterpart, the *Phoenix Gazette*, devoted many lines of copy to covering and editorializing about the Knapp Report over the summer and fall of 1991. The newspapers' interest in the issue appears to have been largely prompted by the response of county prosecutors, who took a strong stance against the report and its conclusions. They were led by Maricopa County Attorney (the elected county prosecutor) Richard Romley, whose office was responsible for the majority of prison sentences in the state. The prosecutors were aided in the debate by a professor of law and economics at the University of Arizona, Michael Block, who criticized the report in the press and who signed on to do a "shadow" report about Arizona's sentencing outcomes for the Arizona Prosecuting Attorney's Advisory Council.

Block had served on the U.S. Sentencing Commission with Knapp and was open about his disdain for her. He publicly accused her of incompetence, suggesting that when she was with the Sentencing Commission she did not know what she was doing, "was a nightmare" as a director, and was biased against punishment (Yozwiak, 1990). Block was a strong proponent of mandatory sentencing, asserting that such sentencing schemes resulted in successful incapacitation. His "findings" on the question of incapacitation were reminiscent of former attorney general Corbin's studies in that he pointed out that as the prison rate had shot up after the 1978 implementation of the criminal code, the crime rate had declined in the state.

Block's findings were cited in several *Arizona Republic* and *Phoenix Gazette* editorials in support of maintaining the existing sentencing code. Indeed, more attention was paid to research findings in these editorials than had ever been displayed on the issue of crime and punishment within the local press. In a state where the political and popular wisdom privileged commonsense understandings of what is the best course of action, it stood out that editorial commentators in the newspapers (and eventually elected officials) cited selected empirical research (however problematic these data were) in support of their position that tough mandatory sentencing worked.

The first of these instances came in a *Phoenix Gazette* staff editorial that cited an article by Bureau of Justice Statistics statistician Patrick Langan published in the "highly respected *Science* magazine" (*Phoenix Gazette*, 1991a). The editorial quoted the *Science* article extensively, including passages that supported the hypothesis that falling crime rates were caused by the rising incarceration rates in the nation. The editorial heralded the value of the "facts" and the "truth" that were offered through such studies in the debate over Arizona's criminal code. That editorial was followed a week later with a piece by the conservative columnist Mark Genrich. Genrich cited earlier proclamations by Block, who had argued in 1989 that the state's mandatory sentencing scheme was not the culprit in the prison overcrowding crisis. Genrich also cited Langan's *Science* article, concluding that with "Michael Block and Patrick Langan running around with facts and statistics, taxpayers might soon get the extraordinary notion that prisons actually work" (Genrich, 1991). Both of these editorials slammed the Knapp Report for getting it all wrong in terms of Arizona's situation.

A third general editorial was published in July that condemned the Knapp Report and urged the governor to forgo a special session on sentencing reform. It referred to the report as the "big bucks" report that was skewed and composed of "questionable research" (*Phoenix Gazette*, 1991b). It also extensively cited the *Science* article as support for the success of incapacitation. This editorial added the insights of another academic, John Dilulio, by describing how his study of Wisconsin's prison system demonstrated the cost savings of locking up offenders when the real costs of crime are factored into the equation.

Two weeks after that editorial, *Arizona Republic* staff editor Ray Archer again countered the commonly expressed view that the sentencing code was a

significant factor in the state's imprisonment boom by citing mainly uniden-
tified research linking the use of imprisonment to lower crime rates and to
overall cost savings, in terms of crime victimization. In the editorial's conclusion, Archer posed this rhetorical question: "Can Arizona afford not to have
mandatory sentencing laws?" (Archer, 1991).

One day later, the paper published a lengthy guest editorial by Maricopa
County Attorney Romley that again used "the facts" to argue against sentencing reforms. He relied heavily on Block's then-current study of Arizona's
code—the one commissioned by the prosecutors' organization—to demonstrate that his office and other prosecutors' offices did not wield their discretion inappropriately, that mandatory sentences provided public safety and
real cost savings, and that the "right" people end up behind bars in the state.
He, too, cited the Wisconsin study as proof that locking up offenders saves
money in the end.

By December, when the final *Phoenix Gazette* editorial about the Knapp
Report appeared, the unnamed staff writer declared that the report no longer
had a "drop of credibility" left, after having been trumped by Block's study as
well as by an analysis by the Barry Goldwater Institute for Public Policy Research (where Block was a consultant). By this time, Attorney General Woods
signed on in support of maintaining the code, stating that "in Arizona the
right people are going to prison" (*Phoenix Gazette*, 1991c).

Each news article and "status quo" editorial that commented on the Knapp
Report in the *Arizona Republic* and *Phoenix Gazette* specifically noted its cost
to taxpayers—$450,000—a tactic that seemed to aim at somehow undermin-
ing its credibility, or at least associating it with fiscal imprudence. Indeed,
in the December editorial, the author suggested that the politicians who had
spent taxpayer money on the study should "run for cover, embarrassed by the
discredited, shriveled document they purchased" (*Phoenix Gazette*, 1991c).

Throughout this period, several columns expressed the opposing view, most
notably a lengthy guest editorial in the *Arizona Republic* by two Phoenix criminal defense attorneys that was published in July 1991. The other commentary
came from *Gazette* staff columnist Richard De Uriarte, who specifically took
on Genrich, whom he accused of "being infatuated with prisons" (De Uriarte,
1991). Yet the print space devoted to the "reform" position was significantly less
than that allocated to arguing for maintaining the code as it existed.

In this case, then, much of the impetus for forestalling sentencing reform
seemed to come from the local news media, specifically the largest and most

influential paper in the state, with significant input from local prosecutors and Block, at the behest of the prosecutors. Over the months that this issue largely played out, none of the state-level political figures or administrators publicly joined in the chorus that sought to maintain the criminal code, not the governor, legislators, attorney general (until later that year), or any Department of Corrections officials. Rather, the issue was made newsworthy by the newspapers themselves, which took a stance on this issue that was decidedly more law and order than they had been at least since mid-century (and probably before). Although the papers were hardly left-leaning publications historically, their editorials on criminal justice issues had generally balanced needing appropriate "toughness" with being fiscally practical and procedurally fair, so their treatment of this issue during the early 1990s stands out as a movement away from such moderation.

SENTENCE REFORM AND POLITICS

Even though public reaction from most state-level elected officials was minimal during the period that the *Arizona Republic* and the *Phoenix Gazette* were editorializing about sentence reform, the papers' interest in and attention to this issue appears ultimately to have influenced the outcome of how the code would be adapted. It had the effect of framing the problem such that support for maintaining the current code was associated with "the facts" and "the truth," with being what was best for victims, and even, ironically, with being the fiscally prudent course of action. By the time the legislature was heading back into session and ready to deal with sentencing, the issue both was much more politicized and had been reduced to a black-and-white contrast in which one's stance was equated with being either soft or tough on crime.

As a result, the prospect of wholesale reform of the code was diminished; instead, the proposals that followed amounted to tinkering with the length of mandated sentences for just a few select offenses. Nonetheless, the legislature took seriously the prospect of making some adjustments in the sentencing statute in order to address the prison population explosion as well as to address what some members saw as some injustices in the current scheme. A joint legislative committee was formed to deal with the code issue, and it empanelled a group of advisors who came up with a set of recommendations for reform.

The first recommendation was to increase the drug amount thresholds that triggered automatic prison sentences in order to remove the lowest level drug offenders from being subject to mandatory minimums. The group also suggested that the existing statute mandating a life sentence for those convicted of a drug offense while on probation be revised to allow for a shorter sentence. The second recommendation would lessen the sentence range for adults who fondled children without intercourse to slightly fewer years than required in such cases involving intercourse. A third recommendation was to allow more judicial discretion in considering prior offenses as sentence enhancements so that the seriousness and temporal distance of priors could be used to determine enhancements. Finally, the group recommended that the breadth of the felony murder rule be narrowed to prevent injustices in its application.

The joint legislative committee took the recommendations to heart and drafted a bill that incorporated many of the advisory group's suggestions. The bill was the product of bipartisan effort among committee members and received bipartisan support among the full legislative bodies in both branches. It was a rare moment in criminal justice legislating during this period—there was a sense of accomplishment in the legislature, as the bill's creation had required "a difficult compromise" among the parties and had ultimately garnered support from many criminal justice practitioners, members of the public, and the attorney general's office (Flannery, 1992a).

Legislative leaders had consulted with Governor Symington to ensure that he had input and would approve the final product. He raised no objections to any elements of the package and told the lawmakers he was leaning toward signing the bill. Yet by the time the bill had passed both houses and reached the governor's desk for approval, Symington had reversed his support and vetoed it. Reportedly, the impetus for his change of heart was hearing from the "detractors" of the bill, namely, county prosecutors Richard Romley and Stephan Neeley, who represented the two most populous counties in the state and together were responsible for close to 80 percent of the state's prison commitments. Symington also claimed that he had received negative letters from victims' groups and "corporations" that opposed the reforms (Flannery, 1992a). His veto was a 13-paragraph diatribe which suggested that if the bill passed, murderers and child molesters would go free. This narrative attack was an added surprise because he had not voiced any problems with it just days earlier (Kolbe, 1992).

There was backlash against the governor's veto from several corners. The legislators who had crafted the bill and successfully promoted it among their peers, which had taken months of work, were understandably angry. Attorney

General Woods also jumped into the public sparring over the governor's veto, accusing Symington of playing politics and "pandering to the right," to which Symington responded by calling Woods "soft on crime" (Kolbe, 1992). This deepened the competitive animosity between the two men, which had already been brewing since both took office.

Symington followed up with his own proposed reforms that fit with his increasingly vocalized tough-on-crime rhetoric. Thus, he unveiled his proposed truth-in-sentencing bill in the late fall of 1992, which as originally conceived would have had the opposite effect on prison populations from the reform bill that he had just vetoed. His package sought to abolish parole and eliminate the remaining early release programs that were in place; allow a maximum of 15 percent credit for "good time" rather than the existing policy of one day of credit for two served; lower the age from 18 to 16 for adult court jurisdiction for those charged with serious felonies (along with several other tougher provisions aimed at juveniles); and make all felonies involving guns ineligible for probation.

Prosecutors and many law enforcement officials praised Symington's proposal, while activists and many criminal justice experts in the state condemned it for its shortsightedness in terms of its potential effect on the prison population and for its abandonment of any principles of rehabilitation. His announcement of the proposal, to an audience of state law enforcement officials, indulged in a full array of tough-on-crime rhetoric, from highlighting a particularly egregious recent crime incident in the state (the rape and murder of a small-town librarian) to accusing juvenile offenders of "laughing at the legal system" because of the leniency of the juvenile system (Pitzl, 1992).

Symington insisted that his office's "analysis" of the proposal's effect indicated that it would not contribute to further prison overcrowding, and he said that Sam Lewis endorsed it, which Lewis would not have done if he felt the proposal would further strain prison capacity in the state. Yet in this unveiling, Symington did not reveal specifically how this could be possible, given that all of the components of his package would sentence more people to prisons, and for longer periods. It turned out that the truth-in-sentencing plan actually included provisions somewhat along the lines of the sentence adjustments in the bill he had vetoed earlier in the year. Under the proposal, sentences for some drug offenses, burglary, manslaughter, possession of obscene materials, and trespassing would be reduced, which would counterbalance the sentence gains through the increase in actual time served for all offenses. Indeed, research analyst Darryl Fischer of the Department of Corrections actually conducted the analysis to come up with the sentence reform recommendations for the governor that would, at least ideally, slow or nearly halt the prison population growth (Fischer interview, 2004). Yet because of the increases proposed and the truth-in-sentencing component, this set of reforms could not lower the prison population, which had been the original goal of sentence reform.

Thus, the proposal was in part an initiative of the Department of Corrections, which had worked closely with the governor's office to devise a plan that could be sold as purely tough on crime without unduly affecting the department in terms of an increase in prison population (Fischer interview, 2004). The attorney general was left out of the process of devising the plan, signaling a hardening of alliance between the governor's office and the Department of Corrections on sentencing and prison issues. Woods learned about the proposal on the same day as the public, which did not appear to please him (Flannery, 1992b); however, he had to mute his criticism so that he did not come off as too soft on crime.

So in a one-year period, the movement to implement fundamental sentencing reform to reduce Arizona's prison population had morphed into a "get-tough" agenda that at best would not exacerbate prison overcrowding. And because of the short cycle for state legislative elections, the passing of that brief time actually allowed for a new audience in the legislature, which meant that some of the impetus for sentence reform was about to disappear. The Democratic majority that was seated in the 1990 elections was unseated in 1992, and Republicans regained control of both houses. This, in turn, made Symington's proposal viable and seemed to erase the bipartisan goodwill that had developed over the process of writing the prior year's sentencing reform bill.

By early 1993, the crime bill under consideration in the legislature had as its basis Symington's truth-in-sentencing package, with some additional reforms that the Senate Judiciary Committee included. The broader discussion about the bill was no longer primarily focused on how it might stem the flow of inmates to Arizona prisons, or how it might correct some of the sentencing inequities that the Knapp Report had highlighted. Rather, it typified the kind of political rhetoric about crime and punishment that had developed during the late 1980s in the state and that was being voiced by state- and national-level politicians around the nation. Sentence reform that would turn back, or even dampen, the incarceration explosion was thus dead in Arizona.

The truth-in-sentencing legislation passed, with several revisions along the way and with strong support from the Republican-dominated legislature, was signed into law by Symington, and went into effect on January 1, 1994. And much to the shock of those who did the analyses, it did not slow the prison population growth whatsoever; instead, the net monthly growth in the system kept shooting up, and indeed escalated faster after the law passed.[3]

Furthermore, it added even more complexity to a sentencing code that was already arcane in its multiple provisions specifying crime classifications, types of enhancements, limits on sentence options, and so on. Thus, it increased the depth and breadth of the prosecutorial arsenal of discretion in how offenses were charged and plea-bargained. In that regard, it exacerbated one of the central problems identified by the Knapp Report—disparate sentence outcomes for similarly situated offenders.[4]

COMPETING TOUGHNESS IN THE POLITICAL REALM:
GRANT WOODS VERSUS FIFE SYMINGTON AND SAM LEWIS

Simultaneous with the sentence reform process, which ultimately contributed to the prison population growth in Arizona, an increasingly publicized and politicized escalation of punitiveness behind bars occurred as well. This seemed to emerge from multiple fronts. Several constituencies within the state took it upon themselves to up the ante on harsh treatment of inmates, and the net result was that those confined to the prison system, as well as those confined to the state's largest (and the nation's third largest) jail system in Maricopa County, were subjected to increasingly uncomfortable and degrading living conditions. And such conditions were experienced by a population that was proportionately made up of less serious offenders than had been the case in prior decades.

Attorney General Grant Woods was an early contributor to this process. Soon after taking office, he decided to stake out prison life as the arena in which to demonstrate his "get-tough" credentials. This likely helped escalate the commitment of the Department of Corrections to making the prison experience even more austere and uncomfortable, if for no other reason than to stay one up on Woods's proposals.

It was widely assumed in the state that Woods had entered state politics with the ultimate plan of running for a major office beyond attorney general. Symington appeared to view him as a likely opponent in the next governor's race, as did commentators in the press (for example, Montini, 1991). From early on in their respective terms, Symington began to exclude Woods from the closed negotiations and policy planning that his office was undertaking, especially on criminal justice issues, which did not sit well with Woods. The sentence reform drama was one of several such exclusions, and one that revealed the animosity between the two men to the public.

Attacking life behind bars as too cushy allowed Woods to simultaneously compete with Symington in the political arena and take aim at Sam Lewis, with whom he also had a strained relationship.[5] Woods began his publicized "get tough on prisoners" campaign just six months into his term. His first call was to remove televisions from inmates' cells as a way to make the prison experience less palatable.

His stance on prisoners seemed all the more politically cynical because he had been a public defender for much of his legal career, where he presumably worked to keep his criminally accused clients out of prison. In fact, as attorney general Woods claimed a particular expertise on prisoners because of this background and justified his evolving stance on the basis of his understanding of those who end up incarcerated. In a media dispute with Lewis over his comments about how prisons should be run, Woods defended his position that prisoners should be denied televisions, stereos, and weight-lifting equipment on these grounds: "I probably know them [inmates] as well as Mr. Lewis. And at least for the ones that I represented, for most of them, it's not a big deal to go back to prison. Recidivism would go down if it wasn't such a vacation for criminals to go to prison" (Griffin, 1991).

A particularly bizarre example of Woods's stance on prisoners occurred in the summer after he took office. An inmate wrote to his office requesting that the state provide sunscreen for inmates who worked outdoors. The prisoner was encouraged to make the request to someone with more authority by an assistant deputy warden, who also offered to move the prisoner to a job that was not outside. Given that Arizona had at the time the highest rates of skin cancer in the nation and summer temperatures could reach 110 to 115 degrees Fahrenheit, it was a "serious medical situation," as the prisoner characterized it, that needed to be addressed within the prisons because some inmates could not afford to purchase sunscreen yet had work assignments outdoors. Woods's written response to the request was as follows: "I am in receipt of your correspondence dated June 9, 1991, wherein you make a demand upon the Department of Corrections to provide sunscreen for use by prisoners. Please advise your 'clients' that if the sun bothers them, perhaps a lock-down for the summer might be a solution" (quoted in Montini, 1991).

The general architecture of Woods's "tough on prisoners" campaign was laid out in a guest editorial that he wrote for the *Arizona Republic*. It utilized many of the now classic 1990s rhetorical tropes about crime and punishment that were the bread and butter of elected officials' public speeches. First, he defined crime as a quality-of-life issue and reiterated his pledge to the state to focus on improving Arizonans' quality of life as attorney general. He then pointed to the state's prison system as the "biggest and most preventable failure in [the] war on crime," adding that the state was just not getting "their money's worth" from the prisons (Woods, 1992). To illustrate the sorry state of the status quo, he quoted from a diary that he claimed belonged to an Arizona prison inmate, which colorfully illustrated Woods's contention that those behind bars spent their time lounging around "watching television, lifting weights, eating three free meals a day . . . while law-abiding families work to pay the upkeep." The alleged diary passage describes a typical weekend day in the Florence prison:

> Another Saturday of total relaxation. People here in South Unit of Arizona State Prison have one thing in common with the very rich. That is, the choice to do exactly what you want with your time. It can be spent any way the spirit moves. Waste it in any way you like. Sleep in, get up, eat or not, watch TV, etc., and know you will not be disturbed in any way. (Woods, 1992)

With that description of prison life, Woods then detailed his plan for reform. He asserted a commitment to the theory of less eligibility—that no prisoner should live in conditions that are better than those of the poorest "law-abiding citizens"—as a basis for determining what prison life should be like in the state. He took a page from Frank Eyman's playbook (as well as Sam Lewis's, to some extent) by proposing that prison labor should be used to help the state's economy and help offset the "monumental" cost of the prison system, which would also, in his view, provide needed discipline to prisoners. Furthermore, he hinted at a proposal to restrict prisoners' access to legal remedies by suggesting that with all the time on their hands, prisoners were clogging the courts with frivolous lawsuits. Thus, his reform plan made a convict labor program the centerpiece of restructuring and curtailed prisoners' access to television, weight-lifting, and the courts as a way of toughenind up life behind bars.

Woods's position garnered support from some of the editorial staff of the *Arizona Republic*, which published several favorable follow-up editorials. In one, the unnamed writer accused Lewis of running "athletic clubs and TV lounges" and urged the legislature to follow Woods's lead by making policy to get the prisoners "off the couch" and into work (*Arizona Republic*, 1992).

Lewis took every public opportunity to point out Woods's ignorance about the state's prison operations. The two debated on a local radio show, and Lewis turned the table on Woods by suggesting he stop worrying about things that were not his business and begin doing his job, including moving along the death penalty process so that the state could begin executing condemned convicts for the first time in decades. Correctional officers also came out against Woods, accusing him of not understanding the tools needed to maintain order inside institutions and not caring about the safety and security of officers.

Over the following few years, Woods worked hard at translating his political agenda into policy and legislation. Along the way, he continued to face strong resistance from Lewis, who repeatedly pointed out to members of the press that Woods did not know what he was talking about. He also faced hostile indifference from Governor Symington, who was launching his own tough-on-crime agenda while strengthening his alliance with Lewis. Consequently, a kind of one-upmanship of punitive policies ensued, and inmates bore the brunt of that escalation.

For instance, in early 1993, Woods wrote a memo to Lewis (which he shared with the press) suggesting that Lewis teach his prisoners a "work ethic" by having them clean up trash and debris that had swept into the Salt River from the garbage landfill near Phoenix as a result of a storm. He of course also sold his "suggestion" on its value as a cost-saving measure for the municipalities that would have to do the cleanup. The Department of Corrections countered Woods's meddling by letting him, and the newspapers, know that prison labor had already been successfully used to clean up after flooding in several other locales in the state.

Woods also crafted legislation in 1992 and again in 1993 that was designed to turn some of his proposals into policy. After a 1992 bill that sought to limit television use in prison, which initially found sponsorship in the legislature but ultimately did not go anywhere, Woods drafted a much more comprehensive bill in early 1993. That bill took on prisoner lawsuits by mandating a filing fee of $40 as well as a potential punishment of the loss of good time credits for inmates who filed "frivolous" lawsuits. It also exempted the state from liability for most inmate injuries, mandated a $4.00 fee for inmate medical visits, banned television watching during the day inside prisons, and required the removal of all weight-lifting equipment inside penal facilities.

The bill was sponsored by a Republican legislator from Phoenix and was vocally opposed by Lewis, not because he thought the provisions were too harsh but because, according to him, they in no way took into account the realities of how prisons operate. Thus, he complained that the lawsuit bill would disproportionately penalize better behaved inmates because they would have good time credits to lose, whereas the troublemakers would not have anything to lose. The television and weight-lifting restrictions were characterized as misguided and detrimental to staff as these activities served as "babysitters" for inmates. When that bill stalled in the legislature, Woods once again proposed a similar bill that would charge inmates the filing fee for lawsuits and the $4.00 fee for medical services.

Just as Woods's efforts to promote such legislation were abandoned, Lewis quietly changed internal policy and gained legislative support for bills that would do many of the same things, although now he could take credit for the changes. For example, in December 1993, the Department of Corrections requested that the legislature allow the department to charge inmates for electricity used in their cells (for televisions and hot pots and the like), as well as a monthly fee of $1.00 for medical care plus an additional $2.00 per doctor visit. The department also sought more discretion in managing inmate funds to be able to assess such fees (*Arizona Capitol Times*, 1993). These measures were eventually passed in a slightly different form, and the department began charging inmates for medical visits in late 1994 and for electricity in 1996. If inmates could not pay the fees, the money was deducted from the general inmate recreational fund to ensure that prisoners were "held responsible," if not individually then collectively, for their debts (McCloy, 1995).

At the end of 1994, the department also removed weight-training equipment from the facilities and donated it to local schools. Although Woods had proposed this about two years earlier, it was now framed exclusively as a policy initiated by the Department of Corrections. It sold the policy as a cost-saving measure, arguing that the state had paid $600,000 the prior year in medical expenses for injuries related to weight training (*Arizona Capitol Times*, 1994). The state boasted of savings in excess of $100,000 in orthopedic surgeries during the six months after the weights had been removed. Similarly, the fee for medical visits was also touted as a major success because within a year of its implementation, prisoners' visits to the doctor were down

40 percent, and the state had collected more than \$100,000 in fees related to health care in the system.

In December 1995, the department implemented new restrictions on inmates' television use, including restricting the hours during which inmates were allowed to watch it and cutting back the variety of channels available to them. Again, restrictions on television had been one of Woods's "headline" policy suggestions in 1992, and Lewis had vigorously opposed it. But in this recycled version, it was framed solely as a departmentally devised policy designed to force inmates into using their time more productively. Incoming department director Terry Stewart framed it this way for the press: "This is a prison system where inmates are going to work and educate themselves. This is not a prison system where inmates can idle their time away watching TV and movies, many of which are filled with violence and sex" (Manson, 1995).

Over the same time, on the heels of his success with the truth-in-sentencing law, Governor Symington also deepened his commitment to "governing through crime" (Simon, 2007) as a political strategy by proposing well-publicized policies to get tough on juvenile offenders and adult prisoners. Indeed, going into his reelection campaign in the fall of 1994, Symington's first attack on his Democratic opponent was to accuse him of being "soft on crime" for supporting long-term solutions to the problem of crime, including prevention strategies. Symington denounced prevention as a goal, because it was not immediate, and declared, "I am proud of the commitment Arizona has made to prisons" (Pitzl, 1994).

That Symington prioritized crime and punishment as the first weapon in his reelection campaign arsenal, above budget, taxes, and government spending (which were his second priority), signifies the perception of its importance to the state electoral political process by this time. He had not focused on crime in his successful run for governor in 1990, and previous candidates for Arizona governor from both parties generally had not placed crime and punishment at the top of the list of issues over which to battle with their opponents during elections. Of course, as we have seen, that does not mean that sitting governors were agnostic about the crime and punishment issue—even Governor Babbitt succumbed to the law-and-order push during his tenure—but it simply had not taken center stage as the central political issue around which candidates campaigned until now.

In the months leading up to his reelection campaign, Symington was in political trouble over a growing set of his own legal problems, including being a defendant in a huge lawsuit related to his role in the collapse of Southwest Savings and Loan and being the subject of a federal grand jury investigation on the same issues (he would eventually be indicted and convicted of fraud for his financial misdeeds while on the board of Southwest). Thus, in 1993 and 1994, his political career seemed likely to be short-lived, so he turned the attention away from himself to "real" criminals during his campaign. Despite trailing by 9 to 12 points in the various polls leading up to the election, he ended up prevailing and retaining his seat as governor until his conviction in 1997.

His crime strategy was outlined in a November 1993 document titled "Governor Fife Symington's Plan to Combat Urban Violence, Gangs, and Juvenile Crime" (Symington, 1993). The plan had 24 proposals, of which 15 involved increased law enforcement and/or advocated harsher penalties for criminal acts. In the months that followed, Symington focused most of his energy on trying to get the harshest of the proposals implemented. He also spent portions of the preelection period grandstanding with Sam Lewis over the federal district court's rulings regarding prison conditions, framing the intervention as a violation of states' rights and as an affront to the law-and-order values of the state (see Chapter 6).

Once into his second term, Symington made good on his tough-on-crime political rhetoric, even as he faced an increasing risk of indictment himself. He followed through on a campaign promise to initiate chain gangs within the prison system, implementing them in May 1995. Consequently, Arizona was a frontrunner in the (re)institution of chain gangs, second only to Alabama's return to this antiquated practice. Approximately six months later, death row chain gangs appeared. Unlike the general population chain gangs, which worked on public works projects outside the prison walls, death row gangs were confined to working in the vegetable gardens within the fortressed grounds of the Florence prison, so this policy clearly was a matter of form over substance.

Symington also focused on juvenile offenders as a target for harsher policies. Most significantly, he authored a ballot initiative, Proposition 102, that required juveniles aged 15 years and older to be tried in adult court and sentenced to adult prisons if charged with and convicted of specified violent felonies and/or if deemed "chronic" offenders. The initiative was funded by a number of large corporations, including America West Airlines, Phelps Dodge Mining, and the Dial Corporation. It was opposed by Attorney General Woods, virtually all of the state's judges, and even some local prosecutors, including Maricopa County's Richard Romley because of its harshness and inflexibility. Nonetheless, it qualified for the November 1996 ballot after paid signature collectors gathered more than 250,000 voter signatures, and it passed by a significant margin in the election. As a consequence, the demand for available prison beds within the system was pushed even farther beyond the net growth that was increasing because of adult sentencing reforms, and many legislators raised concerns about the high cost that came with this new law (Manson, 1996). Symington followed this victory with a proposal for a "three-strikes" law for juveniles that would ensure their prosecution as adults under Proposition 102 if they had committed three or more felonies.

Ironically, in the same election, voters passed an initiative, Proposition 200, by a two-to-one margin that authorized medical use of all Schedule I drugs and that mandated treatment or other alternatives to incarceration for first- and second-time drug offenders. Not surprisingly, Governor Symington was vociferously opposed to this initiative and made his feelings clear to the public. This proposition was primarily funded by large donations from George Soros, Peter Lewis, and John Sperling, a Phoenix resident who also marshaled support for the measure from a number of influential Arizonans.[6] These somewhat contradictory results in the same election seem to indicate that the populace was not monolithically with the governor and legislature on their punitive streak but was perhaps overly fearful of the threat of violent crime committed by youth, pragmatic about responding to drug offenders, and somewhat libertarian about drug use generally, as well as moderately distrustful of the justice system and its ability to manage the crime problem (see Barker, 2006, on this kind of direct democracy criminal justice policymaking).

TOUGH ON CRIME GOES LOCAL

The competition for getting tough on inmates was not restricted to state-level actors. Indeed, Arizona made national headlines for its unusually tough penal practices during the 1990s, yet this was not as a result of anything happening at the state level under Lewis's leadership. The fame and notoriety were brought on soon after the election of the Maricopa County sheriff, Joe Arpaio, in 1993, who not only appeared to borrow from the Department of Corrections in reshaping the county jail system, but also shamelessly publicized his "innovations" as his own unique contributions to the tough-on-crime movement.

"Sheriff Joe," as he is known around the world, was a former federal drug enforcement officer who adopted the kind of "tough-and-cheap" punishment rhetoric that was already flourishing at the state level—although his came with a more outrageous and clownish slant. One of his first innovations was "Tent City," a fenced-in, tightly packed compound of Korean War–era army tents erected side by side in 1993 on the barren landscape of southwest Phoenix. Even though such tent compounds (which subjected their residents to much longer term stays with no climate control) had been used in the state system for more than a decade, Arpaio widely publicized his unit as if it were completely novel. He also slashed the dietary budget, boasting to reporters that he spent 20 cents a day feeding inmates. He became famous for his purchases of post-date provisions, including the "green bologna" he used for sandwich meat. He reduced the number of meals served from three to two a day and eliminated morning coffee for inmates (Cart, 2000; Arpaio interview, 2003). Again, though, this kind of punitive frugality imposed upon food service had already been a norm in the state system, where surplus "seconds" were bought to save money and unpalatable "meatloaf" diets had been used as punishment. In 1995, just as the state introduced chain gangs, Sheriff Joe implemented a chain gang for his male jail inmates, which he followed with the "first ever" female chain gang in 1996 (Arpaio interview, 2003; Lynch, 2004).

Arpaio's "show-stealing" in nationally publicizing these Arizona-style tough-and-cheap penal innovations not only appeared to contribute to the tense relationship that developed between his agency and the Department of Corrections,[7] but also may have helped spur the department's escalation of the assault on prisoners' rights and privileges that occurred during the 1990s despite the already harsh conditions that existed in the state's prisons. Indeed, Arpaio's national profile not only brought attention to the state for its revolutionary penal practices, but it served to legitimize even further the punitive quality that Lewis imposed on Arizona's prison system.

The 1990s escalation was also catalyzed by the close and politically symbiotic relationship Lewis developed with Governor Symington once he took office in 1991. As was illustrated in Chapter 4, Lewis had already begun to revolutionize corrections in the state during the first few years after he took the reins in 1985. His "tough-and-cheap" approach, which was significantly aided by a willing legislature, had transformed life inside Arizona's prisons within the first five years of his tenure: the supermax facility had come on line and was filled to capacity; the "hard labor" legislation of the 1980s had inmates working under often physically demanding conditions at exceedingly low pay rates; prisoners and their families were being held more and more responsible for the costs of basic services and the expenses of prison life, including exorbitant phone charges, room and board, and gate money; and larger numbers of inmates were perennially housed in substandard facilities (as they had been since even before Lewis's time) such as tents, Quonset huts, and warehouse buildings converted into substandard dormitories.

But over the last five years of Lewis's directorship, with the active cooperation and encouragement of Symington (and vice versa), the system became even more austerely punitive. As noted above, the department became a national leader in passing on fees for services to its captive population when it instituted fees for medical services and electricity. In addition, the administration made sustained attempts to outlaw prisoners' access to sexually explicit magazines, to scale back access to legal materials and to the courts, and to cut off holiday packages from families (see Chapter 6).

One arena where the transformation was evident was in Lewis's stance on prison alternatives. During his early years, Lewis encouraged the judicious use of some alternatives to imprisonment as a population management strategy (he was never keen on alternatives for rehabilitative purposes). He supported the investment in house arrest / electronic monitoring and lobbied for increased discretion for his agency to use early release to control overcrowding. Yet once his relationship with Symington was established, he became an across-the-board advocate of longer and more certain prison sentences for offenders, working directly with Symington's office to formulate the truth-in-sentencing scheme, which took effect in 1994 and ensured longer sentences for many convicted felons and severely limited early releases in the state.

In 1995, Symington and Lewis joined to oppose a number of Arizona criminal justice professionals and legislators by turning down private grant money awarded to develop alternatives to prison. The funds, which were being offered by the Edna McConnell Clark Foundation, were to be used to explore alternatives for nonviolent offenders such as home arrest and intensive probation. Lewis flat out opposed receiving the funds, issuing a statement to the press that this foundation "believes that more alternatives and diversion are needed" and that he did not agree, as he felt that prison "is a viable response to all crimes" (Whiting, 1995). Symington wrote a letter of declination to the foundation, indicating that he could not support any program that would keep larger numbers of criminals within communities and out of prison, and suggested that it give its money to a state that would be more receptive to that notion.

Lewis also personally lobbied Arizona's U.S. congressional representatives in support of federal legislation that supported longer prison sentences and harsher treatment of prisoners. For instance, he wrote Representative Jim Kolbe in late 1995 regarding legislation he had recommended to allocate federal funds to states to build more prisons. He urged Kolbe to ignore organizations such as the American Correctional Association and the Association of State Correctional Administrators (professional organizations in his own field) that might voice concerns with the bill and advised him to listen to "the people who think criminals must be punished." He stressed that his department supported the notion that "there is a vital need to be tough on crime. People who commit crimes need to go to prison" (Lewis, 1995c).

In addition, the department and Symington jointly waged their own war against immigrants within the criminal justice system. In 1994, the state engaged in negotiations with government officials in Mexico to send Mexican nationals to Mexican prisons to serve their time. In accordance with international treaties, eligible inmates would need to volunteer for the transfer. The department and Symington predicted that about half of the 800 Mexican nationals who were eligible to participate would choose to be transferred; ultimately, though, very few made that choice. Thus, three years later, the department (under the leadership of Terry Stewart) and Governor Symington came up with another plan to move Mexican nationals out of the state's prisons and back to Mexico. This plan was to contract with a private prison company to build a prison across the border to house such inmates. The prisoners would still be under the jurisdiction of Arizona, and the state would be responsible for its operation through the private prison contract system, but the facility would be in Mexico.

The governor argued that under the North American Free Trade Agreement (NAFTA), such an arrangement should be feasible if both parties agreed to it. The plan was sold as a "win-win" for all, in that it would provide huge savings to the state, given the lower construction and labor costs in Mexico, and the inmates would benefit by being in an institution run in their own language and that would serve Mexican food. The proposal made national newspaper headlines and was a topic of discussion on cable news networks. Indeed, California followed suit soon after Arizona made the proposal by exploring a similar possibility. The Request for Proposals that was issued by the Arizona state government yielded two interested parties—a private prison firm from the United States and one based in Mexico—but the plan was ultimately abandoned because of the lack of an international treaty that would allow such an arrangement across national boundaries (see Fitzpatrick, 2004).[8]

The department also pushed legislation that would make it a felony if previously convicted Mexican nationals returned to Arizona after being deported upon their release from prison. In the same set of proposals, the department sought legislation that would prohibit Mexican nationals from being educated during their time in prison, because in their analysis it would be a waste of resources to teach them since they would be deported upon release anyway. Thus, within an already punitive and nonrehabilitative system, immigrants were singled out as deserving even less of the meager programming offered. This treatment played out as well in terms of legal access to the courts. The Department of Corrections was found to be especially remiss in providing means for those inmates who did not speak English to access the courts, and it fought a long and contentious battle in order to avoid being forced to do so (see Chapter 6).

LEWIS HANDS OVER THE REINS

Lewis decided to step down at the end of 1995 after ten and a half years as director of the Arizona Department of Corrections. His decision to resign was in part a reaction to his ongoing personality conflicts with Attorney General Woods, especially as they came to a head during the rollback litigation movement described in Chapter 6. However, he was also 70 years old, and he said publicly that it was time for him to work on his golf game. Before he openly announced his resignation, though, he ensured that the department would stay on the same course that he had set by arranging with Governor Symington to appoint his second in command and protégé, Terry Stewart, as his successor. Symington agreed to the move, and Stewart's appointment was publicized at the same time as Lewis's retirement announcement (Lewis interview, 2004).

Like Lewis, Stewart was an Arizona native, and his career had been in law enforcement before going to work for the Department of Corrections under Lewis. He was a graduate of Arizona State University, earning both a bachelor's and master's degree while working as a Tempe police officer. As expected, Stewart pledged to continue in the same direction as Lewis, including battling against federal court "intrusion" into prison operations. Stewart kept his word by enthusiastically following through on Lewis-initiated policies and coming up with some of his own innovations. For instance, he oversaw the implementation of the new fees and charges imposed on inmates that resulted from the policies that were devised during Lewis's tenure. Indeed, as second in command, he had already helped shape many of the harsh policies enacted during the early 1990s as he and Lewis generally agreed about penal philosophy. He also partnered with Symington on the continued attack on immigrant inmates, including collaborating on the plan to export Mexican nationals to Mexico and to cut off their access to education within the system.

Early in his tenure, Stewart also "got tough" on prison gangs by using a major portion of the SMU to isolate and house gang members. Inmates who were placed in the SMU had to denounce their gang affiliation and debrief in order to make it out of the unit (although once they debriefed, they often had to stay isolated in protective segregation).[9] In 1999, he upped the ante in his battle against gangs when he implemented a policy to ship problem inmates— primarily those deemed gang leaders—to out-of-state prisons, both private facilities and contracted space with public institutions. This was the first system in the nation to try such a policy and was a particular point of pride for Stewart (Stewart interview, 2004). His policies that aimed to crack down on gangs resulted in death threats against him, one of which was almost carried out in a restaurant where Stewart ate lunch.

Stewart was particularly enamored of the SMU units: early in his tenure, he suggested to a reporter that investing in facilities like the SMU was one of the best uses of prison funding (Relly, 1999). The second supermax unit (SMU II) was completed and opened just as Stewart took over as director, doubling such bed space available to be used at his directive. The conditions of confinement in Arizona's SMUs were generally considered by experts as among the harshest in the nation (Relly, 1999), but those conditions became even more brutal under Stewart's leadership, and the restrictions imposed at SMU II were even more severe than those in operation at SMU I.

In 1997, Stewart moved the death row population of more than 100 men to SMU II. Although this meant that such inmates no longer worked on the death row chain gangs, it also meant a different and probably more severe set of living conditions for that population. Most significantly, the move appears to have led to an increase in execution "volunteers" who no longer wanted to pursue their appeals and whose psychological state had been shaped by the isolated conditions to which they were being subjected (see Ferrier, 2004; Lynch, 2000 and 2005).

The department declined to keep statistics of suicide attempts or incidents of self-mutilation, but mental health workers reported that these were frequent occurrences in the SMUs. The department used SMU II to house disruptive mentally ill inmates; in 1999, nearly 25 percent of the total population of that unit were diagnosed with mental illness, and many more exhibited signs of serious mental disturbance (Relly, 1999). Five inmates in SMU II managed to commit suicide during the first three and a half years of its operation, despite the lack of any viable tools to aid in the suicides, and a number of disturbing incidents of self-mutilations have also occurred there.

Under the Stewart regime, pepper gas and Israeli foggers were routinely used on inmates who refused to cooperate with officers in the unit, and inmates in the cell runs who were not being targeted were not provided with any protection from the gas (Relly, 1999). The use of force was increased even further in 1997 when Stewart authorized a controversial policy to use trained attack dogs in "cell extractions"—violent, involuntary removals of inmates from their cells—when other methods such as gassing failed (Human Rights Watch, 2006; see Haney, 2003, for more on cell extractions). During such extractions, a dog that had been trained to bite the inmate and hold on with its teeth was sent into a cell on a 30-foot leash, at which time the officer holding the leash, outside of the cell, pulled the dog and the inmate being held by the dog's jaw out of the cell.

Although Stewart, like Lewis, justified most of his harsh policies with claims that they were necessary for security (or occasionally for fiscal reasons), it was a huge stretch for credibility in some cases, where the policies simply seemed mean-spirited. Both administrations did oversee a significant drop in escapes within the system as a result of the new security policies, but in some cases, the security claim seems to have been, if not baseless, at least overblown. For example, the department instituted a policy that prohibited same-sex visitors from hugging or kissing inmates unless they were immediate family. The department argued that the ban was for the protection of gay inmates because they might be targeted for abuse from other prisoners if they were seen in displays of affection with same-sex visitors. The policy was challenged in the U.S. district court by the partner of an openly gay prisoner. After the district court dismissed the suit, the Court of Appeals for the Ninth Circuit reversed and remanded. The opinion was quite skeptical about the department's justification for the policy, particularly in this case, in which the inmate himself was open about his sexuality (*Whitmire v. Arizona*, 2002).

Stewart remained the department director until the end of 2002, when he stepped down after arranging (as Lewis had done for him) for his protégé and second in command, Chuck Ryan, to be appointed as interim director by out-going Governor Jane Dee Hull (see the epilogue). Thus, a stable and consistent approach to penology existed within the department for 18 years during the crucial imprisonment boom years. Both political branches responsible for empowering and funding the department were largely in sync with the Lewis-Stewart approach, which helped ensure that continuity. As a result, the kind of punitive institutional philosophy that Lewis ushered in and Stewart carried on (as did Ryan as interim director) was even more potent in its transformational quality. There was little resistance by any constituencies with political power in Arizona to the punitive approach (both in terms of increasing sentences and making prison life more uncomfortable) from the time Lewis was appointed into the twenty-first century. Therefore, rather than operating in an environment in which the purpose of the penal system was both in question and politically contested, as had been the case at several crucial points during the decade preceding Lewis's appointment, under this regime, the assumption undergirding penal operations was that prison was a good first response to crime and was best delivered as a punitive experience.

CONCLUSION

The criminal justice politics that increased in salience in Arizona during the 1990s did not merely culminate in symbolic lawmaking and media-transmitted rhetorical grandstanding by state politicians. It translated into an increasing portion of the state budget being dedicated to building and operating prisons. At the time Lewis took over as director of the Department of Corrections in 1985, the bed capacity of the adult prison system was 6,779; by fiscal year-end 2001, a year before Stewart left, that capacity had grown to 25,452, with an additional 1,450 private prison beds under contract with the department. Thus, the size of the prison system had quadrupled during the Lewis-Stewart regime, necessitating a massive fiscal commitment on the part of state government to the prison as a criminal justice response. Although some of that growth had been planned and authorized before Lewis became director, the bulk of it reflected the concrete-and-steel manifestation of Arizona's tough-on-crime movement that emerged from the Department of Corrections, the governor's office, the legislature, and local prosecutors' offices during this period. Indeed, the legislature, with the governor's approval, committed somewhere around $500 million above and beyond the 1983–84 prison expansion funding commitments to construct new prisons during

the Lewis-Stewart years. Included in that spending was $43 million for build-
ing SMU II and $143 million for building the largest prison in the state, a
4,150-capacity multilevel institution, which opened in 1999, dubbed Arizona
State Prison Complex–Lewis, in honor of Sam Lewis.[10]

Of course, with the expansion of capacity came hugely increased operating costs, which the legislature and governor also supported. Annual expenditures for adult prison operations, excluding prison construction, grew
more than fivefold over the Lewis-Stewart tenure, from around $106 million
in 1985 to about $564 million in 2001. The result was that corrections took a
steadily larger piece of the state general fund pie. In 1979, corrections received
about 4 percent of the state's general fund, and by 1992, its share had doubled
to 8 percent (*Arizona Daily Star,* 1994; Arizona Advocacy Network, 2003). As
of 1999, Arizona ranked among the top three states in the nation in terms of
proportion of the state budget allocated to corrections (Relly, 1999). By 2003,
just after Stewart's tenure ended, the Department of Corrections' share of
the general fund was close to 11 percent (Arizona Advocacy Network, 2003).
Higher-education funding bore the brunt of the cuts necessary to fund the
prison expansion machine over this period of time.

In contrast, particularly during the Symington years, the Department of
Corrections was consistently either fully immune to budget cuts or at least
given the mildest cutbacks of all the state-funded agencies. During the 1990s,
the state was in the bottom quarter of per capita overall spending in the United
States, ranking particularly low relative to the national average in terms of
spending on the poor and on primary and secondary education. Nonetheless, Symington successfully pushed through several major income tax cuts
while in office, as did his successor Governor Hull. And despite the frugal state
spending, the department barely felt the tightened purse strings that came with
it. Higher and elementary and secondary education, heath-care programs for
uninsured children, and assistance for the poor all took hits from the limited
revenue brought by tax cuts, by taking proportionately larger reductions in
allocations (or smaller increases despite state population growth), while the
Department of Corrections was largely spared (Ingley, 1998).[11]

These increased dollar expenditures did not translate into programs or amenities for inmates; rather, the opposite occurred. Largely as a result of the political process described in this chapter, inmates were actually getting the short
end of the stick in terms of benefiting from the governmental largesse bestowed
upon the Department of Corrections. Indeed, they became subject to charges

for basic expenses—such as for health care, electricity, and room and board if they earned money through contracted private-sector jobs—that previously had been the responsibility of the department. Inmates also had fewer opportunities for constructive activities as the prison population swelled but investment in programming did not. In its annual reports, the department prided itself on spending significantly less than the national average on inmates, per capita, and touted the annual savings garnered by policies such as charging for medical care. Nor did corrections spending benefit the frontline correctional officers, who were generally paid significantly less than their law enforcement peers in the state and who did not (and still do not) have the benefit of a strong union to advocate for their benefit.

Terry Stewart provided an example of the underlying philosophy of the Department of Corrections on the matter of spending on inmates under his leadership. He suggested that Minnesota, which he characterized as the most "program-heavy" system in the country, spent double the dollar amount per capita compared with Arizona but that the two systems had the same recidivism rate, demonstrating that programming had little effect on inmates (Stewart interview, 2004). Thus, according to this analysis, the department was justified in spending a proportionately large share of its budget on expenses that did not directly benefit the inmates in either the short or the long term, whether that was in security-related expenses within institutions, upper-level administrative costs, or other such budget items.

The penal administrative bureaucracy itself continued to balloon at an even more accelerated rate over the late 1980s and 1990s, and the department solidified as one of the largest and most politically influential state agencies in Arizona. One physical manifestation of all of this was the quadrupling of bed space, which was kept overfilled by a criminal justice system that mandated prison for an expanded population of nonviolent offenders. The share of annual admissions of drug offenders, for instance, nearly doubled in 11 years, growing from 14 percent in fiscal year 1985–86 to 27 percent in 1996–97, while the relative proportion of violent offender admissions fell from 22 percent to 19 percent over the same time.

A key element of the process that brought both unprecedented growth and increasingly harsh prison conditions during the 1990s was the stepped-up involvement of local actors in the tough-on-crime wave. The crucial role that local prosecutors—and the local press in Phoenix—played in derailing sentence reform at the beginning of that decade was an added galvanizing feature. As Simon (2007) and others have pointed out, local prosecutors gained an enormous amount of power during the 1980s and 1990s by virtue of legislation that shifted decision-making discretion from judges to prosecutors' offices. This has been especially keenly felt in states like Arizona (and California) that have seen a number of criminal justice ballot initiatives directly shift that balance of power. In this case, local prosecutors did not simply settle with their increased discretionary power within the local criminal justice realm; rather, they organized to influence the state legislative process as that body grappled with the problems wrought by a harsh determinate sentencing scheme that had played a significant role in prison population growth from 1978 on.

Even the local jailer in Maricopa County, Sheriff Joe Arpaio, participated in the law-and-order movement by publicizing his harsh and degrading practices in such a way as to bring a national spotlight to the state. There is no way to prove that his antics spurred on more state-level tough-on-prisoners proposals and policies (although it seems plausible), but it added to the totality of penal harshness in Arizona during the 1990s. Although such devolution, especially in terms of what was going on inside penal facilities during the decade, seems like it should have been kept in check in some way, given the increased intervention by federal courts since the early 1970s, part of the movement in Arizona entailed directly facing off with those very institutions in charge of such oversight. As Chapter 6 examines in depth, Arizona truly became a frontrunner in the punitive movement by fighting against the courts and the Justice Department that tried to regulate them through open defiance and proactive litigation.

6 TAKING BACK THE PRISONS

IN ARIZONA, the Department of Corrections and the executive branch, with support from the legislature, eventually coalesced around an emerging strategy designed to "take back" the state prisons from federal oversight, which primarily entailed waging battles with the federal district court on myriad issues related to prison operations. Like most penal systems in the nation, Arizona's prison operations were subject to judicial oversight for much of the 1970s, 1980s, and 1990s. The main prison at Florence operated under various court orders issued primarily by U.S. district court judge Carl Muecke during this period, regulating population counts and housing conditions, the inmate disciplinary system, the mail service and regulations regarding what could and could not be sent from or received by inmates, the rules regarding inmates' personal property, and inmates' access to the courts.

The legal battle over Arizona prisons transpired over several decades, and the state's evolving reaction to prisoner lawsuits reflected larger social shifts in punishment that were under way across the United States. They were also very much a function of specific local processes, in that they were strongly influenced by the changes in power brokers within state government and by long-standing cultural norms about federal government "meddling" in state business. Thus, this set of battles tells a story at two levels: about structural changes in how legal institutions dealt with prisoners' rights and about how local norms, traditions, and expectations were brought out of the cultural "toolkit" (Swidler, 1986) to construct and implement a plan of action in response to the problem of prisoner litigation.

The state underwent a major shift in its response to federal court directives that sought to reform prison operations. After a relatively long period of compliance (under earlier corrections administrations and governorships), during the 1990s the Department of Corrections began to employ a strategy of resistance against court efforts to regulate the state's prisons, followed by an offensive against such oversight in a series of costly and contentious legal battles. Political and institutional actors moved from a stance that was, if not sympathetic, at least somewhat agnostic with regard to the plight of prisoners to one that directly declared war on prisoners as state-controlled subjects. As was detailed in Chapter 5 and will be fleshed out further here, the state put significant energy into taking away prisoners' rights, privileges, and dignities—large and small—beginning with the start of Sam Lewis's tenure as corrections director and accelerating once Fife Symington took office as governor.

THE EARLY CASES AND CONSENT DECREES

The first major successful class action lawsuit filed by Arizona prisoners challenged the disciplinary procedures that were in place at the Florence prison during the early 1970s. The case, *Taylor v. Arizona*, began with two habeas corpus petitions filed in 1972 by inmates who challenged, among other issues, the loss of good time credits during disciplinary proceedings. The two writs were consolidated into one case in the court of U.S. district court judge William Copple. Plaintiff Eddie Taylor's challenge was on behalf of the entire class of inmates affected, so the case had ramifications for all prisoners housed at the Florence prison. During the first evidentiary hearing, the state admitted that its disciplinary procedures were problematic, and the two sides agreed to negotiate a suitable remediation plan. By the end of that year, the stipulated agreement was finalized, and the court entered an order formalizing the new procedures. This order was slightly modified in the summer of 1973 when the prison's new disciplinary rules and regulations were submitted and approved.

Although the suit itself and the order that followed were limited to the issue of disciplinary procedures, in the final order, Judge Copple complimented the state on the numerous changes it had made to improve conditions in the prison, including efforts to upgrade the professionalism of staff and increase their numbers, improve health-care facilities and personnel, devise a better classification system, and address overcrowding. He expressed hope that these efforts would eliminate the "veritable flood of prisoner civil rights complaints" that had been filed with the court during the prior three years (*Taylor v. Arizona*, Memorandum and Order, August 23, 1973).

So in this instance, the state responded quickly and proactively to get the case out of litigation and in the process was amenable to entering into an agreement that allowed for the court to monitor the disciplinary procedures into the future. As a result of the consent decree, all changes to the disciplinary procedures required judicial approval, and in the early years the state dutifully went to court to gain such approval for each substantive modification of policy. This case also foreshadowed the court orders and consent decrees to come, in that Judge Copple used this order to comment about other issues that were not under consideration in *Taylor v. Arizona*—health care, overcrowding, classification—and to subtly suggest that the state would be wise to address such problems before being ordered to do so in subsequent cases.

Yet *Taylor v. Arizona* was by no means the end of successful prisoner litigation. A year after *Taylor* settled, the state entered into a consent decree with the plaintiffs in another case, *Hook v. State of Arizona*, which challenged the prison's mail procedures, particularly its policies of limiting, reading, and censoring incoming and outgoing mail. In this case, which was heard in Judge Muecke's court, the plaintiffs alleged that the ban on certain adult magazines and the restriction of allowing mail to be sent to, and received from, only 10 people who were on an approved list (barring even courts and legal counsel if not on the inmate's approved list) violated the First and Fourteenth amendments of the Constitution. Again, the state was relatively cooperative and swift in settling; the case was resolved within months of its filing.

The consent decree in *Hook* ratified new mail procedures proposed by the department that allowed unlimited mail going out and coming in to inmates (except to and from certain people such as other inmates) and banned the policy of reading and censoring incoming and outgoing correspondence with family members, state or federal officials, legal counsel, and corrections administrators. It reserved the right to censor "up to 10%" of other outgoing mail under specified conditions. The agreement also allowed a broader range of publications to come in through the mail, excluding only those materials that contained instructions about methods that threatened security (such as bomb-making plans) and those that would be deemed obscene under "applicable constitutional standards." Finally, the state allowed for prisoners to receive up to three holiday packages during a three-week window in December, weighing up to 25 pounds each. This provision of the agreement turned out to be the most contested in the years to come, as Sam Lewis fought vigorously to rescind it during the late 1980s and 1990s.

The most comprehensive consent decree resulted from a case, *Harris v. Cardwell*, that challenged overall conditions of confinement in the Florence prison. This suit was originally filed in 1974, then amended in 1975, in propria persona by inmate Muni Fred Harris. Within a year, it was picked up by the Arizona affiliate of the ACLU, with the help of the ACLU's National Prison Project, on behalf of all prisoners confined in the men's units at Florence. A local attorney, Frank Lewis, was the primary litigator for the plaintiffs, on behalf of the ACLU. This case was quite a bit more contested than the previous two and resulted in a series of orders, stipulated agreements, and revisions over the next 10 years.

The first court order was issued by Judge Muecke in 1977 and addressed the overcrowding issue. After an evidentiary hearing and extensive documentation of conditions in the prison, Muecke ordered a population cap to be achieved within a certain time frame and required that the state provide the court with daily counts of the population, as well as reports of all injuries in the prison, to demonstrate its success in achieving the population goal. He asked the state and plaintiffs to come up with a workable plan to address all kinds of corollary issues as well. Judge Muecke then urged the state to consider alternatives to just building more prison cells as a response to the problem, suggesting that it pursue less restrictive options such as halfway houses, community-based facilities, and job and education training centers.

The state scrambled to reduce population numbers in the prison by building new housing units, reclassifying inmates to allow some to be transferred to one of the minimum-security camp-type facilities, tweaking release criteria to allow for more parole eligibility, and so on (see Chapter 3). Although the suit affected only the men's portion of the Florence prison—as it stood in 1975—its influence was huge because that accounted for virtually all of the adult male inmate housing in the state that was not classified as minimum security. And although the primary problem the court identified in this case was the severe overcrowding, counsel for the plaintiffs successfully raised corollary issues at each juncture, inviting Judge Muecke to intervene in matters such as access to health care, quality of diet, and availability of vocational and recreational opportunities.

Almost concurrently with the course of this lawsuit, the U.S. Civil Rights Commission undertook its probe of the prison that focused on allegations of discrimination within the prison, in terms of both the hiring and promotion of staff and the treatment of prisoners of color. This probe grew out of the

1973 study conducted by the Arizona Advisory Committee to the U.S. Commission on Civil Rights to assess prison conditions in the state. In late 1974, the Arizona Advisory Committee issued a nearly 200-page report that found numerous deficiencies and included a wide-ranging set of recommendations for prison reform. Some recommendations focused specifically on remediating the racially discriminatory practices in staffing and in the treatment of inmates, and others dealt with the general policies and practices that shaped prison life, including education, recreational, and work programs; disciplinary procedures; inmate access to legal materials and services; medical care; mail services; and visiting procedures.

Director John Moran responded to the commission recommendations by hiring an Equal Opportunity Programs (EOP) employment specialist, expanding the training for staff on multicultural issues, developing materials in Spanish for inmates who were not English speakers, and improving the school and vocational programs with additional staff and course offerings, among other remedial improvements. Despite his efforts, the U.S. Department of Justice was back in 1976 making inquiries into the treatment of prisoners. In 1977, just weeks after Judge Muecke ordered the parties to devise a plan for reducing the population numbers in the *Harris v. Cardwell* case, the U.S. attorney filed a motion to intervene in the case, alleging that the state had violated the Eighth and Fourteenth amendments through discriminatory practices used against inmates of color. It also raised concerns about the general conditions of confinement and the adequacy of the mental and physical health care in the Florence prison.

Judge Muecke compromised on the federal government's request to intervene by granting it amicus (friend of the court) status while giving the state a chance to fix the racial discrimination problems. Muecke left open the possibility that the federal government's status in the case could be elevated to becoming a party in the suit should the state not respond to the government's concerns. Thus, by the end of 1977, the Department of Corrections was almost completely focused on fixing the myriad problems in Florence in order to satisfy the various interested parties from the federal government, and the state attorney general's office was regularly in court defending the department on multiple fronts.

In response to numerous crises in the prison, including these federal inquiries and the *Harris v. Cardwell* lawsuit, Governor Raul Castro established a Commission on Corrections Planning in early 1977 that, by design, was charged

with the broad duties of providing advice to the governor on correctional issues, commissioning and conducting research and policy analysis for improving procedures and programs, developing strategies for managing prisoner
population growth, and generally reviewing the department's functioning
with an eye toward improvement. The commission was cochaired by attorney
David Tierney, who quickly recognized the need to manage the system so as to
mitigate the level of litigation in which the state would become involved.

What this meant for the commission was that Tierney's energies were
often focused on orchestrating the state response to the litigation, which
largely required him to try to get disparate and often disputing parties within
the state on the same page. Thus, he worked with key legislators who were
relatively hostile to Director Moran to try to persuade them to pony up funds
for corrections, and he corresponded regularly with the attorney general—at
that time, his good friend Bruce Babbitt—about legal strategy and about how
to get Moran to move on the crises in a way that would not create more animosity with legislators (Tierney interview, 2007). The commission lasted just
over a year, being dissolved by Governor Castro's successor, Wesley Bolin, but
Tierney remained an informal mediator on prison issues for years to come.

Thus, at this point, the department and the executive branch were making earnest attempts to address the myriad issues raised in *Harris v. Cardwell*
even though it was an uphill battle, given the breadth of issues and the pace at
which offenders were being sentenced to the overburdened prison system. The
legislature was somewhat less cooperative, especially when it came to allocating funds to pay for the needed reforms, but it was not, as a body, completely
resistant to doing its part in complying. Nonetheless, the litigation in *Harris v.
Cardwell* did not end with Judge Muecke's 1977 population reduction order.

Plaintiffs and the U.S. attorney continued to allege unconstitutional conditions despite the state's efforts at compliance. In early 1978, Muecke gave the
U.S. attorney's office limited power to obtain its own discovery in the case,
and later that spring, the plaintiffs amended their complaint to include allegations of discrimination in line with the U.S. attorney's primary interests.
By year-end 1978, the court ordered the state to further reduce the population
at the prison and to develop a plan for improving the quality of and access
to health care for inmates; this order was drafted and all parties agreed to it
in the fall of 1979. By that time, the department had fully complied with the
population cap in place, so it seemed that the time had come to put this case to
rest. In spring of 1980, all sides agreed to terminate the litigation but could not

agree to the terms of that termination regarding how to deal with future con-duct by the Department of Corrections. By that fall, a negotiated agreement was crafted into a comprehensive order that spelled out the state's duties in terms of maintaining reasonable populations through the use of single-celling and single-bunking in dormitories; providing educational, recreational, and work opportunities to all eligible inmates; developing a rational classification system that did not overclassify inmates and that allowed for periodic reviews; and maintaining an adequate health-care system through a series of directives spelled out in the order. It took another two years, until May 1982, for an agree-ment to be reached on the terms of monitoring compliance with the order, especially on the issue of inmates' rights to file grievances about treatment.

So although this negotiation process was much more drawn out and con-tested than that of the earlier suits, it was nonetheless characterized by a pro-cess of give and take on the part of the plaintiffs and the defendants to further the goal of settlement. Both sides were willing to compromise to some degree in order to reach that goal, and notable changes—most significantly in terms of the overcrowding issue within the Florence men's unit—were made in the system through the process of negotiation. Such an approach to prisoner liti-gation, however, was about to come to an end.

LAWSUITS DURING THE LEWIS ERA

As soon as Sam Lewis took over as director of the Department of Corrections in 1985 and began to implement policy reforms that restricted inmates' rights and privileges, prisoners and their representatives challenged many of those changes in federal and state courts. Suits were filed against the department re-garding the new grooming policies, the new restrictions on personal property, changes in visitor policies, and decreased access to protective custody for in-mates who needed it for safety and survival reasons; there was even a suit chal-lenging the method by which Lewis made policy change, which was alleged to be out of compliance with state law. Indeed, it was a 1986 lawsuit about the abusive, draconian conditions that had developed in the youth facilities under Lewis's directorship that was largely responsible for the state moving toward establishing an independent department of juvenile corrections in 1990.

But before being the principal defendant in such suits, Lewis first became the de facto defendant in several ongoing cases, in which his oppositional stance became a notable new feature of prison litigation in the state. One such lawsuit was *Black v. Ricketts*, which the ACLU had filed toward the end of the tenure of Lewis's predecessor, James Ricketts. The suit challenged the conditions of confinement in CB-6, which was then the highest security housing unit in the system and which had become a particularly harsh place as living conditions had devolved significantly over time.

The 200 inmates confined in CB-6 were locked in solitary cells, many of which had solid metal plates in place of windows, for all but four hours of the week. Guards had virtually stopped any maintenance on the unit so it was filthy, in disrepair, and overrun with trash. Prisoners were subjected to brutal anal cavity searches when they were moved; one such search had been caught on videotape and was in the possession of the plaintiffs' counsel. More generally, many of the inmates were suffering from psychological impairments as a result of the long-term isolated confinement. As noted in Chapter 4, inmates who were deemed disruptive in this unit were also subjected to days or weeks of an unappetizing "meatloaf" diet. Because the inmates challenged this punishment as well as the other conditions, the case became known as the "meatloaf lawsuit."

Ricketts had tried to improve conditions in CB-6 while the case was in litigation, but once Lewis took over the directorship, there was new resistance within the department to complying with the court during the settlement process and beyond. Although the state settled with the plaintiffs in May 1985, just a month after Lewis was named director, Lewis was hardly cooperative during the postsettlement period. His first move, six months after the settlement, was to ban ACLU lawyers from visiting their clients in prison, in the name of order and security. He claimed that the lawyers incited disruptive behavior among inmates and encouraged them to pursue more litigation. Lewis also asserted that the settlement meant that lawyers did not need to converse directly with their clients anymore. Of course, this ban was quickly struck down by Judge Muecke, who had presided over the case. A month later, Lewis refused to accept the progress report submitted by the independent monitor whom the court had appointed to oversee compliance by the department. Such tactics kept the case in court for several years after the settlement. It was officially dismissed in early 1988, yet even after that, the ACLU tried to revisit the case when the department went out of compliance with the mandates of the settlement agreement.

Concurrent with *Black v. Ricketts* was *Gluth v. Arizona*, a 1984 case that was primarily litigated during Lewis's tenure. *Gluth* was a class action suit brought by inmates at the central prison unit in Florence alleging that prisoners were denied meaningful access to courts because of inadequate law library facilities and the total denial of access to those facilities for many prisoners, including those in disciplinary lockdown and those who were mentally disabled or not fluent in English. Under order from the court, the state agreed early on to improve the access and did indeed modify and expand the law library, but the plaintiffs returned to court in 1988 alleging continued violations of prisoners' rights. In 1990, Judge Muecke issued a detailed order that laid out very specific requirements for maintaining a constitutionally acceptable level of legal access at the prison.

By this time, a significant change in the state's posture toward prisoner lawsuits was evident, particularly as embodied by the Department of Corrections. No longer conciliatory and apologetic for not complying more quickly and more fully with the court's directives, in this case, the department, under Lewis's leadership, sought to skate at the edge of the minimal requirements necessary to be in compliance. Indeed, its first "try" at compliance, which resulted in the return to court in 1988, was indicative of a new ethos in reference to prisoner challenges. Although Muecke had ordered that the department supply trained legal assistants to help prisoners who were denied physical access to the library (that is, those in lockdown), the department simply assigned prisoners, many with no legal skills whatsoever, to the job of "legal assistant." Furthermore, inmates were subjected to inadequate and arbitrary hours of access to the library, and many were forced to pay for basic supplies, such as paper and stamps, with which to exercise their legal rights even if it meant that they had to forgo other necessities such as basic toiletries to do so.

In a 1990 memorandum to the partial final decision and order, Judge Muecke expressed his amazement at the Department of Corrections' collective behavior throughout the suit:

> This memorandum and the partial final judgment mark the successful partial completion of a case the likes of which I have never seen before in my twenty-five years on the bench. . . . Despite the seriousness of plaintiffs' complaints, defendants demonstrated, throughout this litigation, a callous unwillingness to face the issues. The Court was forced to take extraordinary measures to compel the Arizona Department of Corrections to focus on the merits. (*Gluth v. Kangas*, 1990: 1309)

Judge Muecke's memorandum also contained a subsection titled "Hysteria and Delay" that directly took on Lewis for his behavior in the case, particularly his tactic of issuing press releases designed to incite the public, rather than dealing directly with the court on issues of concern (*Gluth v. Kangas*, 1990: 1315).

Lewis did indeed take his case to the *Arizona Republic*, which was becoming more staunchly "law and order" in its editorial stance and which was happy to report on the battle of the state versus the feds. Lewis also complained to sympathetic legislators and the governor. One of his major complaints was that Arizona State University law professors and law students were representing inmates in this and other suits. He suggested that it was a conflict of interest for the state-funded law school to represent those who were suing another state agency.

He also protested paying the court-ordered fees for the special master, Dan Pochoda, whom the court had appointed to devise a plan for improvement, and in 1990, Lewis came within hours of being cited for contempt over his refusal to pay those expenses. He told the press that his refusal to pay was both fiscally prudent and necessary because, according to him, the bills submitted did not have sufficient information about the expenses being claimed. Finally, he accused Judge Muecke, via the press, of costing the state "thousands of dollars" to implement the order, at the risk to "good security practices" within the prison (Morrell, 1990), and suggested that the overall cost of compliance would total more than $6 million. Editorials in the *Arizona Republic* and the *Phoenix Gazette* were consistently supportive of Lewis in this battle, and Judge Muecke was increasingly painted as an unreasonable meddler in state business.

Early in his tenure, Lewis also decided to openly defy the earlier consent decrees and judgments. Blaming budgetary constraints, Lewis announced to the legislature in October 1985 that he planned to begin double-bunking maximum-security prisoners at Florence, claiming that the *Harris v. Cardwell* mandate was limited to only a small set of cells. The state ACLU director immediately responded by seeking clarification as to whether this practice would violate the *Harris v. Cardwell* agreement, as it clearly appeared to do, and Lewis had to abort his plan once it was determined that such a move would be a direct violation of the agreement. In the following years, the department was accused of going out of compliance with the health-care provisions of that settlement and violating provisions of the other agreements. Rather than denying such violations, or trying to remedy the situation, Lewis generally maintained the violating behavior until forced to cease.

The first major battle of this sort came over a provision of the consent decree in *Hook v. Arizona* that granted inmates the right to receive three

25-pound holiday packages each December. In the summer of 1990, the Department of Corrections announced a new policy that limited each inmate to only one such package, justified on the grounds of security concerns and fiscal considerations. Inmates sought an injunction to bar the department from implementing the restriction, and in December 1990, just days before the package season was to begin, Judge Muecke ruled in favor of the inmates. He determined that Lewis was in violation of the *Hook* settlement agreement and would need to specifically seek a modification of the order to make the policy change. The department agreed to comply with the three-package rule that year but maintained the position that decreasing the allowance was not in violation of *Hook*. The newspapers were for the most part sympathetic with the Department of Corrections, although several pointed editorials by liberal *Arizona Republic* columnist E. J. Montini were quite critical of Lewis, including one that suggested he was a Scrooge (Montini, 1990a, 1990b, 1990c). Lewis defended himself in a letter to the editor published in the *Republic*, again suggesting that the proposed limitation was done in the name of the safety and security of the prisons and out of fiscal concern for the state (Lewis, 1990c).

The department did not let the issue go, either. The state appealed Judge Muecke's decision to the Court of Appeals for the Ninth Circuit, and in 1992, that court upheld Muecke's decision. Even in the face of that ruling, the department still maintained that it "continues to believe that inmates are not entitled to 75 pounds of food" under the *Hook* decree (Manson, 1992). The department immediately sought to modify the *Hook* consent decree, while simultaneously imposing a new restriction on the gift packages that required inmates to consume all foods received in the packages by a certain date in early January. Judge Muecke refused to expedite the modification request to be heard before the next holiday package season began and ordered the department to lift its newly imposed deadline by which all food had to be eaten.

Lewis then upped the ante and asked for a modification of the policy to outlaw *all* holiday packages and then refused to negotiate with the plaintiffs about a compromise. The hearing on the issue was delayed for two years after Judge Muecke urged the parties to settle; Muecke also appointed a special master to oversee the holiday package distribution and ensure department compliance with the existing policy. After the parties gave up on reaching a settlement, Muecke ruled on the case in late 1995, turning down the department's request to eliminate the packages. He maintained the limit at three

25-pound packages and granted the plaintiffs the right to continue to use hot pots in their cells—a long-standing practice that the department was now also trying to ban.

Once again, the department appealed the decision to the Ninth Circuit Court of Appeals, which in late 1996 reversed Muecke's decision upholding the three-package policy and his decision to contractualize the hot pot privilege (*Hook v. Arizona*, 1997).[1] That court allowed the holiday packages to be received in the 1996 holiday season because the decision came so late in the year, and the case was sent back down to the district court in order to work out a suitable modification to the original agreement. There, a new judge was assigned to the case who fully sided with the Department of Corrections and approved its requested modification to ban all holiday packages, to outlaw the use of hot pots in cells, and to allow in place of these gifts expanded spending privileges in the canteen and monetary gifts from inmate families.

A second showdown erupted over the issue of access to the courts and the requirements of the order in *Gluth*. The issue was raised again in 1990 when inmate Fletcher Casey filed a suit that sought (among other issues that it raised) to extend the legal access rights granted in *Gluth* to Department of Corrections prisoners housed in the prison facilities beyond the Florence central unit (*Casey v. Lewis*, 1992). This case, like most of the other prisoner cases, was heard in Judge Muecke's court, and by late 1992 Muecke granted permanent injunctive relief to the plaintiffs, requiring that the department modify all of the larger facilities' law libraries in line with the *Gluth* requirements. In his opinion, Muecke praised the work that Dan Pochoda had done as special master in *Gluth* and appointed him and his assistant to oversee the compliance process in this case as well.

Muecke held separate hearings on the other allegations raised in this case, including the denial of food-service jobs to HIV-positive inmates and the denial of contact attorney visits for high-security inmates; on both issues, he found in favor of the plaintiffs. The quality of medical, dental, and mental health care was also challenged in this suit, which was litigated separately. In a particularly blistering 273-page ruling following a court trial dealing with the allegations of inadequate medical and mental health care in the prisons, Judge Muecke characterized the current treatment as "appalling" and in violation of the Eighth Amendment ban against cruel and unusual punishment. He issued an injunction requiring remediation plans for improving health care in the system.

The state appealed all of the judgments, except the one addressing health care, to the Ninth Circuit Court. In a single decision, that court reversed Muecke on the plaintiffs' right to have contact visitation with their attorneys and on the food service issue. On Judge Muecke's decision to extend the legal access requirements in *Gluth* to the entire system, the court upheld all causes of action in contention (the plaintiffs did not oppose a few of the more minor requests made by the state), thus backing Judge Muecke on the substance of the injunction. The state then appealed the Ninth Circuit Court's decision to the U.S. Supreme Court, which, at the request of Arizona native Justice Sandra Day O'Connor, issued a stay in May 1994 pending its consideration of the petition for a writ of certiorari filed by the state. A year later, certiorari was granted, and a year after that the Supreme Court announced its decision. Justice Antonin Scalia wrote the majority opinion, which reversed and remanded the case for further proceedings, and seven of the justices concurred in full or in part (only Justice John Paul Stevens dissented). The opinion concluded that Muecke's injunction was improper because plaintiffs had not shown "actual" injury caused by the alleged violations of access to the courts (*Lewis v. Casey*, 1996).

Although the decision did not overturn *Bounds v. Smith* (1977), the U.S. Supreme Court case that had firmly established prisoners' right to adequate law libraries or other legal assistance, it did drastically roll back the scope of that case. Scalia's opinion characterized Judge Muecke's requirements as "inordinately . . . wildly intrusive" into state business and set a new standard for demonstrating a constitutional violation that was, in practical terms, exceptionally difficult to meet for most prisoners, especially because they were facing obstacles in obtaining legal access in the first place. It basically required inmates to do two things before prevailing on a claim of legal access violation: first, the inmate must show widespread actual injury was caused by the lack of access, and second, it required inmates to show that the suit that would have been filed was "nonfrivolous" in nature and only challenging their conviction, sentence, or conditions of confinement. It also reinforced the notion that libraries per se were not necessary to providing access, but some form of access needed to be provided.

This decision was hailed as a monumental victory by the Department of Corrections, the governor, and the state attorney general and promoted an even deeper level of bravado in their ignoring existing orders and pushing the limits of humane treatment of Arizona prisoners.

EXECUTIVE BRANCH COMPLICITY IN THE DEPARTMENT
OF CORRECTIONS VERSUS MUECKE

In the midst of these battles, Lewis decided to directly challenge another pro-vision of the *Hook* agreement, namely, the allowance that prisoners could re-ceive adult magazines such as *Playboy* and *Hustler*. In early 1994, Lewis and Governor Symington issued a joint announcement that in order to enhance the security of female employees, the department would no longer allow pris-oners to receive adult magazines. Inmates challenged the move, and their law-yers suggested to Judge Muecke that Lewis should be found in contempt for the policy change because once again it directly violated the *Hook* consent decree. Lewis withdrew the policy before it was put into practice; nonetheless, Muecke found him in contempt and ordered him to personally pay a $10,000 fine and attorneys' costs associated with the incident.

The adult magazine incident, which appears to be more of a political stunt than thoughtful, considered policy reform, epitomized the relation-ships among the Department of Corrections, the executive branch, and the intertwined politics of states' rights and law and order. Symington used Judge Muecke as his foil to orate about what was wrong with the justice system and what needed to change. Muecke's orders and actions in the prison cases could be used to illustrate the fiscal imprudence of outsiders such as federal judges and special masters who were happy to fritter away Arizonans' tax dollars. The governor certainly held them up as egregious examples of federal govern-ment's meddling in legitimate state business. And the governor's office and its mouthpieces (including at times the *Arizona Republic* editorial staff) painted Muecke as a bleeding heart liberal who coddled criminals and made those on both sides of prison walls less safe.

In June 1994, the governor's office issued a news release after Judge Muecke reappointed the same special master and assistant special master who had worked on the *Gluth* and *Casey* law library compliance processes, and with whom Lewis had sparred over their bills, to oversee the holiday package dis-tribution. Just a month earlier, the special masters were at least temporarily relieved of their duties in the *Casey* compliance efforts with the stay issued by the U.S. Supreme Court, and Symington characterized their appoint-ment in the holiday package matter as a show of vindictiveness against Lewis on the part of Muecke. Symington's news release, and a letter to the editor that he submitted to the *Arizona Republic* just three days later, hit all of the themes designed to outrage Arizonans about Judge Muecke and his ilk—the fiscal waste he had caused, the coddling of criminals that he endorsed, and the inappropriate meddling in the state's matters in which he engaged.

The news release provided quotations from both Lewis and the governor himself to illustrate the points made. It opened with: "In another attempt to micro-manage Arizona's prison system, Judge Carl Muecke yesterday re-hired a previously ousted Special Master. As a result of the granting of a stay by the U.S. Supreme Court, the activities of the Special Master and the Assistant Special Master were suspended last month, denying them of tax-payer-funded positions" (Symington, 1994a). The page-and-a-half-long release went on to mention how much "taxpayer money" the special masters had already received and played up the actions of the Court as pure retaliation for the state's recent victories. In a symbolic move, Symington called for the impeachment of Judge Muecke because of his vindictive actions against Lewis, including the contempt finding on the adult magazine issue and the appointment of Pochoda as a special master once again.

Symington's letter to the editor removed the patina of any objectivity and was politics in its purest form, even as he insisted that it was not "just politics in a political season, [but something] much larger than that." The letter repeatedly cited how many of "our hard earned dollars" Judge Muecke had cost Arizona citizens, including his most recent $10 million "wish list" that would be used in large part to make "murderers, rapists, child molesters, and other felons more comfortable during their stay in our state prisons." He mentioned the costs for ACLU lawyers, the ongoing special masters' fees, and additional nonpublic attorneys' fees the state had paid in defending themselves. Symington then reminded his readers that Judge Muecke was not elected by the people of Arizona and had no right to spend their money. He raised the issue of the sexually explicit materials that Muecke "allowed" prisoners to possess while citing Sam Lewis for contempt for trying to withhold such materials from inmates. He concluded by making his case that this pattern of "malconduct and improper judicial behavior" was sufficient grounds for Muecke's removal (Symington, 1994b).

In 1995, the legislature added fuel to the fire by passing a bill crafted by Symington and Lewis that specifically disallowed state agencies from paying special masters who were appointed by a federal court unless the legislature appropriated special monies for that purpose. The bill was conceived as a way to assert states' rights and to challenge the legitimacy of federal court intervention into prison operations and was also intended to "set up a confrontation on who has the appropriations power" (Senate committee testimony of Ernest Baird, the bill's cosponsor, cited in *Hook v. Arizona*, 1995: 23). As soon as the law went into effect that summer, the Department of Corrections refused to pay the special masters' bills when submitted. Two attorneys representing some of the plaintiffs in the underlying cases, and who were Democratic Party heavyweights in the state, filed a motion asking that Lewis be held in contempt once again, this time for his refusal to pay the special masters. Muecke asked that an out-of-state federal judge hear the case, so it was assigned to a visiting judge, David Ezra, from Hawaii. Judge Ezra ruled that the statute violated the supremacy clause of the U.S. Constitution, thus invalidating it, and held Lewis in contempt. In the decision, he took Lewis to task for his disingenuousness in being a major supporter and architect of this statute, then claiming his inability to pay the special masters' bills because the legislature would not appropriate the funds to do so.

Rather than roll over and pay up, the state continued to fight on this issue—in court, behind the political scenes, and in the public arena. Within two days of Ezra's decision, vague "charges" were made in the press that special master Pochoda was a "reform radical" with a history of supporting prisoner causes, including the prisoners during the Attica prison riot (Coppola, 1995). Washington lawyers retained by the Constitutional Defense Council were paid to write an 11-page report that detailed the background of Pochoda, with a slant toward painting him as a radical, "far-left" agitator who did not share the same values as Arizonans. The report was released to the press and used to discredit Pochoda's appointment and to justify the state's unwillingness to pay him. The state paid the same attorney who wrote the Pochoda report more than $300 per hour to represent Sam Lewis in the contempt penalty hearing.

Several reporters and editors did dare to question the wisdom of the state's strategy of paying so much to fight the court's finding rather than complying with it. For instance, Eric Miller, of the *Arizona Republic*, reported that the state had spent $200,000 to avoid paying a $37,000 special master's bill but then provided extensive quotations from the governor's office and the Department of Corrections spokesperson that defended the action, thus dulling any criticism that the state was being irresponsible (Miller, 1995). Similarly, an editorial in the *Tucson Citizen* chastised Symington for keeping the battle going even though it agreed that he did have a "valid concern" (*Tucson Citizen*, 1995).

In response to these mild criticism, Governor Symington issued a press release that aggressively defended the state's actions by asserting that the "stakes" were not just a $37,000 bill but $11 million in current tax dollars and unlimited millions more in the future if the state went along with the federal courts' interference (Symington, 1995a). He followed this up with a letter to the editor addressed to the *Arizona Republic* that made the same points in detail (Symington, 1995b).

Lewis also wrote a pointed four-page letter to a member of the state's Joint Legislative Budget Committee, copying 19 other legislative leaders, that recounted the battles with the federal courts over the prisons and argued that challenging the courts on these issues was actually cost-effective for the state. He ended by expressing outrage about the uncontrollable "breach of power" exercised by the federal courts that had resulted in Arizona taxpayers' financing of millions of dollars of expenses (Lewis, 1995b).

Although the state did pay the outstanding special master's bill several weeks after Judge Ezra's judgment, Symington also enlisted U.S. senator John Kyl (R-Ariz.) to author and sponsor federal legislation requiring that the federal judiciary pay for the special masters that its judges appoint in prison cases. The proposed provision also capped the hourly pay allowable for special masters and revised the special master selection process to give federal judges less discretion in appointing people to the job. Furthermore, Kyl's office collaborated with Symington's office, the state attorney general's office, and Lewis to create additional legislation that severely restricted inmates' abilities to seek relief from federal courts, that mandated termination of consent decrees after a set period, and that restricted courts' use of such agreements to order the release of prisoners.

Senator Kyl then brought these provisions to the Senate as a single bill designed to restrict prisoner litigation through multiple means, and with co-sponsor Senator Robert Dole, he introduced the bill as the Prisoner Litigation Reform Act (PLRA) in 1995. In 1996, the act, in a slightly modified version, was attached as a little noticed rider to the omnibus appropriations bill HR 3019 (Title VIII) and passed into law that spring. The PLRA has since become an infamous piece of legislation that has radically reshaped the nature of prisoner litigation and severely narrowed the rights afforded to inmates who seek help from federal courts.

The state also went after the lawsuits from the other end. With the support of the Department of Corrections and the governor's office, the legislature passed a bill in 1994 that authorized the direct collection of court filing fees from inmate accounts when lawsuits were filed. This bill's goal was to "reduce frivolous lawsuits filed by inmates" and was trumpeted, a year and a half after it had been implemented as policy, as reducing the number of lawsuits by 12 percent (Stewart, 1996b). A similar provision was also passed at the federal level as part of the PLRA.

SYMINGTON AND LEWIS VERSUS WOODS REDUX

Simultaneous with going on the offensive against federal court intervention, Governor Symington deepened his feud with Attorney General Grant Woods by trying to take complete ownership, in alliance with Sam Lewis, of the battle against the federal courts. Symington and Lewis were engaged in a purely political show over punishment in the state and seemed to want to make sure that Woods had no chance to take credit for any of the offensive efforts made against Judge Muecke or others who tried to intervene on behalf of criminal defendants and prisoners. Thus, in 1993, Symington came up with a plan to establish a Constitutional Defense Council (CDC), which would be a group that worked for the state in its fight against "unfunded federal mandates" such as requirements of the Environmental Protection Agency to clean up pollution and requirements by federal courts to improve conditions in the state prisons. It would also function to take legal action that it felt was appropriate to restore the state's sovereignty in relation to federal intrusion, primarily by hiring private attorneys to represent the state in such litigation.

Symington received legislative support for the plan, and the bill authorizing the CDC's creation, along with $1 million in funding, was passed and signed into law in the spring of 1994. Even though nominally the attorney general was a member of the CDC in its original configuration, it was widely acknowledged that this group was designed to circumvent Woods's authority, and its formation was a symbolic slap in his face. The council members and advisors included personal adversaries of Woods, such as former assistant attorney general Steve Twist, his primary opponent in 1990, and some of the staunchest members of the political right in the state.

The next year, Governor Symington worked with the legislature in an effort to more fully erode the attorney general's power to act on behalf of the state. At Symington's urging, the legislature considered a bill that would substantially de-fund and disband the attorney general's office, moving it into an Office of General Counsel, which would be devised by the governor and would allow all state agencies to hire their own counsel. Lewis was a major player in the process, testifying in the legislature about the troubles he had experienced with the attorney general's representation and in particular his major clashes with Woods. The Senate passed a watered-down version of the original bill, stripping the attorney general's office of the authority to represent the governor's office, the Department of Corrections, and the Department of Environmental Policy. The House failed to pass the measure, but its brief life was a testament to the animosity that both Symington and Lewis felt for Woods.

In 1996, the legislature did amend the law that authorized the CDC by cutting the attorney general out of the council's composition and stripping him of his powers to represent the state on what was deemed to be CDC-relevant business. The amendment added two advisory positions, one from each house of the legislature, in place of the attorney general. With that law change, the CDC hired a private law firm from Washington, D.C., to represent the state on those matters that it deemed to fall under the CDC's mandate, including the prison lawsuits and environmental regulatory matters, directly usurping the attorney general's power in the process.

The insertion of the CDC, and the private firm it hired, into the prison litigation process just complicated matters more. Woods challenged the authority of the CDC to appear in any state cases, and the Arizona Supreme Court agreed to consider his challenge. In the meantime, the CDC-hired lawyers asserted their right to be substituted into the prison litigation cases as counsel for the state, a move to which Woods objected. Thus, fights over the CDC's legitimacy and standing were being waged simultaneously in state and federal courts, and as a result, the already complex and contentious prison litigation became more so.

This process was aptly illustrated in August 1996 when the CDC lawyers filed a notice to appear as counsel of record for the state of Arizona in the long-dormant *Harris v. Cardwell* case. They simultaneously filed a motion to terminate the consent decree in the case, citing provisions of the recently passed federal PLRA as grounds for termination. The attorney general filed an objection to their appearance, claiming that the attorney general's office was the proper counsel in the matter; this was followed, a month later, by its own motion to terminate the consent decree. The CDC lawyers fought back with several motions that worked different angles to allow them to represent the state in the case. Judge Muecke recused himself from participating, and the new judge stayed any decision on the case until the Arizona Supreme Court ruled on the constitutionality of the CDC. In 1997, that court ruled that the revised statute authorizing the CDC was unconstitutional in that it violated the separation of powers clause of the state constitution (because of the inclusion of the legislative leaders), so the CDC had no authority to represent the state or spend state money.

The battle also played out in the *Lewis v. Casey* legal access case, once it was headed to the Supreme Court in 1995. At the start of the case, the Department of Corrections hired a high-powered local private firm to represent the department instead of using the attorney general as counsel. The private firm handled the federal trial court litigation and the appeal process in the Ninth Circuit and filed the appeal of the Ninth Circuit's decision to the U.S. Supreme Court, successfully earning a hearing before that body. Once the case was granted certiorari by the Supreme Court and a hearing was scheduled, Woods stepped into the case, declaring that he would represent the department from there on out. Lewis was livid, and in a letter to Woods, which he shared with the *Phoenix Gazette*, he accused Woods of being ill-prepared and incompetent to take over the case, thus behaving unethically by jeopardizing the best interests of the client. He further accused Woods of "confusing what is in the best interests of the State with what is in the best interests of Grant Woods' political career" (*Phoenix Gazette*, 1995).

The *Phoenix Gazette* editorial sympathized with Lewis and charged Woods with trying to "hog the spotlight" and speculated that he "could start perspiring and stammering like a first year law student" when grilled by the justices (*Phoenix Gazette*, 1995). Woods defended his decision to step in by suggesting that the Court would expect the attorney general to represent the state rather than an outside private attorney. Woods did indeed argue the case in front of the Supreme Court, apparently with success because the Court reversed the decision, making *Lewis v. Casey* a landmark case in the rollback of prisoners' rights on access to the courts.[2]

These battles are of course somewhat idiosyncratic and extreme, but they highlight the political value of using the crime and punishment arena as the venue for (re)asserting more fundamental political values and philosophies. Symington wanted to own this battle of the state versus the federal government, and he used Muecke's handling of prison cases as the public example of the depth of the problem (as he saw it) with federal intervention. He had Lewis to help define the need for bigger legal guns, by implicitly displaying the attorney general's ineffectual representation in such grave matters. Lewis was outspoken in his contempt for both Judge Muecke and Woods, and the personal hits he took in terms of the contempt findings highlighted, in his view, the attorney general's inability to protect him and his agency from legal harms.

In the case of the CDC, even though the council took on much more than prison litigation in its short life—it also was involved in challenging federal environmental regulations and voting rights mandates—the face of the CDC's mission was combating the federal micromanaging of prisons and the excessive costs associated with court-mandated "coddling" of prisoners. Thus, through its creation, Symington was able to manipulate and interweave two salient and powerful political values in the state—those valuing states' rights and being tough on criminals—while simultaneously disempowering his imagined future political opponent, Attorney General Grant Woods. It also highlights the apparent hierarchy of what issues were viewed as sellable to the public and press. Putting the prisoner litigation battle out as the public face of these issues suggests that the political actors involved assumed it would have the most resonance with those public audiences, in a way that fighting against pollution regulations or voting access might not.

TERRY STEWART KEEPS THE MOVEMENT GOING

Sam Lewis had groomed his deputy director, Terry Stewart, to succeed him in the director's position and carry on the penal philosophy and practices that had transformed the state's prison system. This continuity plan extended to the litigation pushback that consumed Lewis's final years as director. Stewart was just as, if not more, proactive in his efforts to undo the federal oversight and flaunt practices that seemed to skirt the very edge of the Constitution, even in the increasingly hands-off atmosphere of the 1990s.

Along with his legacy, Lewis left behind an additional, particularly ugly case that had erupted in the midst of the battles with Judge Muecke, the special masters, and the attorney general's office. In late fall of 1994, the Civil Rights Division of the U.S. Department of Justice was back in Arizona after the *Phoenix Gazette* published a series of stories indicating that 38 correctional employees had been subjects of an internal investigation of alleged sexual misconduct over the previous two years. Donna Hamm, director of the prisoner advocacy group Middle Ground, urged the U.S. attorney's office in Arizona to initiate a federal inquiry, which it elected to do. Simultaneously, 13 victims of the alleged sexual abuse filed suit in state court seeking damages from the Department of Corrections for the harm caused by policies that facilitated such abuses.

The entire exposé and subsequent legal action were catalyzed by a case in which an inmate accused a guard of forcibly raping and mutilating her, yet the guard remained undisciplined and unprosecuted despite the fact that he had failed a polygraph test and she had passed one. The internal department records indicated that none of the accused employees in the larger scandal had been prosecuted although many had been let go or disciplined for their actions. The issue simmered for several months as the Department of Justice began its investigations and while the civil suits were in their early stages, but in the summer of 1995, as Lewis was nearing his retirement, he decided to go on the offensive once more, this time against the U.S. attorney's office for intruding in this case.

First, he crafted amendments to two federal statutes that had major consequences for the treatment of inmates—the Religious Freedom Restoration Act and the Civil Rights of Institutionalized Persons Act (CRIPA)—and sent them to U.S. Senator Kyl to push through the federal legislative process. He argued in his accompanying letter to Kyl that the first piece of legislation inadvertently affected state prisons because it in essence expanded the rights of individuals to religious expression, so he proposed an amendment that would allow a loophole for prison administrators claiming "legitimate" penological interests or concerns.

In the case of CRIPA, Lewis suggested that Congress passed it with the intention to "inhibit federal intrusion into secured State institutions" (Lewis, 1995d) but it was being used "wrongly" by the attorney general and its affiliate offices to intrude at will into state institutional business. Consequently, in 1996, as part of the PLRA, a modification was made to CRIPA to further cut back on federal authority to investigate civil rights violations in state prisons.

Lewis was spurred to take up the task of writing federal legislative amendments to "clarify" Congress's intent because it was under the authority of CRIPA that the Civil Rights Division had initiated its investigation into the Arizona prison sex abuse scandal. He had already written to U.S. Attorney General Janet Reno to complain that her office was behaving in a manner inconsistent with the intent of CRIPA, and he had cut off access to the prisons for the Civil Rights Division investigators earlier in the summer because he believed they had no authority to act in the matter.

Once Stewart took over the department, he maintained this stance and continued the practice of periodically issuing written objections to the U.S. attorney's local office. He agreed to forward reports that the Department of

Corrections generated on allegations of abuse when requested but refused to give Department of Justice investigators access to the prisons. He also maintained the stance that the Department of Justice was acting outside the requirements of CRIPA and had no authority under that act to enter state facilities to investigate alleged civil rights violations (Stewart, 1996a).

The Department of Justice completed its investigation in August 1996 with a report to Governor Symington. The report, issued by then–assistant attorney general Deval Patrick, concluded that female inmates were indeed subject to "an unconstitutional pattern or practice of sexual misconduct and unacceptable invasions of privacy rights" and that the Department of Corrections had not adequately addressed the problems (Patrick, 1996, 1). The report detailed the specific findings of violations in seven pages of text and expressed frustration with the department's refusal to let investigators actually speak with the female inmates and staff, let alone allow them access to the facilities at all. Patrick expressed an interest in resolving the issues cooperatively but warned that his office might decide to file a lawsuit to remediate the problems identified, given the lack of cooperation the department had demonstrated.

The state's initial response was to continue to question the authority of the Civil Rights Division to intervene under CRIPA while making the case that although the sexual abuses alleged might have occurred, they did not add up to a pattern of deliberate indifference on the part of corrections administrators. The two sides negotiated about how to proceed for a few months, but the state insisted that any results of a mutually agreed upon independent investigation would have to remain confidential, a condition to which the federal investigators refused to agree. In March 1997, the U.S. attorney for the Arizona district, Janet Napolitano, formally sued the Department of Corrections for civil rights violations on behalf of the U.S. Department of Justice.

The case was settled two years later after the state agreed to change hiring and training procedures and promised to provide more services to inmate victims of sexual abuse. Ironically, by this time, Napolitano had in essence switched sides from representing the federal government as a U.S. attorney; she had been elected in 1998 as the Arizona attorney general so represented the department in this matter during the final settlement negotiations. Indeed, this may well have been a key catalyst to the case's settlement. The state did not admit any wrongdoing in the settlement and maintained its stance of denial to the local press afterwards. Stewart continued to insist that the lawsuit was groundless and downplayed the seriousness of the allegations by suggesting that some involved only minor violations such as kissing and that some of the incidents were instigated by the inmates themselves (Mattern, 1999).

Stewart also continued the fight in Lewis's other battles. He had held the director position for about six months when the Supreme Court decision in *Lewis v. Casey* came down and was responsible for implementing new policy in accordance with that decision. Stewart's approach to interpreting the *Lewis v. Casey* mandate was aggressively anti–prisoners' rights. Because the *Gluth* decision still stood, he could not immediately touch the law library at the Florence central prison, but he quickly decided to strip all other facilities of their law libraries. Immediately after the decision, when reporters asked him how the department would react to the decision in terms of providing legal access, Stewart's response was that he would replace libraries with "plain English and stubby little pencils," meaning that prisoners could handwrite their complaints in nonlegal terms and mail them to a court of law (Stewart interview, 2004).

And that is what he did throughout the system. By 1997 he had closed 34 of the 35 prison law libraries, leaving only the Florence library (until he could get out from under the *Gluth* requirements). The new "legal access" system mandated that inmates be provided with preformatted legal forms on which they could write their complaints. Those completed forms were then screened by state-hired paralegals, who were to advise whether the cases were meritorious or not. The paralegals were under contractual orders not to assist inmates with the litigation process past the filing of initial petitions.

The administration deemed the new system a success solely because it drastically cut down on the number of prisoner lawsuits filed, but in reality, it was a mess. Middle Ground received a number of complaints from inmates regarding the poor quality of the assistance, so it looked into the qualifications of the paralegals with whom the state had contracted. Two of the three were discovered to have falsified their qualifications in order to appear to meet the job requirements of having a college degree and/or a paralegal degree. The primary contractor, Scott Sirota, whose business did the bulk of the work for the state during the first year of this new operation, had indicated that he was a graduate of Arizona State University in business administration and that he had attended law school. It turned out that he had once attended classes at the university but had not successfully completed a single course; he was on probation for an attempted theft conviction; he had been sued in civil court for a business scam; and he employed his brother, who had been fired as a police officer for various sex and fraud violations on the job. The second contractor lied about having an associate's degree from a community college; she had only a high school diploma. The third paralegal (who was verified to be qualified for the job) quit after the department accused him of overcharging his hours; his contract allowed him to bill only for the time he spent actually meeting with inmates, but he could not bill for time waiting in the prison for inmates to be brought to him, for his travel time to different prisons in his region, or for any work he did on the prisoners' petitions at his own office.

So at the end of the first year of the program, there were no qualified paralegals working with inmates, although the department allowed Sirota (the most egregiously unqualified of the group) to maintain his contract for two months after the discovery of his falsified qualifications and criminal record until they could replace the lot of them. In the end, Sirota's paralegal "business" was paid close to $400,000 for its services. Perhaps the most outrageous aspect of this "legal access" scheme is that, rather than being paid for by the department's budget, it was paid for solely by the inmates' activities and recreation fund, which is composed of profits made when prisoners purchase food and sundries from the inmate store and profits from inmates' phone calls.

Despite this inauspicious start to the post–law library access system, Stewart did not relent. He hired more paralegals to replace the departed ones—including two who had worked for Sirota—who were now under contracts that authorized even fewer hours of service to inmates, and he hired a "monitor" to oversee the paralegal program. Inmates challenged the system in both state and federal courts, but to no avail. To add insult to injury, in the midst of the paralegal scandals, the governor's office awarded the team that implemented the new "Inmate Access to the Courts System" with the Governor's Spirit of Excellence Award in 1998 (Arizona Department of Corrections, Departmental history website). The following year, the department moved to close the lone remaining law library in the central unit at Florence and to replace it with the new legal access system. This change was overseen by a mutually agreed upon monitor and was eventually approved by the district court, which then dissolved the consent decree in *Gluth*.

Stewart also took on a burgeoning issue that Lewis had initiated during the summer before his retirement. Lewis had decided that too many inmates were in protective segregation (PS) within the system and, ostensibly for fiscal reasons, he wanted to try to reclassify some of them so that they could be housed in the less expensive general housing units. Inmates were placed in PS, generally by request, because of a potential for harm resulting from their status as, for example, a snitch, sex offender, or gang member with known enemies in custody. In June 1995, Lewis convened a Special Review Committee composed solely of prison staff and administrators to review each of the cases of the 463 PS inmates in the state, with a goal of reducing the number of such inmates to 200.

The review committee hearings lasted less than 30 minutes each; in the hearings inmates could state their case for why they felt they needed to stay in PS but were not allowed to call witnesses, and the committee did no other investigation in most cases (Hill, Hammond, Skolnik, Martin, and Clement, 2004). As a result of the hearings, only 92 inmates retained their PS status; 274 were involuntarily transferred back to the general population; and 97 agreed to go along with such a transfer.

Given the gravity of this decision for PS inmates, more than 100 of those who were subject to involuntary transfer individually filed suit, without any representation, in U.S. district court. District Court judge Charles Hardy took heed of the seriousness of the issue and asked a well-known local attorney to represent the inmates as a class. Because PS inmates faced very real threats of death or serious harm, the judge ordered the case to be sealed, so the litigation process remained secret for more than two years, through its resolution in the first evidentiary hearing and ruling. At the hearing, numerous witnesses testified about the dangers that PS inmates faced if they were released back into the general population; it was characterized as an even more dangerous situation than the underlying circumstance that required protective segregation in the first place because being in PS was a huge stigma in and of itself. Judge Hardy ruled that the Department of Corrections was deliberately indifferent to the risk of harm faced by the reclassified PS inmates and issued a preliminary injunction barring the department from transferring any inmates out of PS.

Stewart did not attend any part of the evidentiary hearing, and in Lewis's style, he chose to fight (in part through the press) rather than try to work with the plaintiffs on a remedial plan (Hill et al., 2004). He skirted the edges of the judge's strict order to keep the case sealed by issuing a press release after the judge's order came down (it, too, was sealed) that detailed the provisions of the court's order and that lambasted the federal courts for their continued meddling in the state's prison operations. Stewart characterized the decision as "the most egregious intrusion that the courts have been involved with in

Arizona" and suggested that "the only thing . . . accomplished by this ruling is that a federal court has once again flagrantly interfered with my authority" (Pittman, 1996). Judge Hardy issued a second order several months later that more strongly condemned the Department of Corrections and that ordered it to come up with a remediation plan for classifying PS inmates in a manner that did not endanger them.

In 1998, the case went back to court to assess whether the department had revised its policies in compliance with Judge Hardy's order. The case was moved to Judge Richard Bilby's court, where an evidentiary hearing was held to determine whether the department's new plan was acceptable. During that hearing, the plaintiffs presented evidence about the murder of an inmate who should have been in PS but was instead placed in the general population when he was returned to prison on a probation violation. This killing had occurred just one month before the hearing, providing compelling evidence of the department's failure to protect inmates; it was the fourth murder in recent years that appeared to be a result of a PS-eligible inmate being left in the general population. Judge Bilby unsealed the case and in the now-public hearing lambasted Stewart when he testified about the improvements made, citing Stewart's earlier press release as evidence of the department's attitude that it did not care about the safety of inmates. The judge also suggested that the recent inmate murder came "as close to voluntary manslaughter as anything I have ever seen in my life" (Steckner, 1998).

After this hearing and before Judge Bilby ruled, the Department of Corrections quietly agreed to work with the plaintiffs on a settlement while still not admitting that it had engaged in unconstitutional practices. Plaintiffs' attorneys felt that Stewart was prompted in part by the testimony he heard in this hearing about the harsh realities PS inmates faced as well as by the realization that the ruling would not be in the department's favor (Hill et al., 2004). Nonetheless, he did relent, albeit without press releases, from his hard-line stance that he would appeal to higher courts and fight this "intrusion" all the way. The settlement process was also likely aided by a changeover in the state attorney general's office when Janet Napolitano (former U.S. attorney in the Arizona District and future governor of Arizona) was elected attorney general.

Stewart also oversaw the successful appeals processes in the Lewis-era battle stemming from the *Hook v. Arizona* consent decree about the holiday packages and adult magazines. As noted above, in both cases the state pursued reversals on Judge Muecke's rulings with Stewart's active involvement and encouragement. The state had won on the holiday package issue in the Ninth Circuit in 1996, and in the end, instead of allowing a smaller quantity of packages, as it had been willing to do earlier in the decade, the department under Stewart successfully pushed for a policy that outlawed all such packages.

Stewart's major focus, though, in terms of pursuing legal strategy to "take back" the prisons was to work diligently to dissolve the existing consent decrees under which the department was operating. On this, the 1998 Arizona Department of Corrections annual report commented that "the Department is seeking to terminate all of the consent decrees to which it is a party" (Stewart, 1998: 12). The report went on to describe the details of each of these agreements and the strategy used to try to dissolve them. Such efforts were made by both the CDC and the attorney general's office, beginning in 1996 after the passage of the PLRA. The state was first successful in this regard when in late 1996 the district court vacated the consent decree in *Taylor v. Arizona*. This decision was overturned by the Ninth Circuit, which claimed that the order mandating policy in that case was not technically a consent decree so the PLRA provision that allowed for its dissolution did not apply. The *Gluth* consent decree was dissolved in the early 2000s, and the *Hook* consent decree was dissolved by a district court in 2003. In 2004, the district court terminated the action in *Harris v. Cardwell* and closed that file as well.

Like his predecessor and mentor, Stewart also made policy that seemed to push the envelope in terms of challenging the provisions of those consent decrees in effect. For example, prison staff under his leadership routinely confiscated adult magazines on the grounds that they threatened security, even in the face of the *Hook* consent decree. In the changing legal landscape of Arizona's federal district court and emboldened, it seemed, by the victory in *Lewis v. Casey*, such actions by the department were much less likely to result in litigation. In this case, an inmate did file a complaint without the assistance of an attorney, alleging that these actions violated the *Hook* consent decree and that they further violated his First and Fourteenth amendment rights, but the district court found for the defendants on all issues, and the court of appeals denied him relief and refused to award damages (which he sought) on the basis of a series of technicalities. The court did say that the inmate had the right to notice that his mail was being withheld but agreed that the department was justified in withholding the magazines (see *Frost v. Symington*, 1999, 2002).

As already noted, Stewart also instituted even more highly restrictive policies that heightened the harshness of the prison experience beyond what

Lewis had put into place, justifying them on the grounds of security. Thus, among other Stewart-devised policy innovations, restrictions on visiting generally, and contact visits in particular, were increased; policies were drafted to allow the state to send inmates to other states for security reasons; more recreation opportunities were curtailed; more fees were charged to inmates for basic needs and services; the use of the supermax units was intensified; and the conditions within those units were made even more austere.

These policies, when challenged, were generally able to remain in place despite their extreme nature, for at least three reasons. First, Judge Muecke decided to recuse himself in 1996 from any more involvement in the prison cases and retired from the bench in 1997. Thus the inmate challenges in federal court were landing in front of less sympathetic audiences than they had when Muecke played an active role in them. Second, with the passage of the PLRA in 1996, Stewart operated in a legal environment that was so stacked against the inmate that it was a rare and truly disturbing kind of petition that could now inspire intervention (such as the petitions regarding PS). And third, with the implementation of the new legal access system put in place by Stewart, inmates had a much harder time even getting their complaints out and to the court.

CONCLUSION

In the early years of the Arizona Department of Corrections, the state's response to prisoner lawsuits, and the judgments that followed, tended to be conciliatory. The state entered into consent decrees with the plaintiffs with little resistance in order to avoid protracted litigation and worked hard to comply with the orders the court issued. Indeed, the state was willing to work with potential plaintiffs' advocates, most notably the U.S. Commission on Civil Rights during its investigations of the state prison during the 1970s, in order to avoid going to court at all. But this stance changed dramatically by the 1990s. At a more structural level, this effort was helped out by the passage in 1996 of the PLRA, the federal legislation designed to "discourage" litigation by prisoners. Ironically, this legislation was conceived and promoted by Arizona state actors in the midst of this fight.

What seemed to start as an issue of clashing personalities, and consequently a power struggle, between two strong-willed individuals—Judge Carl Muecke and Department of Corrections director Sam Lewis (aided and abetted by Governor Fife Symington)—became a legal revolution that catapulted

Arizona to the forefront of the anti–prisoner litigation movement. Lewis did three things to help catalyze this process. First, he came into the director role untempered by professional penal experience that would have likely modified the nature of his policy approach. Instead, he had no qualms about creating or revising policy in extreme ways that were almost guaranteed to spur a reaction from inmates and their advocates. Second, once challenged, Lewis was open in his expressions of disdain for federal intervention and was bold enough to defy court orders at times. Certainly, he was not predisposed to behave in a cooperative or conciliatory manner, as had former administrators. And third, he went on the offensive against prisoners, and the courts that ruled in their favor, through multiple channels. He willingly sought to challenge district court orders through adversarial litigation; he took it upon himself to draft state and federal legislation that would change the rules that he found problematic (and he found sponsorship for those proposals); and he played politics in the media to sell his combative approach to beating back prisoners' rights as the righteous one to take, and the one that protected Arizona's values.

For his part, Judge Muecke maintained a consistent position that aimed to protect inmates from some of the more severe conditions they faced in Arizona's prisons, but he also seemed to up the ante in terms of the detailed and specific nature of his rulings once he was faced with Lewis's resistance to his authority. He seemed compelled to do so by the frustration he experienced with an obstinate Department of Corrections once Lewis took over, as he commented on more than once in his orders and rulings. This undoubtedly catalyzed some of the spiraling out of these cases from ones that should have been settled with a compromise to ones that stayed in protracted litigation for years. Indeed, the Supreme Court decision in *Lewis v. Casey* would likely not have happened without both sides acting and reacting to each other—Lewis refusing to provide reasonable access to inmates even when told he needed to, and Muecke deciding in the *Gluth* case to dictate down to the most minute detail what adequate legal access would look like in order to ensure compliance, which he then extended to the entire system in *Casey*.

The from-the-ground-up process happening in Arizona on the litigation front transformed the state from being just one of many that grappled with judicial intervention in their prison operations to being a trailblazer that ultimately reshaped the national landscape of prisoner litigation. The most significant effects that Arizona has had in this arena occurred through three processes: direct litigation, particularly through the culmination of *Casey v.*

Lewis; the legislative and political process, especially in terms of its huge role in conceptualizing and promoting what became the PLRA; and mass-mediated politics, as Governor Symington partnered with Lewis and "sold" their message to a much broader audience, including states that adopted the new states' rights rhetoric promoted in Arizona to curtail federal intervention in prisons.

These efforts on the part of the department and the governor not only directly affected the penal system in Arizona and beyond, but also exemplified a broader shift in state executive branch governance through their reprioritizing of the mission and duties of the governor's office. In several ways, this war against federal court intervention captures many aspects of the phenomenon of governing through crime described by Jonathan Simon (2007) that has transformed social and political life today. Thus, despite Symington's gubernatorial campaign line, which used a government-as-business metaphor (with himself as the skilled business manager), he was in office only a matter of months before he shaped his most important political messages around matters related to criminal justice. A key element of that strategy was to wage a publicized battle against those outside meddlers—primarily the federal district court—who would seek to make prison more comfortable and humane.

Additionally, the battles highlighted themes that resonated with several major tenets of Arizona's long-standing political ethos. Fighting the federal courts and the U.S. government over prison issues (although as we saw in one case, the U.S. Supreme Court played the role of an ally rather than enemy and the Ninth Circuit Court of Appeals began siding with the state on several key issues) replayed historical battles that even predate statehood over states' rights and the strong political will to be free from federal intrusion (see Chapter 1). The federal courts' actions were also framed as assaults on the state's commitment to fiscal prudence, especially when it came to spending on the less deserving, because of what was characterized as profligate spending authorized by meddling federal judges. Finally, the long-standing commitment to a theory of less eligibility in penal policy, and a history (outside of the reform experiment from 1968 through the early 1980s) of ensuring that punishment was a deliberately uncomfortable experience for prisoners, were characterized as fundamentally threatened by the intrusive actions of the federal government.

Although the exact shape of the anti–prisoners' rights revolution that developed in Arizona might have looked different had Lewis not been the Department of Corrections director, and indeed, the state might not have been such a leader in that transformation, there were clearly elements in place—deeply rooted ones—that suggest that the state would likely have gone this route even without Lewis's leadership. The federal court "interference" in the state prisons that began in earnest during the 1970s struck an old nerve, and some state legislators had already begun to voice discontent with these developments well before Lewis was on the scene. Once the federal courts began ordering the state to spend money to benefit inmates, an eventual backlash against prisoner litigation seemed to be guaranteed.

The arc of the prisoner litigation movement in Arizona reveals a pattern that can also be seen in other jurisdictions, although it is perhaps not as dramatic as occurred here. The early cases can be credited with professionalizing the corrections enterprise in the state by mandating standardization and procedural regularity for a number of aspects of prison life. Certainly, in states across the nation, including Arizona, disciplinary procedures were considerably reshaped and seemingly made much less arbitrary as a direct result of successful litigation during the 1970s. The deleterious effects of severe overcrowding were also mitigated to some degree in the early years by court orders that specified minimal standards in this regard. In Arizona, the intervention of the Department of Justice helped push for a more professional and diversified workforce, as well as for a more rational system of classification and assignments for inmates.

Yet these gains were relatively short-lived. The backlash that was in full force in this state by the late 1980s culminated in, at minimum, a new "hands-off" jurisprudence that was reluctant to intervene in prison operations by the 1990s. Thus, even if on paper inmates had earned a net gain of rights as a result of the earlier victories, those rights did not mean much in an environment in which they could not be exercised (such as through viable access to the courts) or protected because of a network of procedural blocks mandated by legislation such as the PLRA. And under the Lewis and Stewart administrations, with political support from the governor and the legislature, the state was more than willing to operationally roll back as many of the rights and privileges prisoners gained during the 1970s and 1980s as it could. The end result was that by the 1990s, life inside Arizona's prisons did not differ dramatically from when it was under the authoritarian rule of Superintendent Eyman during the 1950s and early 1960s.

This dramatic change raises the question as to why prisoners' advocates in the state (or advocates from national organizations such as the ACLU's

National Prison Project) had so little power in holding the Lewis-Stewart regime to some minimum bar for standards of treatment. This is likely due to the relatively sparse and weak entrenchment of prisoners' advocates in the state, coupled with structural changes that limited prisoners' ability to seek relief from courts. The state ACLU office, while participating in some of the litigation, did not have the infrastructure to mount major campaigns against the state on these issues, and like many state affiliate offices, it needed to marshal volunteers or seek assistance from the national organization to litigate most cases. More importantly, the Arizona state affiliate's board of directors has traditionally been mainly uninterested in, and at times downright hostile to, focusing on prisoners' rights issues. This was an especially large impediment during the late 1980s and 1990s when Lewis, Stewart, and Sheriff Arpaio in Maricopa County were amping up their punitive policies and publicizing them with pride. The litigation engine thus came in part from outside the state, with both the federal Department of Justice and the national ACLU providing some impetus and support in challenging the state on behalf of prisoners. Of course, local lawyers were key to much of the litigation, particularly Frank Lewis, who worked with the ACLU on much of the litigation in *Harris v. Cardwell*, and several of the high-powered law firms in the state, particularly in Phoenix, which were vital participants in the challenges.

Activist organizations have also been few and far between and only somewhat influential in promoting and protecting prisoners' rights in Arizona. There was a convergence of concern around prisoners' rights during the early and mid-1970s among some activists and several legislators, but by the 1980s, the only two groups in Arizona that were consistently working on prison issues were the American Friends Service Committee affiliate out of Tucson (it also had many other campaigns under way, so its attention to and effect on prison policy were limited) and Middle Ground out of Tempe. Founded in 1983, Middle Ground was for many years primarily a one-person operation led by its founder, Donna Leone Hamm;[3] nonetheless, it has been the most vocal, news media–connected lobbying group (indeed, it says it is the only official prisoners' rights lobbying group in the state) to go up directly against the Department of Corrections since the early 1980s. Hamm has been the spokeswoman to whom local reporters, especially in Phoenix, have turned for an understanding of prisoner concerns. She has also consistently attended legislative sessions in the state to lobby against various sentencing proposals and penal policies, with some notable successes over the years.

Middle Ground has assisted in numerous propria persona prisoner lawsuits and was instrumental in initiating the lawsuit on the holiday packages and adult magazines, finding attorneys, and helping them in the cases. The group was also responsible both for exposing the scandal around the paralegal system initiated in the wake of *Casey v. Lewis* and for getting the U.S. Department of Justice involved in the sex abuse case.

Yet the forces against prisoners' rights within the state—the executive office, the legislative majority, the administration of the Department of Corrections, the bulk of the press, the apathetic (or even propunishment) public, and, after Judge Muecke pulled out of the prison litigation cases, much of the federal judiciary—were too great for prisoners to win many major battles over the long haul.[4] And once *Casey v. Lewis* and then the PLRA reshaped the playing field for prisoners who sought to challenge their conditions of confinement, little hope was left for maintaining the earlier-earned protections, much less for further remedial reform of the system.

7 MAKING MEANING OF THE ARIZONA CASE

THE CASE FOR SUNBELT-STYLE PENALITY

As noted at the beginning of this book, a number of scholars have identified the Sunbelt region as key to the development of "New Right" politics in the United States (for example, Lassiter, 2006; McGirr, 2001). States such as California, Arizona, Nevada, Texas, North Carolina, Georgia, and Florida have all faced rapid growth and transformation since World War II and have been identified as largely responsible for the new breed of political conservatism within the Republican Party that began in the early 1960s and was represented by figures such as Barry Goldwater from Arizona and Richard Nixon and Ronald Reagan from California. The issues of importance during the decades in which the New Right ascended in power included taxation; "big" government and social welfare spending; so-called values issues, such as the disintegration of the traditional family; and national defense. More importantly, in the context of this book, this new brand of conservatism has been credited with bringing law and order to the political foreground at the state and national levels, which in turn played a significant role in (re)shaping penal policy and practices within the Sunbelt and beyond (Flamm, 2005).

Within the New Right law-and-order movement, one can locate the origins of the primary exemplars of late modern penality: mass incarceration resulting from harsh determinate sentencing schemes, "pain and shame" punitive innovations, the no-frills warehouse-style prison, and so on.[1] These late modern penological developments are, in many ways, both ideologically and geographically in opposition to the modern era "penal welfare" (Garland, 2001) innovations that preceded them, which primarily emerged in the

Northeast during the nineteenth and early twentieth centuries. This is not to say that those hallmark penal welfare structures and institutions have been abandoned and replaced. Prisons, probation, parole, and other such institutions continue to live on, yet almost all have been reshaped, in some cases dramatically, in terms of their underlying rationales, philosophies, ideologies, and day-to-day practices, over the past 30 years.

One can map the origins of both sets of reformist developments onto specific, and distinct, regions of the United States. In the early 1800s, Pennsylvania and New York were the first states to build penitentiaries that were explicitly designed to reform convicts;[2] neighboring states in the region and jurisdictions in the northern Midwest soon followed suit. Southern and western states were generally slower to come to this innovation, in some cases trailing the trendsetters by 80 or more years. The form that life took inside the nascent penitentiaries also differed dramatically, depending on region. Southern penitentiaries, particularly after the Civil War, were often brutal places that in many ways served as a proxy for slavery by instituting horrendously exploitative convict leasing programs and offering no pretense of rehabilitation (Lichtenstein, 1996). Indeed, the institutional development of most southern states has been integrally shaped by race relations born from the region's history with slavery, rather than by northern progressive ideals (Lichtenstein, 2006). In many states in the West, including Montana, Nevada, and Arizona, penal institutions were generally run by inexperienced political appointees who had no predilections toward administering rehabilitation programs and who also often resorted to exploiting prison labor for personal or state gain (Edgerton, 2004; Johnson, 1997; Knepper, 1990).[3]

The widespread use of specialized "reform" or "refuge" schools for juveniles followed closely on the heels of the penitentiary movement; like the penitentiaries that preceded them, they originated in the Northeast. The first such institution was built in New York, and the trend spread out from there. In 1899, about 50 years after the emergence of reform schools, the first juvenile court was established in Chicago, transforming the adjudication process for "delinquent" youths. Although all the states eventually adopted such courts, the pattern of adoption generally followed a regionally specific pattern. So although most states had adopted a juvenile court by 1925, Arizona did not establish one until 1940 (Arizona Department of Juvenile Corrections). Florida was even later, establishing its first dedicated juvenile court in 1951 (White, Frazier, and Lanza-Kaduce, 1999).

The practice of parole supervision was also first initiated in the Northeast, beginning in Massachusetts and spreading through that region to the Midwest and eventually to all states (Simon, 1993). Likewise, probation was first enacted as an official criminal justice policy in Massachusetts in the mid-nineteenth century, and it spread as a policy to other states in a similar pattern. Indeterminate sentencing and discretionary parole release boards came somewhat later, originating in New York at the beginning of the twentieth century (Petersilia, 2003) and moving to other states from there.

The decline of the penal welfarist practices has followed a less regionally predictable pattern; however, the new punitive innovations that have supplemented or supplanted them appear to have first emerged generally in states that fall within the southern and western rim of the nation. For instance, the "three-strikes" sentencing policies that proliferated during the 1990s began in the West, with the first such statute being enacted in Washington State in 1993, followed the next year by California. By 2004, 23 states had such laws, but the real story with these laws has been in how they are being enforced within different jurisdictions. Most of the three-strikes states have used the law in just a handful of cases; by 2002, only three states—Florida, Georgia, and California—had incarcerated more than 400 felons under such statutes. California's use has far exceeded all others, in that more than 42,000 offenders were incarcerated under the three-strikes law during the first eight years (Schiraldi, Colburn, and Lotke, 2004).

More generally, although determinate sentencing statutes began to be passed into law in various areas of the country during the late 1970s, generally replacing indeterminate sentencing schemes that were based on a rehabilitative ideal, the size of the punitive hammer built into the new statutes varied significantly. As described in Chapter 3, Arizona's 1978 full-fledged determinate sentencing statute increased felony sentences across the board, and the legislature continued to increase sentences within that sentencing structure during subsequent years, especially through the adoption of harsh mandatory minimum and "prior" enhancement schemes. California's 1977 determinate sentencing law, which, like Arizona's, explicitly eschewed a commitment to rehabilitation, did not in its first incarnation result in huge increases in actual sentence lengths; but within a decade of its introduction, the legislature had ratcheted up statutory sentences such that California had moved from having an incarceration rate below the national average to one that was significantly above it (U.S. Department of Commerce, 1980, 2001; see Zimring and Hawkins, 1991, for further discussion).

In contrast to Arizona's and California's implementation of determinate sentencing, Minnesota's adoption of determinate sentencing guidelines in 1980 resulted first in lowering imprisonment rates and then in maintaining relatively low rates of imprisonment. Indeed, Minnesota continues to have one of the lowest incarceration rates in the nation, even though it has one of the most rigid determinate sentencing schemes. Thus, it is the *way* that the contemporary sentencing reforms—determinate sentencing, mandatory minimums, truth in sentencing, and three-strikes laws—have been implemented, rather than just the *nature* of the reforms that has followed a regionally determined pattern. Specifically, states in the South and Southwest have been much more likely to use such reforms to dramatically increase sentence lengths since the late 1970s than have states in the northern regions of the country.

The (re)adoption of corporal and other harsh corollary punishments in recent decades has also followed a regional pattern. Alabama and Arizona, nearly simultaneously, were the first states to institute modern-day chain gangs; Florida, Iowa, and several other states then followed suit by passing legislation authorizing chain gangs. Contemporary "chemical castration" for sex offenders originated in California, as did sex offender registries (decades before other states followed suit). The modern era of executions is also characterized by a movement from the Sunbelt South to the Southwest, with Florida being the first state (in 1979) to execute a condemned inmate against his will in the post-*Furman* era. Texas, followed by Virginia, leads the retentionist states in the total number of contemporary executions. Abolitionist states (by policy or by practice) are generally concentrated in the Northeast and northern Midwest.[4] Within institutions, the 1990s "no-frills" prison movement (Johnson, Bennett, and Flanagan, 1997), which stripped prisons of basic amenities and often imposed intricate rules on inmates, first emerged in Sunbelt states such as Texas and Arizona, then spread to other states in the region and eventually dispersed to states such as Wisconsin and Ohio. And, as detailed in Chapter 4, the new version of the state-level supermax was born in the Sunbelt, in Arizona, and its most concentrated use has been in the West (King, 1999).[5]

Finally, the contemporary commodified prison—as embodied by the development of private prisons—is still predominantly a southern and western phenomenon, where states have been willing both to allow private companies to build facilities within their jurisdictions and to utilize bed space in private prisons to supplement state penal capacity. At a more micro-level, the trend of charging inmates for things such as medical treatment and electricity also was born in the Sunbelt West. For instance, Nevada was the first state, in 1981, to implement a copayment for medical services within its prison system, followed by Colorado (in 1989) and then Arizona and California (both in 1994). By the beginning of 1996, eight more states had joined the trend, and 26 states either had approved legislation or had legislation in the works to charge inmates for medical care (Gipson and Pierce, 1996).[6]

INSIGHTS FROM ARIZONA

The Arizona case presented here, then, can be seen as an exemplary case of ground-level, late twentieth-century penal change emanating from the Sunbelt. Although the state's political and sociological developments are more representative of those within the southwestern region over the past 50 years (rather than of the entire southern U.S. rim), Arizona's penal narrative reveals how the "new punitive" movement did indeed emerge in opposition to an established penal hegemony that primarily had originated in the Northeast. This opposition was not merely a matter of intrastate or regional friction over the reigning mid-twentieth-century model that emphasized rehabilitation and reintegration of offenders. Rather, Arizona, like many of its southern and western peers (excluding California), had never fully embraced the penal welfare philosophy within its criminal justice system, and the introduction of the philosophy to the jurisdiction during the late 1960s was in many ways doomed by its timing and lack of roots within the state. Furthermore, Arizona had held a more deeply rooted commitment to penal harshness and a philosophy of less eligibility, which then influenced both the legislative process as sentencing reforms were proposed and ratified, and the intrainstitutional policies that shaped prisoners' daily lives, as state actors struggled with the penal crises of the 1970s and 1980s.

The Arizona case also illustrates the interlinked nature of mass incarceration coupled with the qualitative changes that are emblematic of postrehabilitative penality. The catalysts for Arizona's penal expansion, and for its return to "discipline" and punishment as institutional operating philosophies, are both cultural and structural in nature and are not independent of each other. First, and probably most important in influence over most aspects of governance in Arizona, including criminal justice matters, is the deeply rooted political ethos that prioritizes fiscal tightfistedness above most other concerns. This clearly influenced both the long period during which there was little correctional bureaucracy and very limited penal expansion as well as the particular shape that the system's expansion took from the 1970s onward.

As illustrated throughout this book, cost considerations explicitly took precedence in Arizona's criminal justice policymaking, and the commitment to frugality spilled over as an expressive value to administrative operations. So even when *actual* spending was profligate (for example, during the Lewis-Symington "war" on federal courts), such expenditures were sold politically to the populace as both necessary and cost-efficient. Fiscal concerns did not go away in political or media-generated rhetoric in the face of exploding costs associated with penal expansion; rather, they were generally reframed, sometimes in perverse ways, so that investment in building prisons rather than developing alternatives was held up as the fiscally prudent route to take. This partly explains how that important political value was, in reality, so surprisingly and dramatically violated once the investment in system expansion began in earnest.[7]

This value has also been coupled with the state's traditional commitment to punitiveness, creating a singular theme that has driven penal policy during much of the state's history: that it should be cheap and mean. This can be credited for the inmate labor policies that have been instituted (particularly the mandated reliance on inmate labor for construction projects), as well as the meager investments made in inmate programming throughout the state's history; it also provided the underlying rationale for many of the Lewis-Stewart litigated policy reforms, from the banning of holiday packages to the removal of law libraries in the system.

Second, Arizona's historical relationship with the federal government seems to have helped develop a state identity that values its independence, resists outside intervention, and is willing to fight back and rebel when such intervention intrudes on state business. Thus, in a number of battles, as soon as state actors, or the media, framed the underlying issue as a matter of insiders versus outside "meddlers," the fight was nearly won. This is precisely how the "expert" early directors who had been hired from other state systems often lost their legitimacy, and therefore their ability to function in their jobs, and this is how Lewis and Symington were able to garner the resources to wage war on prisoners' rights.

Arizona appeared to have used prison disproportionately as a mechanism of social control against minorities throughout this period of study. In this traditionally punitive state, African American prisoners were consistently overrepresented among prisoners at ratios that were actually higher in the 1950s and 1960s, relative to the overall incarceration rate, than they were in the 1980s and 1990s—the reverse of the national trend (see the appendix and Table 1 in Chapter 1). In other words, the kind of dramatic relative increase in the African American prison population that coincided with the advent of mass incarceration did not happen in Arizona, as it appears to have happened at the national level. Rather, relative to other racial groups, African Americans were especially overrepresented in this system during the years of low incarceration.

Arizona also has traditionally punished Latinos at rates disproportionate to their representation in the general population. It appears that in this state, Latinos have been increasingly subject to imprisonment over time, in that their relative share of the prison population has increased significantly since the late 1980s.[8] This suggests that perhaps in places with long-standing commitments to punitive social control rather than to a correctionalist approach, stark patterns of minority overrepresentation in prison may be the norm for a much longer period. Certainly, many southern prisons, which were notorious for the overrepresentation of African Americans among the convict population for much of the late nineteenth and twentieth centuries as the penal system became something of a functional substitute for slavery (Lichtenstein, 1996), bucked the demographic patterns that were seen in most northern states.

Nonetheless, the general features of penal change in Arizona map fairly well onto the trends happening elsewhere. In other words, this state did not defy the national trends; rather, it both initiated and exaggerated them. The pendulum swung dramatically here once the rehabilitative experiment was abandoned, partly because there was not much historical precedent pushing against it. Ultimately, because the system in Arizona did not have deep roots in the more progressive ideals that shaped older penal systems, particularly in the Northeast and Midwest, change could and did occur rapidly and profoundly, making the transformative processes that much more visible. More importantly, the Arizona case demonstrates how the referent jurisdictions that were looked to for replication shifted from modern rehabilitationist locales, like California and Rhode Island (which was the case for just a brief period during the first 10 to 15 years of the Arizona Department of Corrections), to Sunbelt "peers" that were instituting punitive policies during the late twentieth century. Thus, for example, Governor Wesley Bolin held up Texas as a model system worth emulating during the late 1970s, and Sam Lewis looked to Georgia for inspiration to bring the boot camp concept to the state.

Even more, though, Arizona's political leaders largely created their new punitive system by eschewing outside influences and looking explicitly to their own historical values and practices to inspire penal reform in the state. This ethic was articulated by some political actors (particularly the old-style conservative Democrats) throughout the period under study, but it became a dominant principle of the reform efforts by the mid-1980s, beginning with the appointment of Sam Lewis as chief deputy director, then director, of the Arizona Department of Corrections. Thus, Arizona became a penal leader in its own right by trailblazing a number of postrehabilitative innovations.

Furthermore, *Lewis v. Casey* (1996), which was the crown jewel of the proactive assault on federal intervention that Lewis and Symington launched, has had major ramifications for prisoners' access to the courts in states across the nation. Even more significantly, the legal battles in Arizona helped catalyze the creation and introduction of the federal Prison Litigation Reform Act, which has severely restricted all state prisoners' access to the federal courts and has rolled back previously earned protections by mandating the termination of existing consent decrees under many circumstances. Both Director Lewis and Governor Symington had a hand in conceiving of this federal legislation and suggesting it to Senator John Kyl, who ultimately introduced it, with Bob Dole, in the U.S. Senate. Lewis, Symington, and Attorney General Grant Woods especially pushed for the provisions to restrict the ability of prisoners to sue, to limit the independent ability of federal courts to appoint special masters, and to undermine consent decrees as remedial devices for maintaining agreed-upon conditions.

Not only did Arizona contribute to the national scene in terms of shaping postrehabilitative penal practices; it also has been a player in the global exportation of contemporary U.S.-style punishment. After resigning from the position of director at the Arizona Department of Corrections, Terry Stewart was appointed by then–attorney general John Ashcroft to be one of four corrections advisors for the first International Criminal Investigative Training Assistance Program (ICITAP) in Iraq. In May 2003 he helped set up the Abu Ghraib prison in Iraq and provided training for local corrections officers, along with three other U.S. corrections administrators, all of whom had questionable records in terms of abuses and violations within their respective systems.[9] He was followed in Iraq by his Department of Corrections successor and protégé, Charles Ryan, who was selected to be a member of the second team of corrections consultants to go to Abu Ghraib in the fall of 2003. Their selection by the attorney general to play such integral roles in the George W. Bush administration's imperialistic penal endeavors is a testament to the new hegemony of their brand of "corrections."[10]

Ultimately, though, the Arizona case illustrates the way in which the penal transformations of the past several decades are, in some sense, deeply tied to locale and to history. The histories and locales that are especially important, however, are not the same ones that stand at the center of the preceding penal revolution. Indeed, it becomes clear that penal welfarism (or more specifically, the rehabilitative ideal) was much less hegemonic and much more variegated and regionally specific than has been assumed by many accounts of its rise and fall. Furthermore, this case study provides support for the theory that the newly dominant forms of penal ideals and practices have emerged from locales that were less entrenched in rehabilitation, and where, more broadly, those factors that gave rise to the larger movement of the New Right exist.

I have detailed in particular the historical-cultural predicates to post-rehabilitative penal developments, but equally important (though less fully addressed here) is the effect of massive demographic and economic transformation, which has been a concurrent feature of Arizona's development beginning in the 1950s. As Gilmore (2007) has so well documented in her work on California's prison boom, substantial shifts in the state's political economy created surpluses in labor, land, and capital that converged around the prison as a "solution" to the myriad surplus problems. In Arizona, the postwar transformation of the economy from one primarily rooted in agricultural and mineral extraction industries to one primarily based in a service economy (with a good share of technology manufacturing) undoubtedly contributed to the same kind of surpluses that gave rise to California's prison expansion. As in California, it was often towns in the economically depressed rural regions of Arizona that vied for new prisons during the expansion years to jump-start their economies (see Lynch, 2009). It is likely that these processes particularly contributed to the quantitative side of the penal transformation, in that they created the space within economic structures for the rise of the prison as a fiscal panacea (Gilmore, 2007; King, Mauer, and Huling, 2004).

Furthermore, the social, cultural, and economic upheavals that accompany the kind of population growth that states such as Arizona, California, Nevada, Texas, and Florida underwent after World War II undoubtedly have also shaped statewide politics and political structures, local community dynamics, and the stability and sense of "rootedness" of the citizenry. Transient populations are less likely to invest time and energy in local political issues, allowing for a process of governance that is less engaged with the citizenry and potentially less pragmatic. In states like Arizona, which have a decentralized political structure designed to limit state power, a lack of citizen participation is often associated with a populist form of governance that primarily engages extremists among the public. This model of governance, according to Barker (2006), creates a law-making context that encourages conflict rather than compromise and deepens antipathy and disengagement among the public. Indeed, Barker has argued that just this type of governance has contributed to California's rapidly rising incarceration rates since the late 1960s.

As described in Chapters 3 and 4, this increasingly became the pattern in Arizona. Pragmatism diminished in relation to legislating criminal justice policy, and symbolic politics became the norm, as elected state officials used tough-on-crime stances to bolster their political careers and, through the use of the initiative process, to legislate punitive policies.[11] This was not catalyzed by the citizenry in a from-the-ground-up process, but ultimately the public's role in governance was essential to furthering it. The lack of citizen engagement meant that there was very little organized grassroots community pressure to keep legislators in check, in terms of their representations of what issues were important. Limited civic engagement with the political process also meant that state leaders were not second-guessed by an informed tax-paying public about whether their fiscal investment decisions were wise or whether their proposed policies were truly the most effective ones for a given problem.

Furthermore, by voting for candidates and initiatives on the basis of simplistic tough-on-crime rhetoric (among other simplified messages), the public let the political arena set the agenda for what was important in terms of governance and what kinds of policy actions were necessary. Thus, as Beckett (1997) has demonstrated at the national level, it appears that much of the politics responsible for the punitive escalation in Arizona resulted from a top-down process, initiated by political actors, amplified by the local media, and accepted by the voters of the state. Even the victims' rights "movement" within the state, which one would expect to be primarily the product of grassroots organizing, appears to have been significantly propelled by the state attorney general's office. The most notable community organizing around crime and punishment issues, at least during the period under study, concerned preventing prison facilities from being built in the Phoenix metropolitan area.

There were also several key moments in Arizona where it appeared that anxiety over rapid social and demographic change in the state shaped political and institutional responses. During the 1970s, the framing of the problem population as composed of a "new" kind of undisciplined, drug-addled miscreant was one such moment; 20 years later, the state's aggressive stance on immigrant prisoners was likely tied to the larger brewing "panic" about immigrants that was taking hold in several southwestern states, including Arizona. More broadly, much of the move to return to "discipline" and order within the penal system, begun by conservative legislators in reaction to the penal crises of the 1970s and culminating in Lewis's appointment, tapped into a larger cultural narrative about the disintegration of traditional values and lack of respect for authority that was current in society at large.

Indeed, if we use Swidler's (1986) dynamic conceptualization of how culture shapes action as a framework for tracing penal changes in Arizona, it becomes clear that state actors (occasionally spurred on by local news media) pulled certain cultural norms out of the toolkit at times of upheaval and disorder as a way of providing a decisive ideological solution to the crisis at hand. The period of ideological expansion and experimentation, beginning in the late 1950s with the first attempts by Republicans to modernize the state's penal system and culminating in the establishment of the Department of Corrections a decade later, emerged in a relatively stable social, economic, and political context. During this period, although certain long-standing values continued to have political currency—particularly the value of fiscal conservatism—the past was viewed as something to evolve from, rather than as a place to return to. But by the 1970s, when state actors came to perceive that crisis and chaos were rampant both within criminal justice institutions and more generally in society, the retreat to the past was forthcoming.

This conscious revisiting of old cultural tropes about punishment was, in a sense, a form of "willful nostalgia" (Robertson, 1990).[12] The constructions of the past—of the days when Warden Eyman could literally weld prisoners into their cells to assert state authority and when Superintendent Vukcevich could simply apply some corporal punishment to discipline and reform young wards—seemed to deliberately deny the new challenges faced by the state (and the larger world) while simultaneously pretending that no such challenges existed during those earlier periods. So once the "old" was reinvented during the 1980s, it neither recognized the problems and failures of those earlier practices nor realistically adapted them for a changed legal and political environment in which they would now be used. As a result, the "new-old" regime introduced by Sam Lewis, as described in Chapters 4 and 5, was at once a caricature of the past and something of a revolutionary new way of doing punishment.

In many ways, I seem to be making the case for path dependency in explaining these transformations, in that I stress the importance of certain historical antecedents to the penal change of the past 30 years. Yet it is clear that there is more going on than just historical precedent. First, as discussed in the introduction, and as Zimring and Hawkins (1991) noted early on about the prison boom, despite their differences, all 50 states went through massive incarceration growth over a similar period of time, a phenomenon that would have been very hard to predict even 5 or 10 years before it started. Second, although I have raised the possibility that relative degrees of change among the states are indeed tied to specific subnational histories, cultures, and political structures, it is also clear that even those locales with deep historical commitment to the ideals of penal welfarism have rejected elements of their past and have adopted many of the new punitive ideals that have emerged primarily from the Sunbelt South and West. Furthermore, some of our postrehabilitative penal trends have crossed borders and been adopted (albeit reshaped by local influences) in jurisdictions around the world.

Thus, local history and norms play significant roles in shaping the specificities of change, but there is a porous quality to change, in that trends, innovations, and policies transfer across jurisdictions through a number of means. Indeed, in the case of Arizona, it is clear that directly imported expertise from other jurisdictions played a major role in shaping the first 15 years of the Department of Corrections. Less directly, over the period of the study there was a process of policy and ideology transfer in and out of the state via several routes: nationally based professional organizations that held conferences and trainings for correctional administrators; communication with political peers in other states (Governor Williams in particular looked to California's Governor Ronald Reagan for advice on several penological issues); site visits to other states' facilities and vice versa (which is how California came to build the Pelican Bay supermax facility); and lessons learned through media coverage of larger penal issues across the national landscape (many Arizona governors kept clippings from the national press about penal problems and often communicated with the corrections director about the implications of such problems for the state).

Indeed, we can apply a lesson from Friedman and Percival's (1976) now classic historical comparative study "A Tale of Two Courts," which ponders why two very different courts in 1890—one small and rural and the other urban and complex—grew to operate so similarly over time. As the authors point out, by the end of their period of study, in 1970, the cultural isolation of the rural county had disappeared with the modernization of transportation and mass communications, and the local micro-culture had largely given way to a broader mass urban culture. Thus, it should not surprise us that transfers of norms, innovations, and policies and practices in law, courts, and punishment are an increasingly integrated global process as the geographic distinctions and sovereign boundaries among local jurisdictions dissipate. Of course, the reasons that such innovation transfers "take," or not, are likely products of larger structural forces that open up an opportunity for change in a given locale.

EPILOGUE
Smart on Crime?

IN THE AFTERMATH OF THE ELECTION of Governor Janet Napolitano in November 2002, the director of the Arizona Department of Corrections, Terry
Stewart, resigned his post, which effectively ended almost two decades of departmental stability built around an ethos of harsh, bare-bones custodial control. Stewart's protégé, interim director Charles Ryan, kept the Lewis-Stewart
penal operating philosophy largely intact over the next six months, but that
came to an end when Governor Napolitano named Dora Schriro the new permanent department director in June 2003.[1]

Schriro was widely known in the corrections world as an experienced and
highly educated correctional leader; she holds a doctorate in education, a J.D.,
and a master's degree in psychology. At the time of her appointment, she had
25 years of experience in corrections, including a previous appointment as director of the Missouri Department of Corrections. In a statement to the press
that was somewhat reminiscent of the sentiments accompanying the appointment of Arizona's first director 35 years earlier, Napolitano lauded Schriro as
"one of America's leading minds on modern, effective prison management"
who would be "fresh and innovative" in fixing corrections in the state (Davenport, 2003).

Schriro brought her own brand of reform to Arizona's prison system: a
program she had developed called "the Parallel Universe." The Parallel Universe is essentially built on the concept that prisoners should live life while in
custody in ways that are similar to life outside of prison; thus, the program's
goal is that all inmates work or go to school, make their own financial decisions, and exert more control over their daily lives in order to be prepared

for release. Although Schriro implemented the program in just some of the minimum-security institutions, the thinking behind it represented a major departure from the previous operating philosophy. She also brought a program of restorative justice to the Arizona institutions and created a division of "victims' services" within her administration. Schriro's tenure was jeopardized before she was even confirmed as a result of a January 2004 hostage-taking at the Lewis prison complex—the 15-day standoff is said to be the longest in U.S. prison history—but she subsequently received enough support from the governor's office and the legislature to implement a number of institutional reforms designed to help rehabilitate inmates.

In appointing Schriro, Governor Napolitano was clearly signaling a commitment to move away from the punitive kinds of policies that had dominated over the prior two decades. She specifically voiced support for considering alternatives to incarceration and further investing in reentry programs, rather than the status quo policy of simply locking up offenders, a sentiment that seemed to indicate a political will to reverse the tide of institutional expansion.

Nonetheless, Arizona's prison population continued to grow under Napolitano's governorship and Schriro's directorship, with the incarceration rate reaching 546 per 100,000 citizens by mid-year 2007 (Sabol and Couture, 2008). More than 37,000 inmates were in custody in Arizona by that point, which was 3.3 percent more than were held just six months earlier, while the national average for state prison growth over the same period was 1.4 percent (Sabol and Couture, 2008). The state facilities have maintained populations that are significantly higher than capacity, and the department now sends about 5,000 inmates to private prisons within the state, as well as to ones in Oklahoma and Indiana (Arizona Department of Corrections, website, ADC Prisons). Furthermore, Napolitano's early commitment to "alternatives" to incarceration seemed to vanish almost as soon as it was made.

This was made clear by the political reaction to a perfect storm of crises in the state budget and prison space that occurred during her first year in office and were reminiscent of the 1983 crises during Governor Babbitt's tenure 20 years earlier. The state's fiscal problems hit county-level budgets hard, resulting in cuts to local correctional programs, which in turn pushed courts to send offenders to state facilities at a relatively higher rate than usual. In the case of Maricopa County, which consistently refers more than 50 percent of the state's inmate population to the department, half of the probation staff was cut, so a huge number of offenders who normally would have been in the community on probation were sent to prison. Thus, the department ended up receiving an incoming flow of inmates that was more than double what the state had projected (260 new prisoners net per month instead of the projected 105). The result was an unprecedented overcrowding crisis in the prisons, exacerbated by the defunding of a planned new institution, which was to be built to handle the expected population growth.

Governor Napolitano called for a special session with the legislature in October 2003 to deal with the shortage of prison beds. She preceded the session by issuing a press release that outlined her vision for the resolution. First, she indicated that sentencing reform was not a possibility: "Before talking about the solutions I will propose to the Legislature, I want to make it clear that I do not support changing sentencing guidelines. As a former prosecutor, I believe in our truth-in-sentencing laws and do not support adjustments to them. If you do the crime, you must still do the time, regardless of how crowded our prisons are" (Napolitano, 2003: 1). She then laid out her long- and short-term plans, which primarily involved building more prison beds, the very option that she had advised against just three months earlier. She requested $26.4 million to immediately construct or lease approximately 2,100 temporary beds and to hire additional correctional officers to manage the growing population, and she proposed that $470 million (financed over 15 years) be committed to partially cover the cost to build more than 9,000 beds over the next five years.

The legislature, with a Republican majority, came up with its own set of potential resolutions—a variety of dramatic, often contradictory alternative cost-cutting proposals to close the budget/bed shortfall gap, ranging from a proposed bill to privatize the entire system (except for the death row, super-max, and minimum-security facilities) to proposals that would rely on broad decarceration. A proposal was even made to sell the state's entire collection of prison facilities and other real assets of the department to a private business and then lease them back in order to raise funds to expand prison capacity.

One of the more viable and sensible alternatives emerged from a subcommittee of six Republican and three Democratic House members, the Alternatives to Sentencing Work Group, which had been working for months on a set of proposals to shorten sentence lengths for nonviolent offenders, modify the criminal code by changing the lowest level felonies into misdemeanors, and divert drunk drivers and low-level drug offenders from prison. Republican

Bill Konopnicki headed the group and was ardently committed to reducing the state's overreliance on prisons. He articulated the group's goal as more than a matter of just saving money and managing the fiscal emergency, but also as aiming to help with recidivism by giving offenders "some hope" for the future through the use of less punitive and more constructive alternatives to prison (Marson, 2003). Despite the thought and time that the group had put into developing the recommendations, the special session was dominated by fights over the competing capacity expansion plans, and in particular, the role that private prisons would play. Napolitano pushed hard for more state beds over the short and long term, and several legislators countered with demands that the growth be dominated by the private prison industry.[2] In the end, the Konopnicki working group's proposal went nowhere, and the report it issued a year after it started its work had no effect. Instead, the compromise that emerged from the special session was for a short-term plan to expand the department's bed capacity by 2,000, half of which would be in in-state and out-of-state private prisons. Forty-two million dollars was thus allocated above operating costs to add those beds in 2004; the bulk of that cost was to be covered by tripling the fine for drunk driving offenses.

The only real reform that came out of the 2003 crises was a piece of legislation sponsored by two Republican state senators that offered imprisoned drug offenders job and vocational training in prison and the shortening of their sentences by 30 days if they completed the training. The projection was that the state would net $6 million annually with the plan and the participating inmates might also be less likely to reoffend because of the training opportunity. The legislation passed into law and was made policy in 2004.

The state's criminal justice system was pointedly criticized in Judith Greene and Kevin Pranis's report *Arizona Prison Crisis* (2004). The report documented in detail what most legislators, criminal justice practitioners, and other state actors already knew, but which no branch, including the governor's office, was willing to change: that the 1978 and 1993 alterations to the criminal code, especially the vast and punitive system of mandatory sentence enhancements that the code authorizes, are at the heart of the state's high incarceration rates.[3] The authors directly challenged Governor Napolitano's 2003 proposal that advocated spending $700 million on new prison facilities, saying that it might be "tough, but not necessarily smart, on crime" (Greene and Pranis, 2004: 47). By that time, Arizonans were already spending nearly three times the amount per capita on corrections, after adjusting for inflation, than they had spent in

1978. Like the report of the Alternatives to Sentencing Work Group, though, this report generated a headline or two in the local press but prompted no new smart-on-crime policymaking along the lines recommended.

By 2007, another $205 million had been committed to building a new state institution to house 3,060 inmates; ground was broken on the new facility that fall. And as would be expected with the continued expansion of the penal population, the department also grew considerably larger, appropriations-wise, under Napolitano's executive leadership. In fiscal year 2002, the department's allocation of the state budget for general operating costs (not including any construction) was $553.7 million; in fiscal year 2007, it was 55 percent larger, at $860.8 million. By year-end 2008, Arizona was fourth in the nation in proportion of the state budget spent on corrections (Rotstein, 2009). Thus, it appears that a commitment to a prison strategy once again won out after a period of fiscal crisis, when there was real potential to take a different path. Such a choice is still rooted in partisan politics within the state, although in this round, it appears that the Democratic executive branch was on the side of prison expansion whereas at least a subset of Republican legislators led the effort to try to revisit alternatives to reduce the state's overreliance on incarceration.

Perhaps this shifting of sides is a good sign. It appears that many of the current cycle of state-level reforms across the country that have emerged from the collision between fiscal feasibility and continued prison expansion are products of either bipartisan or Republican efforts. As we saw in national and state-level electoral politics of the 1980s and 1990s, Democrats were particularly vulnerable to charges of being soft on crime, and many responded by an overzealous commitment to law and order. Because Republicans have been less likely to be derailed by such accusations and are more likely to be labeled as fiscally conservative, their criticisms of prison expansion may be perceived as more legitimate than those of Democrats.

As Judith Greene (2003) has pointed out, there are numerous good examples of such change occurring. Since 2000, both Michigan and Ohio achieved major reforms in sentencing and parole policies that reduced their state's prison populations under Republican gubernatorial leadership. Several other states have achieved more modest reforms that have slowed or nearly halted prison growth during the early years of this decade. Indeed, the national rate of prison growth within state institutions slowed to a crawl between 2000 and 2005, with an overall growth rate of just 1.5 percent.[4] More recently, at the national level, Democratic senator Jim Webb, from Virginia, has become a vocal advocate for state and national prison reform, linking the high U.S. incarceration rate to the failures of the war on drugs. He introduced federal legislation in spring 2009 to create a commission charged with developing recommendations for structural reform of the criminal justice system. As the fiscal and human costs of the crime and punishment policies of the 1980s and 1990s become more obviously unsustainable, especially during a period of global economic meltdown (which is the case at the time of this writing), we might expect a continued return to a more pragmatic style of criminal justice policymaking, particularly as it affects lower level, nonviolent offenders.

In Arizona, Janet Napolitano may have felt the need to voice her tough-on-crime credentials early in her first term as a Democratic governor operating in a state with a Republican majority, but with Republican legislators still leading efforts to reduce state reliance on incarceration, such reform may now be politically acceptable. Yet the prospects for substantial reform within the prisons, and in terms of sentencing policy, are still quite uncertain in Arizona. Napolitano left the governor's office in the middle of her second term to join President Barack Obama's cabinet as secretary of homeland security and was replaced by the Republican secretary of state, Jan Brewer. Departing with her was Dora Schriro, who was appointed special advisor on immigration and customs enforcement (ICE) and detention and removal by Napolitano. Governor Brewer immediately named prior interim director Charles Ryan as the new interim director. Consequently, even the ideal of the Parallel Universe in Arizona's prisons has now been abandoned, and the potential for another return to the past is alive.

While it remains to be seen whether the partisan congruence of the executive branch and the legislative majority means even more and meaner prisons, there is at least one indication that Arizona is trying to get smarter on crime to reduce its dependence on incarceration. In 2008, the legislature passed a bill, with bipartisan support, that was designed to give incentives to counties to keep probation violators from being sent to prison. Governor Napolitano signed the bill into law, which went into effect in January 2009. The legislation authorizes the state to pay counties the calculated prison cost savings for their achieved reductions in new offenses or technical violations by probationers, and those funds are then to be reinvested into the county's community supervision, victim services, and drug treatment programs. It also offers an incentive to probationers, in that their supervision periods are shortened by 20 days if they remain violation free. Since about 4,000 felons are sent to prison on probation revocations each year, the law has the potential to make a notable dent in the overall correctional population.

The scheme addresses one of the major structural problems unique to criminal justice in the United States that contributes to our skyrocketing incarceration rates. As Zimring and Hawkins (1991) noted, those jurisdictions that send the vast majority of offenders to state prisons—counties—have no fiscal responsibility for those decisions. Indeed, there is a financial incentive *to* send offenders to prison when finances are tight, since counties have funding responsibility for their local jails, probation departments, and other community corrections options. Although this law does not make Arizona's counties financially liable for overuse of prison sentences even though there is wide variance between counties in the relative use of incarceration (Greene and Pranis, 2004), it opens the door for such a practice. It also indicates a political willingness to move toward meaningful reform that can begin to roll back the excesses of the past three decades.

REFERENCE MATTER

APPENDIX

Incarcerated population in Arizona, 1958–2003

Year	Adult prison population[1]	Incarceration rate (per 100,000)[2]	% White[3]	% African American	% Latino	% American Indian
1958	1,392	117	56	20	20	3
1959	1,493	118	57	22	18	3
1960	1,516	115	55	21	19	4
1961	1,592	113	59*	16*	21*	4*
1962	1,679	115	58	19	20	3
1963	1,728	114	57	18	21	3
1964	1,627	105	58	18	22	3
1965	1,694	108	56	20	21	3
1966	1,627	101	55	22	22	2
1967	1,596	97	—	—	—	—
1968	1,653***	99	55	23	20	2
1969	1,765***	104	55	22	20	2
1970	1,460	81	56	22	20	2
1971	1,401	75	56	24	18	2
1972	1,529	78	56*	21*	20*	3*
1973	1,693	81	56	22	19	3
1974	2,101	97	51**	21**	24**	4**
1975	2,647	120	—	—	—	—
1976	2,850	126	—	—	—	—
1977	2,982	130	—	—	—	—
1978	3,450	137	—	—	—	—
1979	3,478	139	49	20	26	3
1980	4,372	161	50	20	25	3
1981	5,199	184	—	—	—	—
1982	6,048	209	—	—	—	—
1983	6,693	223	55	18	23	3
1984	7,847	255	55	17	24	3
1985	8,518	256	53	16	24	4
1986	9,434	268	54	16	25	4

Year	Adult prison population[1]	Incarceration rate (per 100,000)[2]	% White[3]	% African American	% Latino	% American Indian
1987	10,948	307	52	16	27	4
1988	12,158	329	53	16	27	4
1989	13,251	358	53	16	27	3
1990	14,261	389	51	17	28	3
1991	15419	396	50	17	29	3
1992	16,477	409	49	17	30	3
1993	17,811	430	47	17	31	3
1994	19,746	459	47	17	31	3
1995	21,341	473	48	16	31	4
1996	22,573	481	47	16	32	4
1997	23484	484	47	15	33	4
1998	25,311	507	48	15	33	4
1999	25,986	495	46	15	33	5
2000	26,510	515	46	15	34	5
2001	27,710	492	45	15	34	5
2002	28,008	513	44	14	36	6
2003	29,722	525	45	14	35	5

[1] Year-end incarcerated population totals taken from *Statistical Abstract of the United States, 1958–94* (as reported by the Bureau of Justice Statistics, 1979–93), and from the Bureau of Justice Statistics, *Prisoners in 1994*, and for following years to 2003.

[2] Calculated using data from *Statistical Abstract of the United States, 1958–79*; incarceration rate figures from Bureau of Justice Statistics, 1980–2003.

[3] Population breakdowns by race from Arizona Department of Corrections annual reports (1972–2003) and Arizona State Prison annual and biannual reports (1958–71), unless otherwise noted.

* Derived from total admissions for fiscal year; year-end population figures are not available.

** From Arizona Advisory Committee to the U.S. Commission on Civil Rights (1974).

*** Midyear totals, taken from the Arizona State Prison annual reports, 1968 and 1969.

NOTES

Introduction

1. These figures do not include people incarcerated in local jails.

2. There are geographic, economic, and demographic characteristics that help define Sunbelt states: they are jurisdictions that experience a high percentage of sunshine annually, have experienced relatively high rates of postwar population in-migration, and have had high levels of federal capital outlay during the same period. Thus, these states are concentrated in the Southeast and Southwest but exclude several states in the Deep South that have not experienced population and economic growth.

3. These numbers were calculated for the following 11 Sunbelt states: Arizona, California, Colorado, Florida, Georgia, Nevada, New Mexico, North Carolina, South Carolina, Texas, and Virginia.

4. Arizona exemplifies this process in that it has been among the fastest-growing states in terms of general population since 1950, and it has concurrently been a front-runner nationally in terms of increases in incarceration rate.

5. This is not to say that the existing body of work on mass incarceration is not vital to our understanding of the contours of this phenomenon. A large body of excellent scholarship has documented its extent and its effect on those incarcerated and their families as well as its policy implications (for example, Braman, 2004; Currie, 1998; Mauer and Chesney-Lind, 2002; Tonry, 1995, 2004; Travis and Waul, 2004).

6. See also Chiricos and DeLone (1992), Western (2006), and Western and Beckett (1999) on the relationship between labor market surplus, race, and the use of incarceration.

7. The other side of this coin is a body of scholarship that illustrates the self-perpetuating quality of the imprisonment explosion, in that whole new, lucrative markets have emerged in the corrections field. This market expansion has been labeled by

some as the "corrections-commercial complex" (Lilly and Knepper, 1993: 150) or the "prison-industrial complex" (Davis, 1998–99; Schlosser, 1998).

Chapter 1

1. This is clearly an abbreviated and therefore somewhat simplistic overview of the state's political history. For a more nuanced and detailed account, see Berman (1998).

2. The cell bars and gallows equipment were turned over to the prison museum at Yuma in 1966 when the original Florence death row was demolished (Westerman, 1966).

3. The controversial youth facility, Fort Grant, was converted to an adult minimum-security prison in 1973, and in 1970 the state acquired Job Corps equipment and facilities from the federal government that the Department of Corrections moved and converted into a conservation camp (see Chapter 2).

4. The "big house" prison is the colloquial name for the early to mid-twentieth-century large, industrial prison that used work primarily as a means of maintaining order and discipline. See Bright (1996) for a nuanced case study of the development of one such institution in Michigan.

5. Eyman himself was a native of Illinois and started his law enforcement career as a railroad investigator in Joliet after serving in World War I. No evidence exists that he deliberately adopted the Ragen style of penal authority, but his approach had many similarities to Ragen's (Jacobs, 1977).

6. As much scholarship on southern penal systems suggests, regionally and historically specific cultural factors also have contributed to some idiosyncrasies in how southern prisons have transformed over the twentieth century, further complicating the assumption of the hegemony of the rehabilitative ideal (Lichtenstein, 1996; Myers, 1998; Taylor, 1999).

Chapter 2

1. Members of this same board had actually recommended to the 1967 legislative subcommittee that the age be extended to 21, but this was before they were aware that their board would no longer exist under the legislative plan being devised in that study.

2. Cook had also banned this long-standing practice of renting the boys out to ranchers for $1.00 to $2.00 a day, perhaps deeming it too much like a convict leasing system.

3. MacDougall took over as the Arizona Department of Corrections director in 1978 and was quite controversial and colorful in that position (see Chapter 3).

4. These qualifications appeared to directly describe MacDougall himself; he may have been angling at this point for the job he would eventually hold.

Chapter 3

1. This incident functioned symbolically in a manner similar to that in which the change of punishment policy and "runaway problem" at Fort Grant had functioned during Allen Cook's tenure. Neither was particularly meaningful in terms of harm caused, but both were lightning rods that drew critics to make their cases.

2. Determinate sentencing schemes, like the one enacted in Arizona, generally limit or remove judicial discretion in deciding upon defendants' sentences by explicitly specifying what the required sentence (sometimes with aggravated and mitigated terms) is for convictions of each penal code section.

3. The legislature had passed legislation in 1972 that was worded in such a way as to specifically prevent Fort Grant Superintendent Steve Vukcevich from being eligible for the position of department director (O'Brien, 1978).

4. For example, in one of these handbooks, the committee advises new residents that "equally important in the other Resident's point of view is your cooperation in telling the person in the shower that you are going to flush the toilet or the urinal. The water in the shower gets very hot when the toilets or urinals are flushed. This is not a disciplinary offense. This is usually one of the little things that gets us in a jam that we are all trying to avoid. If the man in the shower is having or has had a bad day . . . you may end up with a bar of soap bouncing off of your head" (Arizona Department of Corrections, 1981: i).

5. Infamous Maricopa County sheriff Joe Arpaio claims this as his own innovation when he erected old military tents in Phoenix in 1993 for local inmates, but both the state and Pinal County beat him to this "innovation" by a decade. He did, however, make the concept famous. See Chapter 5 for more details on Arpaio's rise and his relationship to the Department of Corrections, and Lynch, 2004, for more on Arpaio's penal innovations.

6. Wesley Bolin, who was in office for only about six months during 1977–78, was a Democrat but was not at all progressive.

7. It included directives on everything from health-care requirements and classification systems to access to mental health, substance abuse, educational, and recreational programs (see Chapter 6).

Chapter 4

1. There were two issues with regard to double-bunking. First, the older cell blocks at Florence were still under court order to maintain single occupancy so could not be converted to double cells. Second, by legislation, the Perryville facility was limited to a population cap of 1,400, which dated back to the compromise settlement with area residents, so it could add only a small percentage of beds before it would hit its limit.

2. Beyond that, as Craig Haney (2006) has eloquently described in his book *Reforming Punishment*, this process has resulted in the exacerbation of the racialization of punishment and has intensified the rates of failure for those subject to the "new" style of imprisonment.

3. The first figure is minus the juvenile services budget, as that division of the Department of Corrections became a separate state agency in 1991.

4. Governor Mecham was probably best known outside of Arizona for rescinding a newly enacted law that made Martin Luther King Jr.'s birthday a state holiday. He made this a campaign promise, which he made good on as his first act as governor in January 1987. On this issue, Lewis supported Mecham by withdrawing his invitation to allow tours of SMU I, the new supermax prison, for members of the American Correctional Association and canceling his welcome address to that group when they rescinded their invitation to Mecham to speak at their annual convention, which was taking place in Phoenix that year.

5. Privatization of adult custody actually did not occur for another two years because the 1987 legislation was declared unconstitutional after the public employees' union successfully challenged the law. It wasn't until Democratic governor Rose Mofford, who replaced Mecham after he was put out of office, was replaced by Republican Fife Symington that private prisons were reauthorized.

6. The analogous units under more rehabilitation-oriented systems, called "adjustment centers" or something similar, would be used for particularly troublesome individual inmates but would not be deemed a standard housing unit for a given "level" of population. The supermax is often used as a regular housing unit for inmates with the highest security classification in a system, so many sent there are stuck for huge portions of their sentences, unless they somehow are able to get reclassified at a lower security level.

7. I specifically asked about this in my interview with Sam Lewis, who was director at the time SMU I was built and put into service, and in my interview with Charles Goldsmith, who was warden of the Eyman Complex, of which the SMUs are a part. Neither man indicated that it was seen as anything special; the SMU was just the maximum-security facility that was a part of the large package funded in 1984.

8. The fact that Arizona was the industry leader in the supermax trend was raised in my interviews with current and former administrators, who often expressed resentment that Pelican Bay is more popularly identified (incorrectly) as the first of this breed of new supermax facilities.

Chapter 5

1. Symington was elected governor that year and became the second governor in less than a decade, following Mecham, to be forced out of office for bad behavior. Mecham had been convicted in a 1988 impeachment hearing (which should have dis-

qualified him from even running again under the state constitution). Symington was convicted of criminal charges in 1997, which by constitutional mandate meant he had to resign from office. His conviction was eventually overturned on appeal.

2. Twist remained involved in the movement after he returned to the private sector. As of 2009 he was president of the board of directors for the statewide victims' rights group Arizona Voice for Crime Victims.

3. This may be because of how cases actually are processed in the system, in that norms for dealing cases out are unlikely to change overnight. Furthermore, because this new code did nothing to rein in prosecutorial discretion or power (relative to judicial power), it was naïve to expect prosecutors to automatically and proportionately lower their "going rate" on charges just because maximum sentences were lowered slightly for some crimes in the code. Absent significant alterations in the power structure, or significant cutbacks of crimes that were eligible for prison, it is hard to imagine such subtle reform in a moment of law-and-order frenzy leading to shorter actual sentences for any crimes.

4. See the final chapter of the Greene and Pranis (2004) report, in which attorney Howard Wine provides a detailed 10-page overview of the statutes governing sentencing in the state.

5. Some of that strain was the product of Lewis's alignment with the governor. After a tentative start to their relationship—Lewis was actually planning to retire so as not to have to deal with a new governor when Symington took office—the two men became allied over the sentence reform issue, in large part because the proposal was a jointly developed product.

6. These three men are billionaires (through different means) who have actively supported drug law reform efforts, including Proposition 36 in California, around the country with financial and other forms of support.

7. This poor relationship turned much worse and became downright hostile under the tenure of the next director, Terry Stewart.

8. The idea reemerged as a bill in the Arizona legislature in 2005 but still could not overcome structural barriers to become a reality.

9. To "debrief" is to inform on other gang members to prison officials, by providing names and other information about gang activities. Thus, gang members who made it out of the SMU were assumed to be snitches and therefore faced the possibility of retaliation, sometimes deadly.

10. During the Lewis and Stewart eras, naming facilities and units became a relatively sentimental process. Whereas the names of prior facilities typically reflected pragmatics—prisons were named after their geographic locations (Arizona State Prison–Florence) and units were named for their order of construction (Cell Block 6 or CB-6 for the sixth housing unit built at Florence)—most of the new units built from the mid-1980s on were named after notable people in correctional history. Thus, the

complex that included the two supermax units was dubbed by Sam Lewis as Arizona State Prison Complex–Eyman, after Frank Eyman, even though it was located right up the road from the old Florence prison. Within Eyman, the Meadows unit was named after Eyman's long-time secretary, Della Meadows. A unit that housed sex offenders in that same complex was the Cook unit, named after the department's first director, Allen Cook (it is unclear whether that designation was meant as an honor or a slight). Within the Lewis complex, each housing unit was given the name of a fallen correctional officer, primarily those killed in the line of duty.

11. The funding formula and distribution of funds for elementary and secondary schools had to be revamped after 1994 when the Arizona Supreme Court declared the then-current system of allocating funds, especially for construction, unconstitutional.

Chapter 6

1. The opinion issued on October 25, 1996, was withdrawn and reissued in July 1997 after the inmates were granted their 1996 holiday packages in response to the motion filed on their behalf by their counsel. In both cases, the Ninth Circuit Court reversed Muecke on his denial of the modification of the package policy and remanded the case back to district court for modification.

2. Sam Lewis indicated to me that this incident with Grant Woods was a precipitating factor in his decision to retire, which came just two weeks after Woods argued the case in front of the Supreme Court.

3. Hamm's husband spent 18 years in custody at the prison in Florence for murder. Upon his release in 1992, he became an active partner in the group, and the two continue to be the primary staff of the organization, supplemented by volunteers.

4. The *Phoenix New Times*, an alternative weekly newspaper founded in 1970 by a group of Arizona State University students, has been a consistent and forthright critic of the Department of Corrections and the political actors who have been responsible for the sentencing changes that led to the imprisonment explosion. The paper has been an especially vociferous critic of Sheriff Joe Arpaio.

Chapter 7

1. This also includes the resurgence of capital punishment, although this book does not explicitly address this issue.

2. The transformation of the Walnut Street Jail in Philadelphia into the earliest penitentiary in the late 1700s is the more appropriate "birth" of the penitentiary movement, but the large-scale commitment to the ideals of the penitentiary is most significantly demonstrated by the new construction of major institutions such as the Eastern State Penitentiary in Pennsylvania and Auburn in New York.

3. Of course, life inside most prisons, regardless of locale, has always been characterized by some degree of brutality and violence (see Pisciotta, 1994). My point here

is that the ideals and rationales undergirding an institution's very existence appear to differ significantly as a function of local and regional histories, developmental trajectories, and political cultures.

4. See Zimring (2003) for more on the geographic correlates and historical "path dependence" of contemporary death penalty usage.

5. The conceptual prototype of the supermax is in many ways the United States Penitentiary, Marion, which was retrofitted in the early 1980s to be a maximum-high-security prison, with many of the harsh features and isolation conditions of newer supermaxes.

6. County jails in the United States have almost concurrently developed the same set of policies and typically charge for services that are more directly related to local jail operations, such as transportation and room and board for work release inmates.

7. Of course, most state lawmakers and institutional administrators are driven by budgetary concerns and indeed act in ways that are a direct result of budgetary issues; but in Arizona, as I have pointed out, being frugal, even cheap, in terms of government spending has long been a proud political norm.

8. This upswing coincided with a growing demonization of "illegal immigrants" in the state, both inside and outside the prison walls, as described in Chapter 5.

9. Concerns were raised by Senator Charles Schumer about the selection of the four corrections consultants after the abuses at Abu Ghraib became known to the public in 2004, prompting an inquiry by the U.S. Department of Justice Office of the Inspector General (U.S. Department of Justice, Office of the Inspector General, 2005).

10. Stewart was also appointed by the G. W. Bush administration's Department of State to be a corrections advisor in Haiti.

11. In this regard, Arizona seems to have been following the lead of California, even though the initiative process has been a long-valued component of the state's constitution. California had been passing major legislation by ballot initiative for most of the twentieth century, perhaps most famously in 1978 with the passage of the antitax initiative Proposition 13. Both states have enacted legislation by the initiative process pertaining to the death penalty, victims' rights, juvenile offenders, and sentencing. Both have also passed referenda that decriminalize or otherwise soften laws related to drug use, in keeping with a more libertarian spirit.

12. See also Jonathan Simon's (1995) excellent analysis of the 1980s prison boot-camp trend as a case of willful nostalgia.

Epilogue

1. Ryan applied for the permanent position, but it apparently became clear that he would not get the appointment so he withdrew from consideration.

2. Former director Terry Stewart partnered with his mentor, Sam Lewis, to consult for a company that develops implementation plans for prison privatization. They

worked with several Republican lawmakers in the state legislature during this period to promote the privatization model in Arizona and brought two proposals to the legislature—including one to purchase and run the whole system. They later lobbied hard on behalf of their company to build the largest women's prison in the world—designed to house 3,000 inmates—as a private prison in southern Arizona.

3. Some aspects of the enhancements are currently being challenged on the basis of the holding in *Apprendi v. New Jersey* (2000) that defendants are entitled to a jury for determining findings of fact that would increase the punishment for the offense.

4. The next year, the growth of the state-level incarceration rate was nearly double that, at 2.8 percent, which could indicate that we are heading back into a growth mode.

CASES CITED

Apprendi v. New Jersey, 530 U.S. 466, 2000.

Black v. Ricketts, CA No. 84-11 (D. Ariz.) (unpublished case file), 1984.

Bounds v. Smith, 430 U.S. 817, 1977.

Casey v. Lewis, 834 F. Supp. 1553, 1992.

Frost v. Symington, 197 F.3d 348, 1999.

Frost v. Symington, 31 Fed. Appx. 557, 2002.

Gluth v. Arizona, 84-1626 (D. Ariz.) (unpublished district court case).

Gluth v. Kangas, 773 F. Supp. 1309, 1990.

Gluth v. Kangas, 951 F.2d 1504, 1991.

Harris v. Cardwell, Civ. 75-185 PHX CAM (D. Ariz.) (unpublished case file).

Hook v. State of Arizona, Civ. 73-97 PHX CAM (D. Ariz.) (unpublished district court case).

Hook v. Arizona, 972 F.2d 1012, 1992.

Hook v. Arizona, 907 F. Supp. 1326, 1995.

Hook v. Arizona, 107 F.3d 1397, 1997.

Hook v. Arizona, 188 Fed. Appx. 577, 2006.

Lewis v. Casey, 518 U.S. 343, 1996.

Miranda v. Arizona, 384 U.S. 436, 1966.

Taylor v. Arizona, No. 72-21 (D. Ariz.) (unpublished case file).

Taylor v. Arizona, 972 F. Supp. 1239, 1997.

Whitmire v. Arizona, 298 F.3d 1134, 2002.

REFERENCES

Abbott, C. 1987. *The new urban America: Growth and politics in Sunbelt cities.* Chapel Hill: University of North Carolina Press.

———. 2003. Urbanizing the Sunbelt. *Organization of American Historians Magazine of History.* October, 11–16.

Adams, M. 1976. Justice Department probes state prison on inmate treatment. *Arizona Republic.* September 23, B1.

Allen, F. 1981. *The decline of the rehabilitative ideal.* New Haven, CT: Yale University Press.

Archer, R. 1991. Mandatory sentencing: Can Arizona afford the price? *Arizona Republic.* August 10, A18.

Ariav, A. 1982. Inmates take first peek at new "tin can" abodes. *Arizona Republic.* July 14, B1, B4.

Arizona Advisory Committee to the U.S. Commission on Civil Rights. 1974. December. *Adult corrections in Arizona.*

Arizona Advocacy Network. 2003. April. *Borrowing against the future: The impact of prison expansion on Arizona families, schools and communities.*

Arizona Capitol Times. 1993. Legislative requests would increase power of corrections direction. December 10, 48.

———. 1994. Corrections officials lift prisoners' weights, give them to schools. December 30, 52.

Arizona Daily Star. 1958. No title. December 6, n.p.

———. 1994. Punish. Or rehabilitate? February 14, n.p.

Arizona Department of Corrections. 1970. *Progress report of the Arizona State Department of Corrections.* Phoenix: Arizona Department of Corrections.

———. 1981. *Resident orientation for residents housed in the South Unit.* 1981. Revised edition.

———. 1990. *Arizona Department of Corrections 10 year plan, 1991–2000.* Phoenix: Arizona Department of Corrections.

———. 1992. February. Mandatory sentencing study.

———. Website. A history of the Arizona State Prison–Safford. http://www.azcorrec tions.gov/adc/prisons/camp2complex.asp.

———. Website. ADC prisons. http://www.azcorrections.gov/adc/prisons_1.asp.

———. Website. Departmental history, ADC historic legal issues. http://www.azcor rections.gov/adc/history/legal_issues.asp.

Arizona Department of Juvenile Corrections. History of the agency. http://www .juvenile.state.az.us/AgencyInfo/History.htm.

Arizona Republic. 1958. Uprising quelled by bullets, December 5, 1–2.

———. 1968. Gone the "razor strap" discipline for youths at Industrial School. December 17, n.p.

———. 1971a. Ft. Grant situation [editorial]. February 26, n.p.

———. 1971b. Vukcevich hails return of Ft. Grant discipline. March 7, n.p.

———. 1972a. Prison chief calls for inmate reform. May 5, A8.

———. 1972b. Warden warns prisoners he won't tolerate violence. May 11, A8.

———. 1984. Ex-ASP Warden Eyman dies. June 17, n.p.

———. 1987. Prison agency would shut down halfway houses. January 21, B1.

———. 1992. Life behind bars; couch-potato felons [editorial]. September 23, A10.

Arizona Revised Statutes. 1978. Final draft of statute as passed by the Arizona State Legislature. Phoenix: State of Arizona Legislative Archives, 13–101.

Arizona Town Hall. 1966. *Crime, juvenile delinquency and corrective measures in Arizona.* Phoenix: Arizona Academy.

Armstrong, H. 1972. Rights agency to investigate prisons. *Phoenix Gazette.* December 5, n.p.

Arpaio, Joe. 2003. Author interview. Telephone, July 23.

Arrington, L. 1987. Arizona: Better design means better management. *Corrections Today* 49 (April), 84, 86.

Barker, V. 2006. The politics of punishing: Building a state governance theory of American imprisonment variation. *Punishment and Society* 8, 5–33.

Beck, A., and P. Harrison. 2001. *Prisoners in 2000.* Washington, DC: U.S. Department of Justice, Bureau of Justice Statistics.

Beck, A., and C. Mumola. 1999. *Prisoners in 1998.* Washington, DC: U.S. Department of Justice, Bureau of Justice Statistics.

Beckett, K. 1997. *Making crime pay: Law and order in contemporary American politics.* New York: Oxford University Press.

Beckett, K., and B. Western. 2001. Governing social marginality: Welfare, incarceration, and the transformation of state policy. *Punishment and Society* 3, 43–59.

Berman, D. 1998. *Arizona politics and government.* Lincoln: University of Nebraska Press.

Bernard, R., and B. Rice. 1983. *Sunbelt cities: Politics and growth since World War II.* Austin: University of Texas Press.

Blumstein, A., and A. Beck. 1999. Population growth in U.S. prisons, 1980–1996. *Crime and Justice* 26, 17–61.

Bolin, W. 1977. Statement by Governor Wesley Bolin—November 29, 1977, Arizona State Archives, Box 30, Commission on Corrections, Department of Corrections Folder, 1977–78.

Bolles, D. 1971. $30 million gift out for correction chief. *Arizona Republic.* December 26, n.p.

Bottoms, A. 1983. Neglected features of contemporary penal systems. In *The power to punish,* D. Garland and P. Young, eds. London: Heinemann.

Boyles, L. 1970. Work-furlough plan offered convicts. *Phoenix Gazette.* May 16, n.p.

———. 1971. Dual public role stirs controversy. *Phoenix Gazette.* October 13, n.p.

———. 1973. Corrections director says prison "worst" he's seen. *Phoenix Gazette.* May 14, n.p.

———. 1979. Prison gets new beds, but still not enough. *Phoenix Gazette.* December 10, A18.

Braman, D. 2004. *Doing time on the outside: Incarceration and family life in urban America.* Ann Arbor: University of Michigan Press.

Bright, C. 1996. *The powers that punish: Prison and politics in the era of the "Big House," 1920–1955.* Ann Arbor: University of Michigan Press.

Browning, C., and W. Gesler. 1979. The sun belt–snow belt: A case of sloppy regionalizing. *Professional Geographer* 31, 66–74.

Buchen, C. 1959. Will ask for a program. *Arizona Republic.* August 20, 1.

Bureau of Justice Statistics. 1998. *Sourcebook of criminal justice statistics, 1997.* Washington, DC: U.S. Department of Justice.

Cart, J. 2000. Sheriff draws ire for new "jail cam," special inmate diet. *Milwaukee Journal Sentinel.* September 10, 12A.

Cavanaugh, W. 1964. Prison dental lab due for June debut. *Arizona Republic.* April 23, 41.

Chiricos, T., and M. DeLone. 1992. Labor surplus and punishment: A review and assessment of theory and evidence. *Social Problems* 39, 421–46.

Cohen, S. 1979. The punitive city: Notes on the dispersal of social control. *Contemporary Crises* 3, 339–63.

———. 1985. *Visions of social control.* New York: Polity.

Cook, A. 1968. Letter to J. Williams, Arizona State Archives, Governor Williams Papers, Box 429.

———. 1970. Letter to J. Ford Smith, August 28. Arizona State Archives, Governor Williams Papers, Box 515.

———. 1971. Letter to Attorney General G. Nelson, April 26. Arizona State Archives, Governor Williams Papers, Box 590.

———. 1972a. Letter to J. Williams, January 17. Arizona State Archives, Governor Williams Papers, Box 355.

———. 1972b. Letter to J. Williams, June 13. Arizona State Archives, Governor Williams Papers, Box 639.

———. 1972c. Letter to J. Williams, November 22. Arizona State Archives, Governor Williams Papers, Box 639.

Coppola, C. 1995. Arizona officials slam "master" as reform radical. *Tribune*. October 20, n.p.

Corrections Today. 1988a. Haver, Nunn, and Collamer advertisement. July, n.p.

———. 1988b. Stewart-Decatur advertisement. July, n.p.

Currie, E. 1998. *Crime and punishment in America*. New York: Metropolitan Books.

Daien, A. 1975. Supreme Court justice urges dismissal of corrections chief. *Arizona Republic*. November 15, n.p.

Davenport, P. 2003. Napolitano names new director for prison system in "crisis." *Associated Press State and Local Wire*. June 13, n.p.

Davies, J. 1966. Letter to J. McFarland, June 14. Arizona State Archives, Governor Goddard Papers, Series 1, Box 33.

Davis, A. 1998–99. Globalism and the prison industrial complex: An interview with Angela Davis. *Race and Class* 40, 145–57.

———. 2003. *Are prisons obsolete?* New York: Seven Stories.

Davis, M. 1986. *Prisoners of the American dream*. London: Verso.

De Giorgi, A. 2006. *Re-thinking the political economy of punishment: Perspectives on Post-Fordism and penal politics*. Burlington, VT: Ashgate.

De Uriarte, R. 1991. Opening the door; intensive probation a sensible alternative. *Phoenix Gazette*. September 2, A13.

Denny, B. 1984. Letter to B. Babbitt, May 2. Arizona State Archives, Governor Babbitt Papers, Box 429, Folder 4550.

Directions. 1985. A prison is a prison. June, 2.

———. 1993. Arizona Department of Corrections: 25 years of service to the state. June, 1, 7.

Donziger, S. 1996. *The real war on crime*. New York: HarperCollins.

Economist. 1999. A hydra in the desert: Phoenix's urban sprawl. July, 26–27.

Edgerton, K. 2004. *Montana justice: Power, punishment, and the penitentiary*. Seattle: University of Washington Press.

Edwards, K. 1968. *Report on homosexuality in the Arizona State Prison*. Arizona State Archives, Governor Williams Papers, Box 491.

Evaluation report No. 76-5. 1976. April 9. Arizona State Archives, Governor Castro Papers, Box 82.

Eyman, F. 1958. *Annual report: Arizona State Prison, July 1, 1957–June 30, 1958.*

———. 1960. *Bi-annual report: Arizona State Prison, July 1, 1958–June 30, 1960.*

———. 1962. *Bi-annual report: Arizona State Prison, July 1, 1960–June 30, 1962.*

———. 1967. Letter to J. Williams, April 13. Arizona State Archives, Governor Williams Papers, Box 418.

Feeley, M., and E. Rubin. 1998. *Judicial policy making and the modern state: How courts reformed America's prisons.* Cambridge: Cambridge University Press.

Feeley, M., and J. Simon. 1992. The new penology: Notes on the emerging strategy of corrections and its implications. *Criminology* 30, 449–74.

Ferrier, R. 2004. Note: "An atypical and significant hardship": The supermax confinement of death row prisoners based purely on status--A plea for procedural due process. *Arizona Law Review* 46, 291–315.

Fifer, O. 1962. Murderers best prison workers. Arizona Republic. March 26, n.p.

Findlay, J. M. 1992. *Magic lands: Western cityscapes and American culture after 1940.* Berkeley: University of California Press.

Fischer, Darryl. 2004. Author interview. Phoenix, Arizona, April 6.

Fitzpatrick, P. 2004. Terminal legality? Human rights and critical being. In *Critical beings: Law, nation, and the global subject,* P. Fitzpatrick and P. Tuitt, eds. Aldershott, UK: Ashgate.

Flamm, M. 2005. *Law and order: Street crime, civil unrest, and the crisis of liberalism in the 1960s.* New York: Columbia University Press.

Flanagan, T., D. Clark, D. Aziz, and B. Szelest. 1990. Compositional changes in a long-term prisoner population: 1956–89. *Prison Journal* 70, 15–34.

Flannery, P. 1992a. Crime bill vetoed by Symington; lawmakers angry he gave no warning. *Phoenix Gazette.* July 11, B1.

———. 1992b. Justice system reform questioned: Explosion in prison population feared. *Phoenix Gazette.* November 21, A1.

Fort Grant Centennial. 1972. *Fort Grant centennial: 1872–1972.*

Frey, W. 2002. Three Americas: The rising significance of regions. *American Planning Association Journal* 68, 349–55.

———. 2005. Research brief, May. The electoral college moves to the Sun Belt. Washington, DC: Brookings Institution. http://www.frey-demographer.org/reports/BROOK 2005.pdf.

Friedman, L., and R. Percival. 1976. A tale of two courts: Litigation in Alameda and San Benito counties. *Law and Society Review* 10, 267–301.

Gaffaney, T. 1999. Citizens of the market: The un-political theory of the New Right. *Polity* 32, 179–202.

Garland, D. 1990. *Punishment and modern society: A study in social theory.* Chicago: University of Chicago Press.

———. 1996. The limits of the sovereign state: Strategies of crime control in contemporary society. *British Journal of Criminology* 36, 445–71.

———. 2001. *The culture of control: Crime and social order in contemporary society.* Chicago: University of Chicago Press.

Genrich, M. 1991. Prison overcrowding costly? Compared to national crime increase, Arizona saves money. *Phoenix Gazette.* June 5, A11.

Gilliard, D., and A. Beck. 1995. *Prisoners in 1994.* Washington, DC: U.S. Department of Justice, Bureau of Justice Statistics.

Gilmore, R. 2007. *Golden gulag: Prisons, surplus, crisis, and opposition in globalizing California.* Berkeley: University of California Press.

Gipson, F., and E. Pierce. 1996. Current trends in state inmate user fee programs for health services. *Journal of Correctional Health Care* 3, 159–78.

Goddard, S. 1966a. Letter to F. Eyman, January 13. Arizona State Archives, Governor Goddard Papers, Series 1, Box 33.

———. 1966b. Letter to S. Vukcevich, May 23. Arizona State Archives, Governor Goddard Papers, Series 1, Box 32.

Goldfield, D., and H. Rabinowitz. 1990. The vanishing Sunbelt. In *Searching for the Sunbelt: Historical perspectives on a region,* R. Mohl, ed. Knoxville: University of Tennessee Press.

Goldsmith, Charles. 2002. Author interview. Florence, Arizona, August 6.

Gottschalk, M. 2006. *The prison and the gallows: The politics of mass incarceration in America.* Cambridge: Cambridge University Press.

Greene, J. 2003. *Smart on crime: Positive trends in state-level sentencing and corrections policy.* Washington, DC: Families against Mandatory Minimums.

Greene, J., and K. Pranis. 2004. *Arizona prison crisis: A call for smart on crime solutions, May 11, 2004.* Washington, DC: Families against Mandatory Minimums.

Griffin, S. 1991. Woods: Arizona desperate for prison overhaul, Lewis surprised; angry at criticism. *Phoenix Gazette.* September 20, B1.

Hack, S. 1987. Special Management Unit opens in Florence. *Directions,* 1.

———. 1988. Officers receive training for shock incarceration. *Directions,* 1.

Hait, P. 1981. "The Santa Fe riots cannot happen here": Ellis MacDougall assesses Arizona's prison situation. *Scottsdale Progress.* June 13, 4–5.

Hamm, Donna. 2004. Author interview. Tempe, Arizona, April 5.

Haney, C. 1998. Riding the punishment wave: On the origins of our devolving standards of decency. *Hastings Women's Law Journal* 9, 27–78.

———. 2003. Mental health issues in long-term solitary and "supermax" confinement. *Crime and Delinquency* 49, 124–56.

———. 2006. *Reforming punishment: Psychological limits to the pains of imprisonment.* Washington, DC: APA Books.

Harrigan, J. 1970. "Better bad boys" can be sent now to facility near Alpine. *Arizona Republic*. February 15, n.p.

Harris, J. 1973. *Crisis in corrections*. New York: McGraw-Hill.

Haskell, J. 2001. *Direct democracy or representative government? Dispelling the populist myth*. Boulder, CO: Westview Press.

Hill, D., L. Hammond, B. Skolnik, S. Martin, and D. Clement. 2004. Effective post-PLRA settlement models: A case study of Arizona's protective segregation lawsuit. *Pace Law Review* 24, 743–68.

Human Rights Watch. 2006. Report: How dogs are used in cell extractions. http://www.hrw.org/en/node/11143/section/4.

Ingley, K. 1998. Amount Arizona spent per person in 1994: $2339. *Arizona Republic*. March 8, A1.

Institute for Rational Public Policy. 1991. *Arizona criminal code and corrections study: Final report to the legislative council*.

Jacobs, J. 1977. *Stateville: The penitentiary in mass society*. Chicago: University of Chicago Press.

Jeffrey, J. M. 1969. *Adobe and iron: The story of Arizona Territorial Prison at Yuma*. La Jolla, CA: Prospect Avenue Press.

Johnson, J. 1997. The penitentiaries in Arizona, Nevada, New Mexico, and Utah from 1900–1980. Lewiston, NY: Edwin Mellen Press.

Johnson, W., K. Bennett, and T. Flanagan. 1997. Getting tough on prisoners: Results from the National Corrections Executive Survey, 1995. *Crime and Delinquency* 43, 24–40.

Joint Interim Committee on Corrections. 1975. November 6. Rough draft No. 4. Arizona State Archives, Governor Castro Papers, Departments, Boards, and Commissions Subgroup, Box 7.

Joint Study Committee on Juvenile Institutions. 1968. *Report to the Arizona Legislature: Proposed structural reorganization of correctional programs in Arizona*, January. Phoenix, AZ.

King, R. D. 1999. The rise and rise of supermax: An American solution in search of a problem? *Punishment and Society* 1, 163–86.

King, R. S., M. Mauer, and T. Huling. 2004. An analysis of the economics of prison siting in rural communities. *Criminology and Public Policy* 3, 453–80.

Knepper, P. 1990. *Imprisonment and society in Arizona territory*. PhD diss., Arizona State University.

Kolbe, J. 1992. The curious case of Symington's unexpected veto. *Phoenix Gazette*. July 26, G2.

LaJeunesse, W. 1985. "Betrayed" Ricketts quits prisons helm. *Arizona Republic*. March 26, A1.

Lassiter, M. 2006. *The silent majority: Suburban politics in the Sunbelt South*. Princeton, NJ: Princeton University Press.

Legislative Proposals of the Arizona Department of Corrections. 1970. Arizona State Archives, Governor Williams Papers, Box 515.

Leonard, S. 1993. Death's price: 3 killers cost $155,000 to execute. *Arizona Republic.* April 18, B1.

Lewis, S. 1985a. *Arizona Department of Corrections 1984–85 annual report.* Phoenix: Department of Corrections.

———. 1985b. Letter to B. Babbitt, July 25, Arizona State Archives, Governor Babbitt Papers, Box 430, folder 4554.

———. 1985c. Letter to B. Babbitt, September 7, Arizona State Archives, Governor Babbitt Papers, Box 489.

———. 1986. *Fiscal year 1985–86 annual report.* Phoenix: Arizona Department of Corrections.

———. 1987. *Arizona Department of Corrections fiscal year 1986–87 annual report.* Phoenix: Arizona Department of Corrections.

———. 1989a. *Arizona Department of Corrections 1989 annual report.* Phoenix: Arizona Department of Corrections.

———. 1989b. Proceedings of the Symposium on Corrections, November 15, 16, and 17, 1988. Prepared by Samuel Lewis, February.

———. 1990a. *Arizona Department of Corrections 1990 annual report.* Phoenix: Arizona Department of Corrections.

———. 1990b. Director's perspective. *Directions.* June, 3.

———. 1990c. Letter to the editor: Prisons' goal is a safe Christmas. *Arizona Republic.* December 19, B1.

———. 1995a. *Arizona Department of Corrections 1994 annual report.* Phoenix: Arizona Department of Corrections.

———. 1995b. Letter to G. Richardson, November 6. Arizona State Archives, Governor Symington Papers, Series 3, Box 2, 1994–96.

———. 1995c. Letter to J. Kolbe, November 22. Arizona State Archives, Governor Symington papers, Maria Baier files, Corrections Folder, Series 3, Box 2, 1994–96.

———. 1995d. Letter to J. Kyl, August 10. Arizona State Archives, Governor Symington Papers, Series 3, Box 2, 1994–96.

Lewis, Samuel. 2004. Author interview. Phoenix, Arizona, January 6.

Lichtenstein, A. 1996. *Twice the work of free labor: The political economy of convict labor in the New South.* Brooklyn, NY: Verso Books.

———. 2006. Looking beyond the walls. *Punishment and Society* 8, 117–23.

Lilly, J. R., and P. Knepper. 1993. The corrections-commercial complex. *Crime and Delinquency* 39, 150–66.

Lopez, L. 1985. State officials losing faith in prisons chief's abilities. *Arizona Republic.* February 10, B2.

Lynch, M. 2000. The disposal of inmate #85271: Notes on a routine execution. *Studies in Law, Politics, and Society* 20, 3–34.

———. 2002. Selling "securityware": Transformations in prison commodities advertising, 1949–1999. *Punishment and Society* 4, 305–20.

———. 2004. Punishing images: Jail cam and the changing penal enterprise. *Punishment and Society* 6, 255–70.

———. 2005. Supermax meets death row: Legal struggles around the new punitiveness in the USA. In *The new punitiveness: Current trends, theories, perspectives*, J. Pratt, D. Brown, S. Hallsworth, M. Brown, and W. Morrison, eds. Devon, UK: Willan.

———. 2008. The contemporary penal subject(s). In *After the war on crime: Race, democracy, and a new reconstruction*, J. Simon, I. Haney López, and M. L. Frampton, eds. New York: NYU Press.

———. 2009. Punishment, purpose and place: A case study of Arizona's prison siting decisions. *Studies in Law, Politics, and Society*, forthcoming.

MacDougall, E. 1972. *Arizona Department of Corrections report*, October 20. Arizona State Archives, Governor Williams Papers, Box 639.

———. 1980. *State of Arizona Department of Corrections 1979–1980 annual report*. Phoenix: Arizona Department of Corrections.

Manson, P. 1992. Curb on gifts to inmates rejected: Prison sought 25-pound limit over holidays. *Arizona Republic*. July 29, B3.

———. 1995. Policy will cut inmates' TV time. *Arizona Republic*. December 30, B1.

———. 1996. Prop. 102 prison costs questioned. *Arizona Republic*. December 21, B1–B2.

Marson, B. 2003. Group seeks fix of prison crunch. *Arizona Daily Star*. August 18, A1.

Martinson, R. 1974. What works? Questions and answers about prison reform. *Public Interest* 36, 22–54.

Mattern, H. 1999. DOC sex abuse suit is settled: State admits no wrong, but will toughen policies. *Arizona Republic*. March 13, B1.

Mauer, M. 1999. *Race to incarcerate*. New York: New Press.

Mauer, M., and M. Chesney-Lind, eds. 2002. *Invisible punishment: The collateral consequences of mass imprisonment*. New York: New Press.

Mazurek, N. 1973. Convicts given bill of rights at state prison. *Arizona Republic*. August 31, B-1.

McCloy, M. 1995. Prisoners may sue over medical charge; recreation fund used for unpaid bills. *Phoenix Gazette*. August 5, B1.

McGirr, L. 2001. *Suburban warriors: The origins of the new American right*. Princeton, NJ: Princeton University Press.

Meadows, Della. 2002. Author interview. Florence, Arizona, January 25.

Melossi, D. 1993. Gazette of morality and social whip: Punishment, hegemony, and the case of the USA 1970–1992. *Social and Legal Studies* 2, 259–79.

Miller, E. 1995. Corrections battle proves costly: State spends $200,000 to avoid $37,000 bill. *Arizona Republic.* November 16, A1.

Montini, E. J. 1990a. Prison pinch on yule gifts cruel to cons. *Arizona Republic.* August 17, B1.

———. 1990b. Prison chief has a failure to heed order. *Arizona Republic.* December 7, B1.

———. 1990c. Prisons chief teaching cons a real lesson. *Arizona Republic.* December 16, B1.

———. 1991. Woods on risk of con cancer: Tough, guy. *Arizona Republic.* July 3, B1.

Morgan, R. 2000. Developing prison standards compared. *Punishment and Society* 2, 325–42.

Morrell, L. 1990. Injunction on prisons agency OK'd. *Arizona Republic.* April 27, C5.

Myers, M. 1998. *Race, labor and punishment in the New South.* Columbus: Ohio State University Press.

Napolitano, J. 2003. News conference to announce corrections reforms in special session, October 1. http://azgovernor.gov/dms/upload/03-10-01%20Corrections%20 Special%20Session.pdf. Downloaded February 8, 2008.

National Probation and Parole Association. 1958. *Correctional services in Arizona.* New York: National Probation and Parole Association.

Nicolaides, B. 2003. Suburbia and the Sunbelt. *Organization of American Historians Magazine of History.* October, 21–26.

Nilsson, J. 1983a. State senate panel OKs prison multiple bunking. *Arizona Republic.* February 9, B-4.

———. 1983b. Babbitt urges criminal-law revisions to ease overcrowding of prisons. *Arizona Republic.* March 18, A1.

Norrander, B., and C. Wilcox. 2005. *State residency, state laws, and public opinion.* Paper presented at the State Politics and Policy Conference, Michigan State University, May 13–14, 2005. http://polisci.msu.edu/sppc2005/papers/satpm/norrander,% 20stpolconf.pdf.

O'Brien, G. 1978. Panel favors bill to ease penal-chief standards. *Arizona Republic.* February 1, B4.

———. 1979. Legislature is rallying behind state's corrections director. *Arizona Republic.* February 4, B1–B2.

O'Malley, P. 1992. Risk, power and crime prevention. *Economy and Society* 21, 252–75.

Pappas, T. 1980. Remarks, Prison Site Controversy. Arizona State Archives, Governor Babbitt Papers, Corrections Series, Box 11.

Patrick, D. 1996. Letter and report to Fife Symington regarding CRIPA investigation of Arizona's women's prisons, August 8.

Perry, D., and A. Watkins. 1977. *The rise of Sunbelt cities.* Beverly Hills, CA: Sage.

Petersilia, J. 2003. *When prisoners come home: Parole and prisoner reentry.* New York: Oxford University Press.

Phoenix Gazette. 1971a. U.S. grant gives boost to facility. March 4, n.p.

———. 1971b. Report cites lack of communication. June 17, n.p.

———. 1972a. Justice Holohan assails Department of Corrections. July 21, n.p.

———. 1972b. Legislator raps corrections unit [editorial]. September 14, n.p.

———. 1974. Judge orders reinstatement of Vukcevich. January 12, 7.

———. 1988. Lewis drops a bombshell at Ev's trial. March 4, A1.

———. 1991a. Excuse us; truth on mandatory sentences. May 28, A14.

———. 1991b. Special session: Governor Symington, just say no. July 26, A14.

———. 1991c. Drip, drip, drip, no credibility on sentencing [editorial]. December 13, A22.

———. 1995. A spotlight Mr. Woods doesn't need to hog [editorial]. October 3, B4.

Pisciotta, A. 1994. *Benevolent repression: Social control and the American reformatory-prison movement.* New York: New York University Press.

Pittman, D. 1996. Protective-custody ruling irks Arizona prisons boss. *Tucson Citizen.* December 26, 1B.

Pitzl, M. 1992. Governor targets teen crime; general crackdown urged on use of guns. *Arizona Republic.* November 21, A1.

———. 1994. Paints rival as liberal soft on crime; foe condemns portrayal. *Arizona Republic.* September 16, B1.

Pratt, J., D. Brown, S. Hallsworth, M. Brown, and W. Morrison, eds. 2005. *The new punitiveness: Current trends, theories, perspectives.* Devon, UK: Willan.

Preliminary Plan of the Arizona Correctional Training Facility. 1973. Updated November 1. Arizona State Archives, Governor Williams Papers, Box 748.

Provine, D. M. 2007. *Unequal under law: Race in the war on drugs.* Chicago: University of Chicago Press.

Reichman, N. 1986. Managing crime risks: Toward an insurance based model of social control. *Research in Law and Social Control* 8, 151–72.

Relly, J. E. 1999. Supermax: Inside, no one can hear you scream. *Tucson Weekly.* May 3. [electronic version]. http://weeklywire.com/ww/05-03-99/tw_feat.html.

Rhodes, L. 2004. *Total confinement: Madness and reason in the maximum security prison.* Berkeley: University of California Press.

Ricketts, J. 1984. *Arizona Department of Corrections, 1983–1984 annual report.* Phoenix: Arizona Department of Corrections.

———. n.d. *Arizona Department of Corrections: Adult institutional and community inmate work programs.* Phoenix: Arizona Department of Corrections.

Rivera, S., and B. Norrander. 2002. Parties and politics in Arizona. In *Politics and policy in Arizona,* Z. Smith, ed. Westport, CT: Greenwood, 9–30.

Robertson, J. 1997. Houses of the dead: Warehouse prisons, paradigm change, and the Supreme Court. *Houston Law Review* 34, 1003–63.

Robertson, R. 1990. After nostalgia? Willful nostalgia and the phases of globalization. In *Theories of modernity and postmodernity*, Bryan Turner, ed. London: Sage.

Rothman, H. 2002. *Neon metropolis: How Las Vegas started the 21st century*. New York: Routledge.

Rotstein, A. 2009. Arizona ranks 4th in measure of corrections spending. *Arizona Daily Star*, March 3.

Sabol, W., and H. Couture. 2008. *Prisoner inmates at mid-year 2007*. Washington, DC: U.S. Department of Justice, Bureau of Justice Statistics.

Sabol, W., H. Couture, and P. Harrison. 2007. *Prisoners in 2006*. Washington, DC: U.S. Department of Justice, Bureau of Justice Statistics.

Salt, J. 1989. Sunbelt capital and conservative political realignment in the 1970s and 1980s. *Critical Sociology* 16, 145–63.

Savelsberg, J. 1994. Knowledge, domination, and criminal punishment. *American Journal of Sociology* 99, 911–43.

Scheingold, S. 1998. Constructing the new political criminology: Power, authority, and the post-liberal state. *Law and Social Inquiry* 23, 857–95.

Schiraldi, V., J. Colburn, and E. Lotke. 2004. *Three strikes and you're out: An examination of the impact of 3-strike laws, 10 years after their enactment*. Washington, DC: Justice Policy Institute.

Schlosser, E. 1998. The prison-industrial complex. *Atlantic Monthly*. December, 51–77.

Schmandt, M. 1995. Post-modern Phoenix. *Geographical Review* 85, 349–63.

Schulman, B. 1991. *From cotton belt to sunbelt: Federal policy, economic development and the transformation of the South, 1938–1980*. New York: Oxford University Press.

———. 1993. Politics in the New South: Republicanism, race, and leadership in the twentieth century. *Reviews in American History* 21, 340–45.

Schwartz, J. 1974. Prison hearing termed a farce by legislator. *Arizona Republic*. March 20, B1–B2.

Scull, A. 1977. *Decarceration: Community treatment and the deviant*. London: Prentice Hall.

———. 1983. Community corrections: Panacea, progress or pretence? In *The power to punish*, D. Garland and P. Young, eds. London: Heinemann.

Shoults, S. 1968. Telegram to J. Williams. Arizona State Archives, Governor Williams Papers, Box 429.

Simon, J. 1993. *Poor discipline: Parole and the social underclass, 1890–1990*. Chicago: University of Chicago Press.

———. 1995. They died with their boots on: The boot camp and the limits of modern penality. *Social Justice* 22, 25–48.

―――. 2007. *Governing through crime: How the war on crime transformed American democracy and created a culture of fear.* New York: Oxford University Press.

Simon, J., and M. Feeley. 1995. True crime: The new penology and public discourse on crime. In *Punishment and Social Control: Essays in Honor of Sheldon L. Messinger.* T. Blomberg and S. Cohen, eds. New York: Aldine de Gruyter, 147–80.

Sloop, J. 1996. *The cultural prison: Discourse, prisoners, and punishment.* Tuscaloosa: University of Alabama Press.

Smith, D. 1998. *Tax crusaders and the politics of direct democracy.* New York: Routledge.

Smith, J. F. 1970. Letter to A. Cook, August 26. Arizona State Archives, Governor Williams Papers, Box 515.

Sommer, A. 1974. Both good news, bad news for prison operation. *Phoenix Gazette.* May 22, B1–B2.

Sowers, C. 1983. Babbitt to propose expansion of prisons. *Arizona Republic.* September 8, B2.

Special Committee on Health and Sanitation. 1953. Arizona State Prison Report, September 13, Arizona State Archives, Governor Pyle Papers.

Special Legislative Study Committee. 1967. Final report. Arizona State Archives, Governor Williams Papers, Box 407.

Starrett, P. 1966. Letter to F. Eyman, May 10. Arizona State Archives, Governor Goddard Papers, Series 1, Box 33.

Steckner, S. 1998. Prisoner's death outrages judge, calls system's attitude scary, calls for changes. *Arizona Republic.* February 28, A1.

Stewart, T. 1996a. Letter to J. Napolitano, July 17, Arizona State Archives, Governor Symington Papers, Corrections Folder, Series 3, Box 2, 1994–96.

―――. 1996b. Press release, August 7, Arizona State Archives, Governor Symington Papers, Corrections Folder, Series 3, Box 2, 1994–96.

―――. 1998. *Annual report, fiscal year 1998. Arizona Department of Corrections.* Phoenix: Arizona Department of Corrections.

Stewart, Terry. 2004. Author interview. Tempe, Arizona, January 7.

Sweitzer, P. 1966. Routine marks daily living in prison. *Arizona Daily Star.* June 4, n.p.

Swidler, A. 1986. Culture in action: Symbols and strategies. *American Sociological Review* 51, 273–86.

Symington, F. 1993. November. *Governor Fife Symington's plan to combat urban violence, gangs, and juvenile crime.* Arizona State Archives, Governor Symington Papers, Boards and Commissions Subgroup, Box 4, 1991–1993.

―――. 1994a. News release, June 9, Arizona State Archives, Governor Symington Papers, Corrections Folder, Series 3, Box 2, 1994–96.

―――. 1994b. Letter to Editor, June 12, Arizona State Archives, Governor Symington Papers, Corrections Folder, Series 3, Box 2, 1994–96.

———. 1995a. Press release, circa November, Arizona State Archives, Governor Symington Papers, Series 3, Box 2, 1994–96.

———. 1995b. Letter to Editor, November 24, Arizona State Archives, Governor Symington Papers, Series 3, Box 2, 1994–96.

Taylor, M. 1982. Prison furloughs face critical test in house hearing. *Arizona Republic.* February 15, B1–B2.

Taylor, V. 1968. State prison accepts challenge to reduce guard problems. *Arizona Republic.* September 28, n.p.

Taylor, W. B. 1999. *Down on Parchman Farm.* Columbus: Ohio State University Press.

Thompson, C. 1985. Church leaders scorn proposed prison chaplains cutback. *Phoenix Gazette.* March 22, n.p.

Tierney, David. 2007. Author interview. Telephone, June 14.

Time. 1952. Reasonable punishment? March 10, 56.

Tonry, M. 1995. *Malign neglect: Race, crime and punishment in America.* New York: Oxford University Press.

———. 2004. *Thinking about crime: Sense and sensibility in American penal culture.* New York: Oxford University Press.

Torrey, J. F. 1986. Prisons chief exempt in rule-making steps; lawmaker surprised. *Arizona Republic.* July 19, B-1.

Tragash, S. 1976. Dem labels corrections chief an inept and lax "political hack." *Arizona Republic.* January 7, B1, B3.

Travis, J., and M. Waul. 2004. *Prisoners once removed: The impact of incarceration and reentry on children, families, and communities.* Washington, DC: Urban Institute.

Trubowitz, P. 1992. Sectionalism and American foreign policy: The political geography of consensus and conflict. *International Studies Quarterly* 36, 173–90.

Tucson Citizen. 1995. Governor should give up and pay "special masters" [editorial]. October 20, 16A.

U.S. Department of Commerce, Bureau of the Census. 1951. *Statistical Abstract of the United States, 1951.* Washington, DC: GPO.

———. 1954. *Statistical Abstract of the United States, 1954.* Washington, DC: GPO.

———. 1958. *Statistical Abstract of the United States, 1958.* Washington, DC: GPO.

———. 1962. *Statistical Abstract of the United States, 1962.* Washington, DC: GPO.

———. 1972. *Statistical Abstract of the United States, 1972.* Washington, DC: GPO.

———. 1976. *Statistical Abstract of the United States, 1976.* Washington, DC: GPO.

———. 1980. *Statistical Abstract of the United States, 1980.* Washington, DC: GPO.

———. 1982. *Statistical Abstract of the United States, 1982.* Washington, DC: GPO.

———. 1992. *Statistical Abstract of the United States, 1992.* Washington, DC: GPO.

———. 2001. *Statistical Abstract of the United States, 2001.* Washington, DC: GPO.

———. 2003. *Statistical Abstract of the United States, 2003.* Washington, DC: GPO.

———. 2005. *Statistical Abstract of the United States, 2004–05.* Washington, DC: GPO.

U.S. Department of Justice, Office of the Inspector General. 2005. February. *A review of ICITAP's screening procedures for contractors sent to Iraq as correctional advisors.* http://www.usdoj.gov/oig/special/0502/final.pdf.

Van Der Werf, M. 1989. Prison calls to be taped, monitored. *Arizona Republic.* April 25, B1.

Vukcevich, S. 1959. *1958–1959 annual report to the Board of Directors of State Institutions for Juveniles: Arizona State Industrial School.*

Wacquant, L. 2000. The new "peculiar institution": On the prison as surrogate ghetto. *Theoretical Criminology* 4, 377–89.

Warne, D. 1971. State prison to keep stiff rules, chief says. *Arizona Republic.* August 25, n.p.

———. 1972a. New prison study avoids "sensational." *Phoenix Gazette.* August 8, n.p.

———. 1972b. Corrections chief raps suits against personnel. *Phoenix Gazette.* August 28, n.p.

Westerman, A. 1966. Demise of death row. *Arizona Republic.* November 27, 14B.

Western, B. 2006. *Punishment and inequality in America.* New York: Russell Sage Foundation.

Western, B., and K. Beckett. 1999. How unregulated is the U.S. labor market? The penal system as a labor market institution. *American Journal of Sociology* 104, 1030–60.

White, H., C. Frazier, and L. Lanza-Kaduce. 1999. A socio-legal history of Florida's juvenile transfer reforms. *Journal of Law and Public Policy* 10, 249–75.

Whiting, B. 1995. Symington snubs prison alternatives; refuses funding to study options. *Arizona Republic.* June 11, A1.

Whitman, J. 2003. *Harsh justice: Criminal policy and the widening divide between America and Europe.* New York: Oxford University Press.

Willey, K. A. 1983. Republicans ram through prison bills, dare Babbitt. *Arizona Republic.* December 22, A1–A2.

Williams, J. 1967. Letter to F. Eyman, September 24. Arizona State Archives, Governor Williams Papers, Box 418.

———. 1971. Letter to A. Cook, September 24. Arizona State Archives, Governor Williams Papers, Box 590.

———. 1972a. Letter to H. Fleischman, June 14. Arizona State Archives, Governor Williams Papers, Box 639.

———. 1972b. Letter to A. Cook, July 6. Arizona State Archives, Governor Williams Papers, Box 639.

Woods, G. 1992. Focus on state prisons; Arizona is not getting its money's worth [editorial]. *Arizona Republic.* January 11, A17.

Wynn, B. 1963. House passes resurrected prison advisory board bill. *Arizona Republic.* March 6, n.p.

———. 1983. Plush state prison takes Constitution step too far. *Arizona Republic.* November 26, B1.

Yozwiak, S. 1990. Prisons to get major review; biggest study since revamp of code in '77. *Arizona Republic.* March 15, B1.

———. 1991. Criminal code berated; rules are crowding prisons, study says. *Arizona Republic.* July 2, B1.

Zimring, F. 2003. *The contradictions of American capital punishment.* New York: Oxford University Press.

Zimring, F., and G. Hawkins. 1991. *The scale of imprisonment.* Chicago: University of Chicago Press.

INDEX

Note: Page numbers in italic type indicate photographs, figures, or tables.

Critical Perspectives on Crime and Law
Edited by Markus D. Dubber